Hardback edition:
Dar el Kutub No. 27481/17
ISBN 978 977 416 884 0

Dar el Kutub Cataloging-in-Publication Data

Humphreys, Andrew
     The American University in Cairo: 100 Years, 100 Stories / Andrew Humphreys.—
Cairo: The American University in Cairo Press, 2020.
     p.   cm.
     ISBN 978 977 416 884 0
     1. American University in Cairo—Anniversaries
     394.2

Paperback edition:
Dar el Kutub No. 27485/17
ISBN 978 977 416 888 8

Dar el Kutub Cataloging-in-Publication Data

Humphreys, Andrew
     The American University in Cairo: 100 Years, 100 Stories / Andrew Humphreys.
Cairo: The American University in Cairo Press, 2020.
     p.   cm.
     ISBN 978 977 416 888 8
     1. American University in Cairo—Anniversaries
     394.2

1 2 3 4 5   24 23 22 21 20

Designed by Gadi Farfour
Printed in China

THE AMERICAN UNIVERSITY IN CAIRO

AUC
100 YEARS I 100 STORIES

ANDREW HUMPHREYS

The American University in Cairo Press
Cairo New York

CONTENTS

HISTORY

WARS & REVOLUTIONS

FACULTY & STAFF

STUDENTS

ALUMNI

SOCIAL LIFE

AUC IN EGYPT

VISITORS

A GLOBAL
UNIVERSITY

NEW CAIRO
CAMPUS

WHAT NEXT?

ABOUT THIS BOOK

▲ Almost the beginning: the staff of 1921 (minus founder and first president Charles Watson), on the steps in front of the main building entrance

This book is not a history of AUC. For that there is Lawrence R. Murphy's *The American University in Cairo: 1919–1987* and Thomas A. Lamont's *The American University in Cairo 1987–1995*. If you want to know who was dean of faculties in 1967, Murphy is your man. Who stepped down as board chairman in 1990? Consult Lamont. Instead, this book is a celebration of AUC. It is one hundred short stories (some are historical in focus, many are not)—one hundred snapshots, all of which, it is hoped, taken together combine to capture something of the spirit of this unique American–Egyptian educational and cultural institution. It collects voices and memories, raids the archive for key documents and intriguing items of ephemera, and showcases evocative imagery, some vintage, some photographed only recently. It also draws on a century of published work about AUC, from brochures and letters to student newspapers, magazines, and online posts.

This is not a book to be read from front to back (or back to front), it is a book to be dipped into. It is not comprehensive—and, indeed, could never be—but if you have been a student at AUC, if you have taught or worked here, if you attended movies or theatre here, if you browsed the Bookstore and read your purchases in the shade of the garden trees, then you are part of the family, and this book is about you. ❁

1

A CENTURY IN THE LIFE OF AUC

A lot has happened between the founding of the university in 1919 and today

THE FOUNDING

1854 The American Mission begins its work in Egypt

1871 17 July, birth of Charles Watson, in Egypt to American Presbytarian missionary parents

1899 Three American missionaries call for the establishment of an English-language Christian college in Cairo, similar to those already in existence in Beirut and Istanbul

1912 Charles Watson completes a report outlining a vision for a "Christian University in Cairo" (pp12–15)

1913 Fundraising begins in the United States for the new university

1919 Purchase completed of the Khairy Palace on what is now Tahrir Square (pp24–27). 11 July, the American University at Cairo is incorporated in Washington DC (p18)

Prince Ahmed Fouad at the Khairy Palace in 1909, ten years before its purchase by AUC

THE 1920s

1920 5 October, the university opens its College of Arts and Sciences. Tuition is set at LE16 a year, while compulsory midday lunches cost a further LE13.50 a year

1921 An existing missionary school, called the Cairo Study Center, is integrated into AUC and renamed the School of Oriental Studies

1923 AUC holds its first commencement, with diplomas awarded to twenty graduates

1924 AUC degrees recognized by the New York State Board of Regents as equivalent to junior college degrees. A third unit is added to AUC, called the Division of Extension (now the School of Continuing Education). The first campus newspaper, *The AUC Review*, is issued (pp122–25)

1925 Land is purchased on Pyramids Road as the site for a future campus (pp20–23). The first university-level courses are offered

1926 The Old Boys' Club is created to keep alumni involved with the university

1928 AUC welcomes first female student, Eva Habib al-Masri (pp106–07). First university-level bachelor's degrees awarded to three students. Ewart Hall is opened (pp182–85)

"The American University at Cairo is a Bridge of Friendliness between America and Egypt, between the West and the East."

Charles Watson, AUC founder and first president

CHARLES WATSON
1919–44
See page 13

THE 1930s

Spiffy looking students of the 1930s

1931 The university gains a fourth unit, the Department of Education. *The AUC Review* sponsors Miss AUC (pp110–13). The Old Boys' Club develops into the Alumni Association

1932 Dedication of a new School of Oriental Studies building, which includes Oriental Hall

1934 AUC enrollment reaches 155; fifteen are women (pp108–09)

1937 AUC begins courses in journalism. Umm Kulthoum gives a series of performances at Ewart Hall broadcast on Egyptian radio (pp212–13)

1938 *Campus Caravan* replaces *The AUC Review*

1939 The Second World War begins and the AUC community forms an Air Raid Protection Committee

THE 1940s

1940 King Abdullah of Jordan visits AUC

1941 AUC hosts classes and special concerts in Ewart Hall for American soldiers in Egypt

1942 Foreign faculty are evacuated, some to Khartoum (pp50–53). Students petition the Ministry of War to allow an instructor to teach them military formations

1944 The Lincoln School is founded to handle preparatory classes, leaving AUC to operate primarily as a university

1945 Charles Watson retires and is honored by King Farouk with the Order of Ismail—the first time this honor has been confered on an American

1948 Charles Watson dies in Bryn Mawr, Pennsylvania on 11 January

Saturday afternoon callisthenics

THE 1950s

1950 First graduate degree awarded at June commencement, an MA in Arabic language and literature from the School of Oriental Studies. Having failed to get funding for a new campus on Pyramids Road, the university abandons the plan

1951 Last preparatory class graduates from Lincoln School, making AUC strictly a university-level institution. Ford Foundation grants $85,000 to launch the Social Research Center (pp188–91), which opens two years later

1953 Hill House is formally dedicated as the first student dormitory on campus

1954 Former Egyptian president Mohamed Naguib and newly inaugurated president Gamal Abdel Nasser attend AUC's Arabic Language Day Convocation

1955 The US office of AUC moves from Philadelphia to New York

1956 The School of Oriental Studies becomes the Center for Arabic Studies

1957 Political science and psychology majors are introduced

1959 Hill House is rededicated as a library

"An American University located at Cairo has an unparalleled responsibility and opportunity."

John Badeau, AUC's second president

JOHN BADEAU
1944–53
See page 35

RAYMOND McLAIN
1954–63
See page 57

THE 1960s

Science blossomed at AUC in the sixties

1960 Dr Hanna Rizk is named vice-president, becoming the first Egyptian to hold a top post at AUC. The AUC Press is established (pp44–47). The Ford Foundation grants $100,000 for an ethnological survey of Nubia (pp182–85)

1961 AUC's name changes from "at" Cairo to "in" Cairo (p19)

1963 For the first time Muslim and Christian students are about equal in numbers on campus

1964 AUC buys two schools from the Greek community, land on Sharia Falaki for a hostel, and residential properties in Maadi

1966 Completion of the Science Building

1967 The universtiy is closed by war and sequestered (pp58–61). Center for Arabic Study Abroad is established (pp234–36)

THE 1970s

1972 AUC Press obtains English-language rights to nine novels by Naguib Mahfouz (pp240–42)

1973 Classes are briefly suspended again by war with Israel

1974 Egypt's Ministry of Higher Education recognizes all but three AUC degrees as equivalent to those offered by Egyptian universities

1975 Egyptian government relinquishes control of AUC. Protocol issued between AUC and the Egyptian government (pp48–49). Introduction of a minor in computer science

1976 Fire halts work on the building of a new $3.25m library on the Greek Campus and damages the adjacent theater

1978 AUC Press publishes its first Naguib Mahfouz novel in English (*Miramar*)

Study abroad students on campus

THE 1980s

1980 AUC's Center for Middle East Management Studies opens

1982 Construction is completed on the new library on the Greek Campus. AUC receives its largest single donation ($5,500,000) from Yousef Jameel ('68)

1983 Students strike over tuition fees (pp114–16)

1984 AUC creates a stand-alone engineering department. AUC awards first honorary doctorate degree to architect Hassan Fathy

1985 A training project initiated in 1979 is given permanent status and renamed the Desert Development Center (pp202–05)

1986 An Egyptology major is established (pp153–55)

1987 Publication of Lawrence Murphy's *The American University in Cairo: 1919–1987*

1988 Naguib Mahfouz is awarded the Nobel Prize for literature and credits the AUC Press with helping him achieve global recognition (pp240–42)

1989 A new Core Curriculum is introduced (pp38–41). The Model United Nations is launched (pp246–48)

THOMAS BARTLETT
1963–69
See page 60

CHRISTOPHER THORON
1969–74
See page 81

CECIL BYRD
1974–77
See page 49

RICHARD PEDERSEN
1977–90
See page 187

THE 1990s

1992 The Rare Books and Special Collections Library opens in a villa Downtown (pp198–201)

1993 All academic departments are reorganized as units of one of three schools: the School of Business, Economics and, Communication; the School of Humanities and Social Sciences; and the School of Sciences and Engineering. Noam Chomsky speaks at AUC (p220)

1994 AUC celebrates its 75th anniversary with Suzanne Mubarak, United States vice-president Al Gore, the Grand Mufti, Pope Shenouda, and foreign minister Amr Moussa

1995 Professor of Egyptology Kent Weeks announces the rediscovery of tomb KV5 in Valley of the Kings (pp243–45)

1996 AUC's Century Committee recommends that the university needs a new campus to secure its future (pp252–53). AUC Press announces the Naguib Mahfouz Medal for Literature

1997 AUC purchases 100 hectares in New Cairo for a new campus

1999 United States first lady Hillary Clinton speaks at Ewart Hall (p218). AUC alumna Rania al-Abdallah ('91) becomes queen of Jordan

THE 2000s

2003 The design of the New Cairo Campus is completed and the cornerstone laid by first lady Suzanne Mubarak ('77, '82)

2004 AUC signs a construction contract for the New Cairo Campus and building begins (pp256–61)

2006 John D Gerhart Center for Philanthropy and Civic Engagement founded (pp303–05)

2007 The library is the first building to be completed on the new campus. AUC Press publishes its thousandth book

2008 7 September, the first day of classes is held on the New Cairo Campus

2009 Egypt's first lady Suzanne Mubarak ('77, '82) inaugurates the New Cairo Campus

A new intake on the New Cairo Campus

THE 2010s

The 2012 shut-out by protesting students

2010 Launch of the School of Business, School of Global Affairs and Public Policy (pp249–51)

2011 Demonstrations on Tahrir Square close the Downtown campus (pp64–77)

2012 The graduation of the first class to study entirely on the New Cairo Campus. A student strike closes campus (pp114–16)

2013 D-Kimia, Egypt's first university spinoff, markets affordable hepatitis C tests (pp88–91)

2015 AUC partners with Magdi Yacoub Foundation on cardiac research (p221)

2018 AUC establishes the Tahrir Cultural Center in AUC Tahrir (p296–99)

2019 Celebrations begin marking one hundred years of AUC

DONALD McDONALD
1990–97
See page 244

JOHN GERHART
1998–2003
See page 304

DAVID ARNOLD
2003–10
See page 259

LISA ANDERSON
2011–15
See page 67

FRANCIS RICCIARDONE
2016–PRESENT
See page 294

2

WHAT'S THE BIG IDEA?

The fact of AUC is taken for granted, but why one hundred years ago did anyone feel the need to set up an American university in Egypt?

What would become AUC was born out of the ministrations of the American Mission. This was a religious charity affiliated with the United Presbyterian Church of North America, which operated in Egypt from the mid-1850s. It aimed to both evangelize Muslims and convert Copts to a more American way of the worship of Jesus Christ, otherwise known as Protestantism. On 17 July 1871, one particular missionary family, the Watsons, working in the Nile Valley, was blessed with the arrival of a third son, who they named Charles. The boy was brought up in Egypt until the age of eighteen, at which point he was sent to the United States to complete his education. In 1902 he was asked by the United Presbyterian Board of Foreign Missions to direct its activities in the Middle East and India. Among his responsibilities were 171 missionary-run schools in Egypt, including a notably successful secondary college in Assiut. Watson regretted that no similar institution existed in Cairo and in 1912, accompanied by the Assiut College principal Robert McClenahan and a professor from Columbia University, he spent four months in Egypt looking to see if something could be done to rectify this. He returned to the United States convinced of the viability of launching an American-sponsored university in Cairo.

Cairo already had two universities: al-Azhar, which had been the center of Muslim learning already for nine centuries, and the substantially more recent Egyptian National University (later Cairo University), which had awarded its first degree just the previous year, in 1911. Watson believed there was a need for a third institution, a college and university that prepared boys (sorry, no girls) for further education in Europe or America, while promoting Christian ideals. The basics of the scheme were spelled out in a promotional pamphlet handed to potential sponsors at a black-tie banquet at the Hotel Schenley in Pittsburgh in April 1914—the first occasion on which the project was presented publicly. Entitled *Christian University at Cairo*, the pamphlet explained that the new institution was to be a place that carried to "the Moslem Orient the »

A Proposition I'll Endorse

PRESIDENT #1
CHARLES WATSON
(1919–44)
The child of missionaries, Charles Watson was born and schooled in Egypt, before attending college in the United States. He worked at a mission in Pittsburgh and pastored a church in St. Louis before returning to Egypt to found a university in Cairo. He was a cosmopolitan man who talked a missionary language when it suited his goals—notably when fund-raising—but otherwise disliked polemics. He campaigned for funds in America, cultivating an association with the Hill family, who eventually made AUC possible through their generous contributions. He died within four years of retiring from the presidency.

72:—Hotel Schenley, Pittsburgh, Pa.

▲ The Hotel Schenley in Pittsburgh, where in April 1914 the vision for what would become AUC was presented publicly for the first time. The hotel is now the Student Union building of the University of Pittsburgh main campus

richest content of the faith and life of Western Christendom." Future AUC guest speaker Edward Said might have had some fun with that, but it was exactly what Watson's audience of wealthy, philanthropic bankers and industrialists needed to hear if they were to be persuaded to help finance the venture.

As the campaigning for funds continued, the message was tweaked for maximum effect. In 1916, with the United States on the verge of entering the First World War, Watson was suggesting that founding a new university at what he described as the heart of the Muslim world was a "strike for leadership." The Orient of the future, he wrote, was in the hands of a rising generation and it was wise statesmanship to make allies of those who might one day hold power by assisting in their education.

Donations came in slowly but steadily, and by 1919 Watson and his colleagues were able to buy land for the new institution. The newly named "American University at Cairo" was incorporated in Washington on 11 July 1919 and opened the doors to its first intake on 5 October 1920. Now began the main task that was to occupy Charles Watson for the next twenty-five years, that of managing relations with the bodies whose actions could impinge on the running of his university. The Egyptian government was naturally suspicious of this foreign institution and wary of what its presence implied—could Egypt not educate its own citizens? Even trickier was the relationship with the Christian missionary organizations, especially the American Mission.

For the university to flourish, it needed Muslim students. But no Muslim parent was going to send their children to a college that failed to respect their religion. The university addressed this matter in a pamphlet entitled *Our Religious Policies: What Are They?* "We have come from America to give you a number of things we have found useful," it said. "Some of these values lie in the sphere of chemistry and physics; but some of them are in the sphere of moral and religious ideals. Of course, if you do not find them useful, you do not need to appropriate them."

This was a prudent message to send to Muslim Egyptians, but it did not go down well with the evangelical Christians. The American Mission saw the university as out of alignment with its own work in Egypt and, in response, pushed for a greater say in its running. Watson's response was decisive: in 1923, he declared AUC independent of any religious organization. The university retained its essentially Christian character: trustees were subject to the approval of the church; Christian missionaries were looked on favorably when it came to filling faculty positions; and teachings on Christianity remained on the curriculum. However, there was to be no proselytizing on campus. This was not always believed by those outside the university. In 1931, when a young Muslim former student converted to Christianity without the permission of his parents the university was condemned—even though its staff had nothing to do with the conversion. More criticism came when one Egyptian newspaper printed excerpts from a university library book that allegedly mocked Islam.

Throughout the presidency of Charles Watson, the dilemma would remain: too much emphasis on Christianity risked offending potential Egyptian students. On the other hand, religious interests motivated many of the Americans who financed the university and a too secular approach risked losing their support. Watson's two immediate successors also had strong church connections, but they were pragmatists. They understood that if the American University was going to succeed, it needed to serve the interests of Egyptians above all. Other sources of revenue were eventually found—although these came with their own problems—and by the 1950s the overtly Christian tone of the early days had almost completely disappeared. ❀

> ## "We have been praised because we do not teach religion and damned because we do."
>
> AUC president
> Charles Watson

The

BIG IDEA

AMERICAN UNIVERSITY AT CAIRO

▲ President Charles Watson explains the reasoning behind AUC in this brochure from the 1930s

3

WHAT'S IN A NAME?

Setting up a new university involves making many critical decisions, not least choosing a name

In 1919, as the final papers were about to be filed for the incorporation of what until then was being referred to as the Christian University at Cairo, the important matter of a permanent name needed to be settled. Many on the Board of Trustees—formed in November 1914—felt that the word "Christian" might invite prejudice from Muslims and should be avoided. Others felt the institution should be upfront about its core nature so that students and their parents would be under no misapprehensions. A list of potential names was circulated offering subtle but meaningful variations on a theme. Eventually one name was chosen: American University at Cairo. However, the debate was far from over.

"AMERICAN"

There were cautions against including the word "American" in the name because it might be seen to have imperialist overtones. The counter-argument was that unlike the major European powers, America was untainted by any colonial past. It was itself a former colony that had successfully fought the British—currently, let's remember, occupying Egypt—to secure its independence. Only the previous year, American president Woodrow Wilson had outlined a statement of principles to be used for peace negotiations to bring to an end the First World War that had supported national self-determination for all colonial countries, winning America millions of friends in Egypt. And with its dynamic, immigrant culture it stood as the healthy, spiritually pure embodiment of the industrial, scientific, and technological possibilities of the new century. So "American" it was.

"UNIVERSITY"

In 1916, the British high commissioner, Sir Reginald Wingate—effectively the administrator of Egypt—appointed a committee to consider the American proposal for a new university. The British were planning to expand the privately-run Egyptian University and thought a

≫

▶ The main entrance of AUC in the 1950s, when the university was still "at" Cairo rather than "in"

84

ARTICLES OF INCORPORATION
OF
THE AMERICAN UNIVERSITY AT CAIRO

WE, the undersigned, persons of full age, and citizens of the United States, and a majority of whom are citizens of the District of Columbia, being desirous to establish and maintain an association for establishing and maintaining in Egypt an institution of learning of the highest standard of educational efficiency do hereby associate as a body corporated for said purpose, under An Act to establish a Code of Law for the District of Columbia, approved March third, nineteen hundred and one; and we do hereby certify in pursuance of said act as follows:

FIRST: The name or title by which such corporation shall be known in law is THE AMERICAN UNIVERSITY AT CAIRO.

SECOND: The term for which said corporation is organized is perpetual.

THIRD: The object of the corporation is to promote Christian education for the youth of Egypt and adjacent lands by the establishment of an institution of learning of the highest standards of educational efficiency so as to discover to the Moslem world those living springs which are to be found in Christ and which alone suffice for the energizing of the intellectual life, the regeneration of society and the redemption of the individual life.

FOURTH: The University shall have power to acquire by grant, gift, purchase, devise, bequest, or otherwise, and hold and dispose of such real and personal property as the purpose of the corporation shall require.

FIFTH: The University may have departments of elementary, secondary, higher and professional education, and establish and maintain accredited academic affiliation with other institutions giving instruction in any of the said departments, and may make to these or other institutions grants in aid for educational purposes. It shall have the right to carry on publication work, lectureships, exhibits, and other forms of University Extension work. It shall have right to grant such certification of educational or other proficiency as is in harmony with the Government regulations in Egypt relating to Education.

SIXTH: The number of Trustees for the first year shall be fifteen, Their names are: Harlan Page Beach, William Isaac Chamberlain, William Henry Steele Demarest, Ralph Warner Harbison, William Bancroft Hill, George Innes, Melvin Grove Kyle, James Henry Lockhart, John Knox McClurkin, Eben Erskine Olcott, George Milliken Paden, George Livingstone Robinson, Fred Omer Shane, Henry Cantwell Wallace, Charles Roger Watson. The said trustees may enlarge their number to twenty-one, of whom the persons named shall at the first constitute the Board of Trustees of said University, to hold in the order of their naming, the first named five shall hold office until November first, 1919, the second named five until November first, 1920, and the last named five until November first, 1921. The election of additional trustees up to a total of twenty-one shall be made by the Board itself, two to hold office until November First, 1920, two until

competitive foreign institution would be a nuisance. The committee also questioned the Americans' use of the term "university" for what it considered such a modest institution. It is true that in the early years AUC was not solely a university. It was intended to be both a secondary school and university. It offered four years of preparatory schooling following Egypt's standard government course and four years in the College of Arts and Sciences. The first intake in 1920 saw eighty-three students enrolled for the government course and fifty-nine for the arts section. The final year of the arts section was equivalent to sophomore year at an American college. When the university held its first commencement in June 1923, the diplomas were considered equivalent to an American junior college degree. It was not until 1928 that AUC's college department had progressed to the point where it could offer a university-level degree of Bachelor of Arts or of Science. In 1944, an administrative divorce took place that saw the preparatory section of AUC separated from the university and renamed the Lincoln School. Just a few years later, the Lincoln stopped accepting any new intake. Its last class graduated in 1951 and from that point on AUC was wholly a university.

"CAIRO"

When Charles Watson was first soliciting support for his university in Egypt, the eminencies of the United Presbyterian Board of Foreign Missions asked whether the proposed college might find more students if it were located in the more cosmopolitan city of Alexandria. Later, the British, who were invested in the support of the Egyptian National University recently founded in Cairo, also directed Watson toward Alexandria, or even Helwan or Heliopolis. The British also took issue with the Americans using the word "Cairo" in the name of their new institution, arguing that it wrongly suggested municipal sponsorship. Watson remained resolute and eventually the British relented. American University at Cairo it was.

Or it was until 1961. In that year AUC received a complaint from the Egyptian minister of education. According to the minister, describing the American University as "at" Cairo suggested that the university was more important than the place, like "Sinatra at the Sands" or "Abdel Halim Hafez at the Royal Albert Hall" (the minister did not use either of those comparisons). The correct English, it was suggested, was "in." Relations between AUC and the new post-Revolutionary Egyptian government were delicate, and the university's Board of Trustees felt that it was not worth further inflaming matters over a two-letter preposition. And so forty-two years after the discussion first began, the name finally settled on American University *in* Cairo. ❧

NEAR BUT NOT QUITE
Some of the names that were considered for the new university:

- American Foundation for Christians in Egypt and the Near East
- American Educational Foundation for Egypt and the Near East
- Cairo Educational Foundation
- Cairo Associated College
- Cairo College
- Cairo Union Colleges
- Cairo United Colleges
- Cairo American College
- Cairo American Colleges
- Cairo American Associated College
- Cairo American United College
- Cairo American United Colleges
- Cairo Institute
- Cairo American Institute

◀ The Articles of Incorporation for the American University at Cairo, were signed in Washington, DC on 11 July 1919

4

A CAMPUS AT THE PYRAMIDS

The move out to a new desert campus in 2008 was radical, but the idea of a suburban site predates even the founding of AUC

BIRDSEYE SKETCH
PROPOSED UNIVERSITY
IN THE NEAR EAST

MURPHY & DANA: ARCHITECTS
331 MADISON AVE: NEW YORK

When founder and future first president Charles Watson was raising funds for a proposed Christian University in Cairo, he had a clear vision of the kind of establishment he was looking to build. It needed to be self-contained to provide a suitably moral and healthy environment for students; it had to have facilities for boarding, and it needed to provide for future expansion. To meet these criteria, Watson's preference was to site his new university far away from the city center. At the first meeting of the Board of Trustees in 1914, several sites were

put forward for consideration. Two that were strongly favored were land in the newly created suburb of Heliopolis and the Mena House hotel property at the Pyramids; the idea in the case of the latter was to demolish the hotel and replace it with the university. At some point Heliopolis was discarded and Watson's attention was fully fixed on the Pyramids. In 1916, the American architectural firm of Murphy and Dana, which had experience working on overseas colleges, was commissioned to draw up designs. >>

▲ A bird's-eye view of the proposed Pyramids Road campus designed by New York architectural practice Murphy and Dana around 1916/17

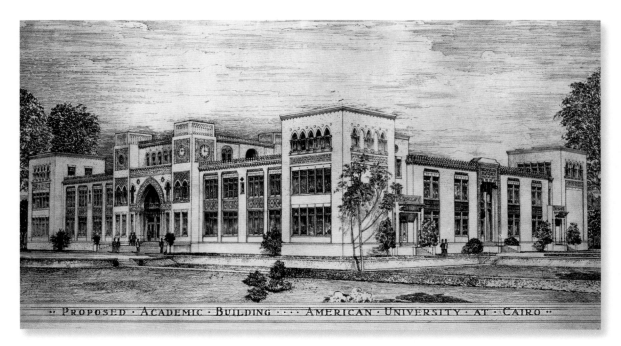

·· PROPOSED · ACADEMIC · BUILDING ···· AMERICAN · UNIVERSITY · AT · CAIRO ··

▲ A campus building from the 1944 masterplan by New York architect Jens Frederick Larson. This had two vast dormitories at the center, ringed by faculty buildings, and a tree-lined drive arcing around the perimeter

On the face of it, this seems an odd decision, to build a university so far from where its potential students lived. At this time Cairo had barely begun to spread onto the west bank of the Nile and there was ample land available closer to the city. Perhaps Watson believed that having the Pyramids for neighbors would inspire students to similarly superlative feats? More likely the notion of a university beside the ancient monuments made for a great fund-raising pitch in the industrial cities of America, where it is likely that the only thing people knew about Egypt were its Pyramids. But Watson was to be disappointed: the government vetoed any proposed development of a site in such close proximity to the Pyramids. (They may or may not have been influenced in this by a letter that appeared in the *Egyptian Gazette* complaining that in locating a large institution so near to the Pyramids the Americans were attempting to make capital out of them.) A second option, to purchase land along the Pyramids Road, faltered when the landlords could not produce the necessary papers proving ownership.

The search for a new site resumed, quickly settling on a small former palace and its grounds on what was then Ismailia Square, now Tahrir Square (see pp24–27). It was here that the university opened its gates in 1920, but the idea of a Pyramids campus never went away. In 1925, an Ohio businessman, W.S. George, pledged $50,000 to AUC specifically for the purpose of purchasing real estate. With this, the university revived its interest along the Pyramids Road and now successfully began the acquisition of what would amount to around one hundred acres about eight kilometers from central Cairo and five kilometers from the Pyramids. For the moment the university lacked the funds to build and so, in the meantime, the land was leased to small farmers. Toward the end of the 1930s it seemed as if it would finally be possible to move forward and a construction plan was put in place with a scheduled move date of 1943, only for the Second World War to intervene.

With the end of the war the scheme was revived. By now, Charles Watson had retired to be replaced as AUC president by John Badeau, but the desire to build a suburban campus, as per Watson's vision, remained undiminished. An internal document quoted one member of faculty as saying, "Unless we can move, we have no future." In the minds of some, added incentive to leave the center of Cairo might have come from the deep anti-American feeling aroused in many Egyptians at this time by the role of the United States in supporting the independence claims of Israel.

With help from American architect Jens Frederick Larson (who had earned himself a dashing reputation in the First World War as an ace fighter pilot) plans were revised. There were several innovative ideas around the new campus, chief of which was that a part of the land should be used to produce as much of the food as possible that would be consumed on site, to the extent of including a dairy. There was also a suggestion that a part of the grounds might be given over to villas and houses that could be rented to alumni and their families, with a primary school for their children. This would not just be a campus but something close to a self-sufficient community with AUC graduates forming its nucleus. As for the Downtown campus, the university would retain only some of the buildings, which would be used for general adult education programs, and the rest would be sold off.

A new fund-raising drive was begun with a target of $1,322,000. Charles Watson was to return to the United States to spearhead this campaign but he died in January 1948. Little money was pledged and, in fact, the university was so short of funds at this time that it was failing even to meet its day-to-day general running expenses. In late 1949 the AUC council recommended that the plans for the Pyramids Road campus be abandoned and the land sold to cover the university's debts. A commitment was made to remaining in Downtown Cairo, made concrete by investment in new buildings, notably a purpose-built student hostel on campus grounds that was inaugurated in January 1953 as Hill House.

Except the dream of a suburban campus never really went away, it would just take another half-century to be realized. ❀

> **"Land in this country is held by so many heirs that one despairs of ever getting anything accomplished in a purchase of real estate."**
>
> AUC co-founder
> Robert McClenahan

23

5

THE PALACE ON THE SQUARE

A pasha's residence turned cigarette factory becomes AUC's first home

It's hard to imagine it now, but wind the clock back just over a century and what is now Tahrir Square (then known as Ismailiya Square) was ringed with low-rise palaces and villas, each with its own walled garden. The area beside the Nile was favored by the ruling royal family, who, from the time of Mohamed Ali but particularly during the era of Khedive Ismail, built their gracious residences here and to the south in what is now Garden City. They are all gone. Well, not quite all. Near the lions of Qasr al-Nil Bridge, a villa once belonging to the sister of Abbas Hilmi II survives in the care of the Foreign Ministry. And then there is the former palace of Ahmed Khairy Pasha, who was a minister during the time of Ismail. The palace, which dates to the early 1870s, was probably built by the pasha on land granted to him by the khedive, although there is a more gossipy tale that says it was built by Ismail for a wife of whom he then tired, and he gave both the palace and the lady to Khairy Pasha. Whatever the case, the palace remained in the pasha's family for more than three decades until in 1899 they sold it to a Greek businessman named Nestor Gianaclis.

Gianaclis ran the oldest and most widely-known cigarette-manufacturing business in Egypt, exporting his products around the world, but particularly to Britain and Germany. His original factory was on Muski Street in the old quarter of the city but success enabled him to relocate to this far more prestigious location on Ismailiya Square. State-rooms were converted to offices, while new buildings were erected at the rear, where the cigarettes would be rolled and packaged. In addition to the practical alterations, Gianaclis indulged in a lavish makeover of his new property, transforming what had been a modest, classically-styled building into a neo-Islamic fantasy, adding crenellated parapets, stalactites in the recesses of the façades, and all manner of frills inspired by the Mamluk architecture of medieval Cairo. Some

▲ A cigarette tin made for the Gianaclis company, which was an occupant of the former Khairy Pasha palace building on Tahrir Square before it was purchased by AUC

sources suggest he was assisted in this by the Austrian architect Max Herz, a former director of the National Museum of Islamic Art (later the Islamic Museum).

Toward the end of 1907, perhaps in need of larger premises, Gianaclis moved his operation to Shubra. He leased the now-vacant former palace to the privately owned Egyptian National University, the honorary president of which was Prince Ahmed Fouad, who would later become king of Egypt and father to King Farouk. In 1910, by invitation from Fouad, recent US president Theodore Roosevelt delivered a famously controversial speech in the main assembly hall. In 1914 the university granted one of its first doctoral degrees to a blind student named Taha Hussein. Despite its successes, by 1915 the university could no longer afford the rent and moved out. The premises were subsequently occupied by a government commercial college but it proved to be a short-term tenant, displaced in 1919 when Charles Watson's search for a suitable site for his new university alighted on the buildings and grounds at 113 Sharia Qasr al-Aini. "By all means get that land on the square," urged early AUC trustee M.G. Kyle. "It may determine the location for all time of the university."

Initially Gianaclis refused the Americans' offer of LE5 per square meter for the parts of the property with buildings and LE3 per square meter for the parts of the property that were vacant. However, unrest ➤➤

▲ The original palace building is the part topped by the two flags. The wing to the right was added in 1927. The gate onto Tahrir Square used to be the main entrance to the university. Note the tram tracks

> **"By all means get that land on the square. It may determine the location for all time of the university."**
>
> AUC trustee M.G. Kyle

resulting from Saad Zaghloul's 1919 revolution caused real estate values to plummet and Gianaclis caved. A deal for the property was signed on 18 April 1919. Surprisingly little work was required to convert the property to AUC's needs. There were twenty-five sizeable rooms suited to classrooms and offices, a large hall perfect for student assemblies, and gardens for recreation. At the end of September 1920, after minimal refurbishing, AUC dean Robert McClenahan boasted to an absent Charles Watson, "I wish you might see the entrance of the building. The colors and especially the subdued lights make it, I believe, the most beautiful place in Cairo."

Not only was it beautiful, but the prime location on the city's central square, surrounded by buildings housing royalty, government, and foreign legations (see the map to the right), not to mention the palace's own pedigree, conferred on AUC right from its earliest days a yet to-be-earned exalted status.

Historians believe that Gianaclis was responsible for commissioning the palace's finest feature, which is the former main entrance facing Tahrir Square, with its graceful arched doorway leading through to a grand processional marble staircase beneath decorative ceilings. For approximately ninety years this stair led up to the president's office (in the room once occupied by Prince Fouad), trustees' room, and other elements of the administration. Impressive as the staircase is, not everyone has been a fan. As vice-provost, Mahmoud Farag had to climb the staircase far too often for his liking. "I climbed it at least twice a day, twenty days a month, ten months a year." Farag calculates that he climbed up and down the stairs somewhere around 7,680 times. "That makes 76,800 meters climbed and descended. Compare that with the 8,848-meter elevation of Mount Everest and I have climbed the equivalent of the world's tallest mountain almost nine times."

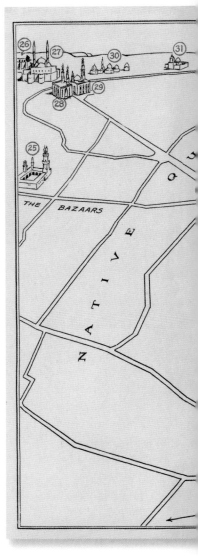

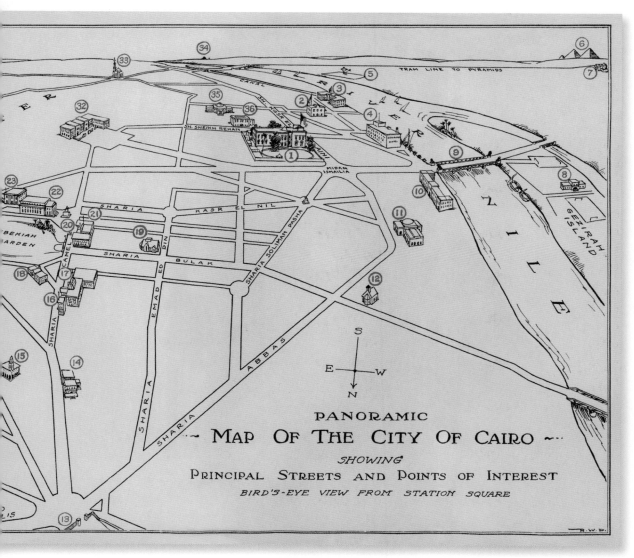

PANORAMIC
~ MAP OF THE CITY OF CAIRO ~
SHOWING
PRINCIPAL STREETS AND POINTS OF INTEREST
BIRD'S-EYE VIEW FROM STATION SQUARE

Personal reservations aside, the occupation of the palace of Ahmed Khairy Pasha by AUC has been an entirely happy one. Without question, if the university had not purchased the palace in 1919, the building would not have survived until today. As recently as the 1970s, a nearby beautiful neo-Islamic villa once occupied by the feminist Hoda Shaarawi was demolished to make way for a parking lot. AUC has not only preserved the old palace but expanded it in sympathetic style, notably by the addition of Ewart Hall and the buildings lining Sheikh Rihan Street, including Oriental Hall. Egypt could not have wished for a better guardian for this fine bit of its architectural heritage. ⚙

▲ A map issued by AUC soon after settling on Tahrir Square, celebrating its prime location (1), next door to Parliament (35), and close by the American legation (2) and British residency (3). Many of the illustrated buildings are now gone, including the British Army barracks (10), old Shepheard's Hotel (17), American Mission (18), and original Opera House (22)

27

6

THE DOWNTOWN CAMPUS

From the old palace building, AUC spread to more than a dozen buildings Downtown

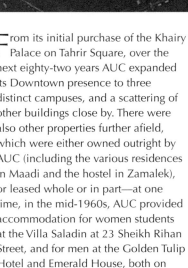

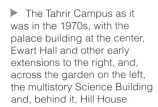

▶ The Tahrir Campus as it was in the 1970s, with the palace building at the center, Ewart Hall and other early extensions to the right, and, across the garden on the left, the multistory Science Building and, behind it, Hill House

From its initial purchase of the Khairy Palace on Tahrir Square, over the next eighty-two years AUC expanded its Downtown presence to three distinct campuses, and a scattering of other buildings close by. There were also other properties further afield, which were either owned outright by AUC (including the various residences in Maadi and the hostel in Zamalek), or leased whole or in part—at one time, in the mid-1960s, AUC provided accommodation for women students at the Villa Saladin at 23 Sheikh Rihan Street, and for men at the Golden Tulip Hotel and Emerald House, both on Talaat Harb.

MAIN CAMPUS

For the first forty-five years of its life, all university activities were located on the main campus, centered on the old palace building. All early expansion was accommodated on the grounds of this campus, including the additions of the Ewart and Oriental halls, Hill House, and the Science Building. The first expansion beyond the main campus did not come until the purchase of what would become the Greek Campus in 1964.

KHAIRY PALACE

This is where AUC began, in the beautiful Islamic-styled building that

faces Tahrir Square. It dates from the early 1870s and was originally occupied by Ahmed Khairy Pasha, a minister during the time of Khedive Ismail. It was extensively remodeled in the first years of the twentieth century by its new owner, the cigarette manufacturer Nestor Gianaclis. The building and its grounds were then purchased by AUC in 1919. The full story is told on pp24–27.

EWART HALL
Inaugurated in 1928, this two-level hall, which seats over eleven hundred people, was originally intended for use by the university's Extension Division for public lectures, film screenings, and cultural performances—the story is told on pp182–85. Among those who have trodden its stage are Umm Kulthoum (see p212–13), Edith Piaf, and Hillary Clinton, and many other exalted guests, as well as countless thousands of graduates who over the decades attended the commencements that were held here every year until 1989.

ORIENTAL HALL
The second major extension to the original Khairy Palace was the Oriental Hall and the buildings of the School of Oriental Studies, which is the whole of the block along Sheikh Rihan Street. This was added in 1932, constructed with the help of a grant from Mrs. David Gillespie and her daughter Mabel. The architect was the British-educated Greek Ariston St. John Diamant, who had previously designed Ewart Hall. He decorated this new, smaller hall in traditional Islamic style. Inscribed on the rear wall and in the lobby are the names of world-renowned intellectuals and literary figures. For many years, the Center for Arabic Studies Abroad (CASA, »

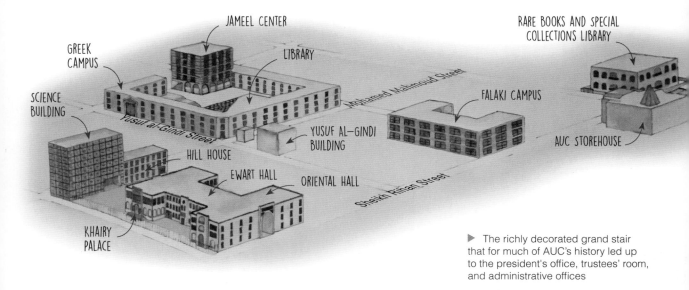

GREEK CAMPUS

SCIENCE BUILDING

JAMEEL CENTER

LIBRARY

Yusuf al-Gindi Street

YUSUF AL–GINDI BUILDING

HILL HOUSE

EWART HALL

ORIENTAL HALL

KHAIRY PALACE

Mohamed Mahmoud Street

FALAKI CAMPUS

Sheikh Rihan Street

RARE BOOKS AND SPECIAL COLLECTIONS LIBRARY

AUC STOREHOUSE

▶ The richly decorated grand stair that for much of AUC's history led up to the president's office, trustees' room, and administrative offices

> "It was a rambling kind of institution, like nobody had planned it. I mean, it was a campus here, a campus there . . . You had to wander through the streets and you might get hit by a car going to class."

Stancil Campbell, faculty member in the theatre department, 2000–2015

see p234–36) and English Language Institute (ELI) used the second and third floors for classes.

HILL HOUSE

Dedicated in January 1953 and named for William Bancroft Hill, chairman of the Board of Trustees from 1921 to 1941, and his wife Elise Weyerhaeuser Hill, Hill House was originally a student dormitory. It was designed by the Cairo architectural firm of Sami Hassid & Yousef Shafik. In 1959 it was converted for use as the university library, although it retained some accommodation on the sixth floor for

members of staff. In 1985, when the library moved to the Greek Campus, Hill House became the offices of student and alumni affairs, and home to the Student Union and a student lounge; the ground floor was the AUC Press bookstore.

SCIENCE BUILDING

This was completed in 1966 thanks to a grant from the US government. The first three floors of the building housed chemistry, physics, math, and solid state science units. The sixth floor housed research labs and the computer center. Floors four and five were completed after 1970 to

house the expanded science units and the new materials science and engineering unit. It was also notable for being the ugliest building not only on the main campus but on Tahrir Square in general, and few can have mourned its passing when it was pulled down in 2015.

FOUNTAIN AREA

The small court behind Ewart Hall derives its name from the small Islamic fountain at its center, donated by former AUC president Thomas Bartlett. This was always one of the main centers of AUC social life.

»

AUC PRESS OFFICE

From approximately 1990 to 2009, AUC owned an apartment building on the north side of Mohamed Mahmoud Street (No.33). This housed the offices of the AUC Press and had stairwell murals by the artist Anna Boghiguian (see pp280–89).

GREEK CAMPUS

The site of the Greek Campus is located a half block east of the main campus and was purchased in 1965 during the presidency of Thomas Bartlett. This was long before the days of bank transfers and, for some reason, even checks were not an option, so Bartlett and the university accountant had to hand over LE409,500 in ten-pound notes, delivered in suitcases. The grounds included two old Greek schools, which were adapted for use, becoming the Social Sciences Building, eventually housing the sociology, anthropology, psychology, Egyptology, mass communications, economics, and political science departments, and a day-care center for the children of university employees. More new buildings were added to the site at later dates.

WALLACE THEATRE

This was originally the gymnasium of the Greek School. It was named after Laila DeWitt Wallace, co-founder of *Reader's Digest*, who provided the restoration funds after the theatre's destruction by fire in 1977. The Wallace was part of the DPS Building, which housed Continuing Education programs.

LIBRARY

The first library was established in 1920 and was housed on the second floor of the Khairy Palace. As the library grew, it was moved to the ground floor in the 1940s and to Hill House in 1959. A new library on the Greek Campus was begun in the 1970s but it took several years to complete because of difficulties with the construction, including a fire. Once the building was completed *(see picture below)*, in 1982, the books were hand-carried in plastic bags from Hill House by volunteers, requiring Mohamed Mahmoud Street to be closed during the operation. Behind the library was a raised courtyard, known as the "plat" *(see picture left)*, which was another major university social hub. Under the plat was the printshop.

JAMEEL CENTER

For short, the JC, but properly known as the Abdul Latif Jameel Center for Middle East Management, named for its generous Saudi Arabian benefactor, whose son was an AUC alumnus. The center was completed in 1989 and housed the rapidly expanding management and business administration programs.

FALAKI CAMPUS

With the continuing expansion of the university, additional property was purchased on Falaki Street, a little further east again of the Greek Campus. The main purpose at the time was to build a dormitory and a sports facility. The first building (the dormitory, *see picture above*) was completed in 1968. The ground floor housed the indoor sports facility and an apartment for the university registrar who was also the supervisor of the dormitory. The grounds contained tennis and volleyball courts as well as a garden. Later, when the Zamalek hostel was completed in 1991, the Falaki Building was turned into departmental offices and classrooms. It was eventually demolished and replaced by the Academic Center, which was completed in 2001 to house the departments of engineering, computer science, and performing and visual arts.

YUSUF AL-GINDI BUILDING

Acquired in the 1960s, this was an apartment block mostly converted to faculty and administrative offices, with a clinic on the ground floor. AUC also maintained some accommodation in the building.

RARE BOOKS AND SPECIAL COLLECTIONS LIBRARY

The attractive villa, *pictured below*, in which the Rare Books and Special Collections Library was housed (until it moved to the New Campus) was originally built in 1900 by the architect Ali Fahmy as his residence. It was acquired by the university in 1977 and classes were held here for a time, until a new purpose was conceived for the building during the administration of AUC president Richard Pedersen. A project of renovation was inaugurated in 1990 and the library opened in 1992. The building also housed a number of faculty offices, including those for Islamic art and architecture, and Egyptology.

AUC STOREHOUSE

On the corner of Sheikh Rihan and Mansour streets is a villa that wlooks like the Haunted Mansion in a Disney theme park. It was built by Faizi Pasha, a minister in the government of Khedive Abbas Hilmi, and is commonly known, after his son, as Villa Saladin. The family leased the house to AUC in the 1960s and it served as a dormitory, then a nursery for the children of AUC staff and faculty. At one point, some of its smaller spaces were pressed into service as overspill classrooms. Eventually it was a store for the university housing department—this was where any faculty member in need of a piece of furniture could come and rummage to see what they could find. ✸

7

HOW AMERICAN IS THE AMERICAN UNIVERSITY?

AUC benefits from close associations with America but that has not always been the case

There is a neat phrase that appears in a 1926 issue of *The AUC Review*, where AUC is referred to as "the American institution which binds Egypt with America." There was a lot of truth in this at the time. America figured little in Egypt in a political sense in the early twentieth century. The United States appointed a first consul-general to Egypt in 1848, upgrading to a formal legation in 1922, but its most influential presence remained its church missions, most notably the American Mission. The missionaries thought of themselves not only as Christian evangelists, but also as ambassadors for the United States and promoters of American culture. It followed that the missionary-founded AUC, with its central Cairo campus, imported American teachers, and American-style syllabus, was seen as a flag-bearer for America in Egypt.

While the funding and methodology of the university were American, the content of the teaching was deliberately free of national bias. The curriculum did not place any emphasis on American history, literature, or culture. Asked why this was, AUC president John Badeau once answered, "We don't want to be thought of like a French, or a British, or an Italian school, with a kind of cultural superiority. We didn't come to Americanize Egypt. We came to serve the country."

For the most part, being closely associated with America was generally to the university's benefit but, inevitably, policy makers in the White House were not always going to have the same outlook on the Middle East as an independent establishment rooted in Egypt. And not all Egyptians would be able to discern the difference. In December 1947, for example, crowds protesting the United Nations decision to partition Palestine gathered in front of AUC chanting, "Down with the United States. Down with the American University." When the following year the United States government was quick to recognize the newly formed state of Israel, AUC president Badeau sent American president Harry Truman a cable of protest, reflecting not only his own views but those of many of the faculty and students. »

CAIRO

AN ACRE OF AMERICA

◀ When this promotional brochure was printed in the 1920s, AUC was very literally "an acre of America." Under the terms of the Capitulations foreigners in Egypt enjoyed extra-territorial rights, so the land occupied by AUC was American, subject to American law

PRESIDENT #2
JOHN BADEAU
(1944–53)
Badeau followed up a degree in civil engineering with a master's in sacred theology from Columbia University, where he also studied Arabic and Muslim philosophy. He began his career in the Middle East in 1928, spending seven years as a missionary in Mosul and Baghdad. He came to AUC in 1936 as a professor of ethics, becoming a dean before he succeeded Charles Watson as president. Wonderfully fluent in Arabic he was widely admired by all. In the early 1960s he served as the American ambassador to Egypt and became a personal friend of President Nasser.

▶ Never used, as far as we know, this oddity from the AUC archives is an original piece of artwork that combines the Statue of Liberty with a procession of pharaonic figures. Who designed it and for what purpose remains a mystery

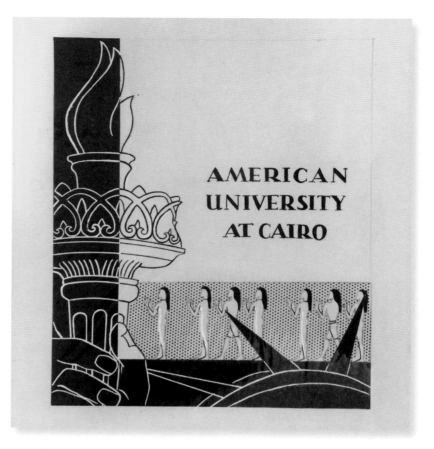

These events occurred at a time when AUC was by necessity drawing closer to the US government. AUC founder and first president Charles Watson had always argued that the university's name did not imply national allegiance. But during the Second World War, many AUCians felt it impossible to remain neutral—which was the official position of the Egyptian government—and supported the American forces in Egypt how ever they could. With the onset of the Cold War, keeping the Soviet Union out of the Middle East became a touchstone American policy. Diplomatic ties were strengthened and funding made available to friendly countries in the region, and to institutions in those countries that were favorable to long-term American interests. Watson had always resisted seeking American government funding, concerned that it might come with knotty strings attached, but he was not around any more and, anyway, these were different times.

When Raymond McLain became president in 1954 he found AUC had a policy of actively avoiding contact with the American Embassy; the embassy reciprocated with what McLain saw as a "hostile" attitude to the university allied to a skeptical view of its educational offerings. This had to change: AUC was a growing university and it needed to source funds where it could. McLain made sure that AUC became the beneficiary of State Department funding and in the early 1960s secured a long-term program of government funding through the United States Agency for International Development (USAID).

If AUC and the embassy drew a little closer when John Badeau (who stepped down from the AUC presidency in 1953) became American ambassador to Egypt in 1961, just a few years later the university took hurried steps backward when the United States again backed Israel, this time in a war with Egypt. AUC's president at the time was Thomas Bartlett, who was insistent in his message that AUC was not an arm of the United States nor was it under the influence of the US government at any time. "The Egyptians must know that. It must be both the reality and the perception."

What Bartlett characterized as a "delicate dance"—the relationship between AUC and the US government—became far less prone to disharmony when President Sadat shrewdly embraced Washington over Moscow. The new, warmer bilateral ties between Egypt and America found an echo in those between AUC and America. Since the 1970s the university has benefitted immensely from that relationship, not least in the $100 million contribution made by USAID to the building of the New Cairo Campus.

"What we do is find that sweet spot," says current chairman of the AUC Board of Trustees Richard Bartlett (who is the son of Thomas Bartlett), "where the interests of the American government and our mission intersect. But we remain very conscious of being independent and we have worked hard to make sure it is true."

"We have cordial relations with American diplomats," says current AUC president Francis Ricciardone (himself a former United States ambassador to Egypt). "We love it when their cultural programmers want to use our Downtown campus for events, and we make it freely available, but we do the same thing with the Dutch, or Italian, or the German embassies."

For Ricciardone, the "American" in AUC has a very specific meaning: "John Waterbury of the American University of Beirut said that the word 'American' is to education what 'Swiss' is to watches." In that sense, says Ricciardone, the "American" in AUC is "an unalloyed good thing." ✺

▲ Because of its unique status as an independent American institution in Egypt, AUC has often been viewed, as this AUC graphic puts it, as "a bridge of friendliness"

"AUC is American with an Egyptian twist rather than Egyptian with an American twist."

Presidential associate Grant Smith (2018–19)

8

WHY A LIBERAL ARTS COLLEGE?

The idea of a liberal arts education has been central to the identity of AUC since its founding

On a lightly warmed March morning on AUC's New Cairo Campus, a group of first-year students fills two rows of seating at the outdoor Allam Amphitheater. Addressing them from the "stage" is a tutor from the Celebrating Ideas program, his subject for today, Sophocles's *Antigone*, a Greek tragedy about a sister who values her dead brothers more than her life. Perhaps some of those in attendance will be enrolled for literature, but most will be majoring in theater, graphic design, architecture, engineering, business, just about any subject AUC has to offer. Some will inevitably be wondering why they are here.

The answer goes back to the earliest days of AUC. This may be an oversimplification but Egypt is a country that is most comfortable with conformity. Education, for example, has traditionally been based on the concept of rote learning. Tutors lecture and students memorize. Plagiarism is condoned, originality penalized. From the beginning AUC offered an alternative. One objective of the university when it launched was to introduce to Egypt new instructional techniques, much like those found in many American-style liberal arts and sciences universities. For anyone who has never encountered a liberal arts–based program before, what this means is that in addition to pursuing a major, students also attend classes in literature, history, philosophy, and other humanities-based subjects, all designed to round out the educational experience by developing valuable "habits of mind."

Former AUC president Thomas Bartlett put it this way: "A liberal arts education is a celebration of learning that encompasses pretty much everything: the arts and the humanities, the social sciences and the hard sciences, business training, and other professional studies. It grounds us in a sound understanding of our own culture and history, but also makes us aware and tolerant of the histories and cultures of others. Liberal learning seeks to emphasize the growth of intellectual self-reliance and independence while encouraging cooperative endeavors. It is the competence to think, analyze, and understand independently."

Part of the original thinking behind AUC's liberal arts approach was to differentiate the fledgling institution from other universities in the region. But there was also a genuine belief that this sort of education better prepared students for a lifetime of critical thinking and independent thought. In the years that followed, the approach served AUC well. When questions were asked in the Egyptian government—which they were, on more than one occasion—along the lines of why the country needed a foreign university, the answer was always that it provided something that Egyptian universities did not, which was its liberal arts teaching. (So foreign is the concept of liberal arts to Egypt, and the Middle East and North African region generally, that Arabic does not have a term that captures its meaning.) The flip side was that the university was often taken less seriously than it warranted. The humanities were typically regarded as frivolous and unlikely to lead to a serious profession and, because of this, AUC was for long »

▲ Part of the Core Curriculum program, the Celebrating Ideas lectures introduce students to books, films, theater, and speeches that have influenced our way of thinking

> **"Liberal learning is the competence to think, analyze, and understand independently."**
>
> Former AUC president
> Thomas Bartlett

periods of its history viewed as a college most suitable for girls, a sort of finishing school.

After the university decided to reposition its educational offering in the 1970s by boosting its engineering, sciences, and business schools, the liberal arts aspect was perhaps downplayed. While this was responded to positively by students more inclined toward the pre-professional majors, among some faculty there was concern that AUC was losing sight of its distinctive mission. In the words of one professor, it was in danger of turning into a "polytechnic." These concerns informed a letter that was submitted to AUC president Donald McDonald in 1995. His response was emphatic: McDonald asked his provost to lead a Commission on Liberal Education, three taskforces were established, and 1996–97 was declared AUC's Year of Liberal Education.

The practical outcome of all this was a new Core Curriculum. The re-envisioned program, which underpins AUC's teaching until today, brought with it an increased sense of purpose, integrating American liberal arts values with Egyptian and Middle Eastern themes, and bringing about closer integration with the majors. On a more fundamental level, it was designed to boost basic skills, notably reading, writing, and speaking fluently.

"At AUC," says Robert Switzer, dean of the School of Humanities and Social Sciences, "you should graduate completely proficient in English. We also have an Arabic program for students who don't have Arabic. The problem is that all too often students leave here functionally illiterate in two languages." Even students of engineering, science, business, and accounting need to know how to write a memo.

To underline the new program, the university came up with a neat tagline: "Teaching people how to think, not what to think." This is where the ancient Greeks, including Sophocles, come in. Switzer teaches a course called Philosophical Thinking, which, as part of the Core Curriculum, is required of all students. Far from being ancient and abstract history, he argues, Greek philosophy is central to AUC's mission. "The most important thing is Plato talking about Socrates. There is Socrates, what is his philosophy? He doesn't have one. His whole life was about just asking questions. Having the courage to ask questions and thinking for yourself."

It is true to say that many AUC students, who are introduced to the Core Curriculum during orientation and the Freshman Program, see it as an imposition that they have to tolerate, rather than a valuable educational opportunity. It is often only after graduating, having experienced the personal and intellectual growth it helps to foster, that they begin to see the merits.

This may take time. The transition from (hopefully) free-thinking, free-speaking liberal arts graduate to the often authoritarian and patriarchal Egyptian workplace can be jarring. But Egypt is changing and changing rapidly. In many respects, a liberal arts education provides the best tools to stay ahead of the game, whatever the field may be. For confirmation of this, look no further than the man who was so far ahead of the game he rewrote its rules, co-founder, chairman, and CEO of Apple Steve Jobs, who in 2011 summarized his company strategy this way: "It is in Apple's DNA that technology alone is not enough—it's technology married with liberal arts, married with the humanities, that yields us the results that make our heart sing."

And next time around, should the lecturer expounding on *Antigone*, or some other Greek classic, find his or her students' attention straying too often to their iPhones, he or she might try challenging them with the question, "What do the billionaire American investors and philanthropists Bill Miller, George Soros, and Carl Icahn have in common?" The answer: they all studied philosophy. ◉

▲ AUC's approach to education can be summed up by a quote from American strategic thinker Alvin Toffler, who said, "The illiterate of the twenty-first century will not be those who cannot read and write, but those who cannot learn, unlearn, and relearn"

9

BRANDING AUC

Every major institution needs an easily identifiable logo, universities included

▲ In 1982 someone at the AUC Press decided the logo looked like a rose and added AUCP leaves and a stem

▶ Sketches from 1966 by Barbara Leslie Cortesi

An instantly recognizable logo keeps an institution in the public eye without the need for words. Think the golden arches of a popular fast-food chain, the swoosh associated with sportswear, or the apple with a bite taken out of it that brands some best-selling technology. As Aristotle said, "the soul cannot think without an image."

AUC's logo took a long time coming. For forty years the university made do with a monogram of the three letters A, U, and C intertwined in indecipherable fashion. It was Christopher Thoron, a future AUC president, but then the executive secretary of the Board of Trustees in the New York office, who instigated a change. He felt that the way AUC presented itself to potential donors was vitally important and the university needed to smarten up its act. He wanted a professional-looking letterhead and he wanted a decent logo, one that was reflective of the region but also showed that AUC was part of the new era—this being the progressive mid-Sixties. The youthful Thoron, who was well connected and stylish (he sped around town in a chic little Mini Cooper, imported from Britain) commissioned a friend, Barbara Leslie Cortesi, to undertake the work. She crafted letterheads in Roman and Arabic type, did some interior design for the New York office, and sketched up a "corporate symbol" of a "pentagon based on Islamic decorative motif," reputedly lifted from a Persian rug.

Take-up of the new logo was slow. It had to wait until Thoron became president in 1969, at which time he enlisted the help of AUC printshop designer Naim Fahmi to polish up the Cortesi designs and adapt them for use. The logo appeared on the spine of an AUC Press book for the first time in 1973. Initially, it was always in black and red; design consultants later changed it to ochre and burgundy, and it has continued to evolve.

Cortesi's invoice from December 1966 survives in the AUC archives. For designing the logo she charged $500—the equivalent of $3,700 today. Cheap for such a key element of the university's identity. ☻

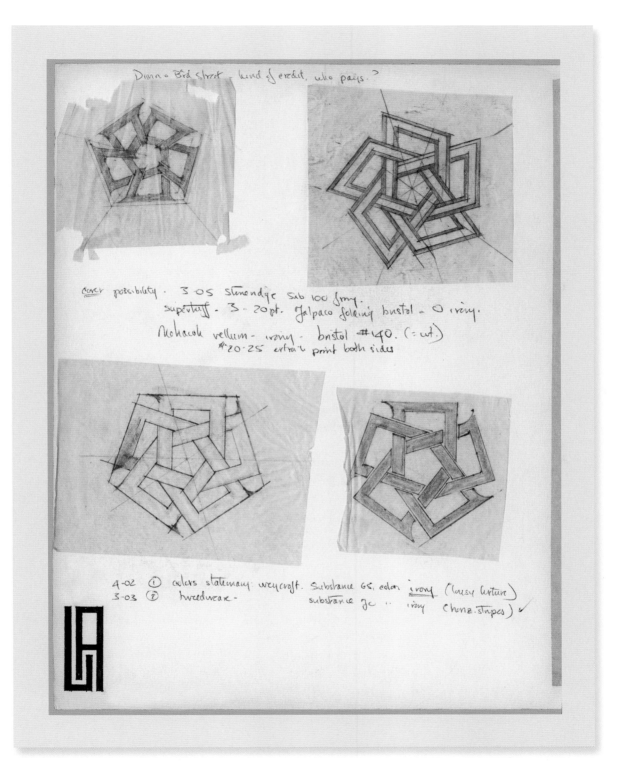

Dunn o Brd street - kind of credit, who pays?

cover possibility - 3-05 Stonendge Sub 100 grmy.
superstuff - 3- 20 pt. galpaco folding bristol - 0 irony.
Mohawk vellum - irony - bristol #140. (= wt.)
$20-25 extra to print both sides

4-02 ① colors stationary: weycroft. Substance 65, color irony ("lousy texture)
3-03 ② tweedwear -   substance 70 " irony (horiz. stripes) ✓

10

THE FREEDOM OF THE PRESS

Publishing books is only one of the roles played by the American University in Cairo Press

University publishing is nearly as old as printing. Just twenty-three years after Gutenberg finished his Bible in Mainz in 1455, Oxford University published a commentary by the fourth-century theologian Rufinus. Cambridge University obtained a licence for its own press in 1534, while in America Harvard began printing a few years after its founding in 1636. The American University in Cairo Press came along a little later, in 1960.

Why found a university press? Traditionally university presses have published work that commercial publishers will not take on. As the majority of mainstream publishers engage in a race to the bottom, fueled by self-help titles, celebrity memoirs, and cookbooks, university presses steadily get on with the business of turning out academic and other specialized works that are often the product of decades of research. As Daniel Coit Gilman, founder of the university press at Johns Hopkins put it, "It is one of the noblest duties of a university to advance knowledge, and to diffuse it not merely among those who can attend the daily lectures but far and wide."

The first task of the newly founded AUC Press was to supervise the publication of K.A.C. Cresswell's monumental (704 pages) and uncompromisingly non-commercial *Bibliography of the Architecture, Arts and Crafts of Islam*, which the university's Islamic studies professor had been preparing for thirty-eight years. At the time the staff of the Press totaled a director, Joe Grady Lehman, and his secretary, who operated out of a single room. Almost sixty years on, AUC Press now boasts a staff of around sixty-five, has five bookshops, publishes on average fifty to sixty titles a year, and currently has about eight hundred books in print.

The growth of the Press has been neither smooth nor steady, wrote historian Carolyn Niethammer in a small booklet celebrating its first twenty-five years. In fact, after the first fourteen years the Press's annual financial deficit was so dire that it faced closure. For much of its early

history, the Press had to cope with chronic shortages of the basic elements of paper and ink, and it made do with equipment so outdated even the manufacturer expressed disbelief it was still functioning. One book was passed to a large local printer—this was in the days of setting type by hand—which then confessed it had lost its letter T and suggested that the press reedit the manuscript to remove the letter from the book. Help occasionally came from unexpected quarters. In 1967, Egypt and the United States severed diplomatic relations over Israel, and the US Embassy closed down, donating the contents of its own printshop, along with its own experienced foreman to run it all, to the AUC Press.

As with the Cresswell book, other early AUC Press titles were never likely to trouble the bestseller lists, although there were books that remain consistent sellers until today, notably Ahmed Fakhry's *The Oases of Egypt* and Richard Parker's *A Practical Guide to Islamic Monuments in Cairo*. It was the latter that, in spring 1974, gave newly appointed AUC Press director John Rodenbeck the idea for a publication. For some years, university wives had produced *Hand Me Downs*, a small volume of advice on living in Egypt for incoming faculty. Rodenbeck had several local and expatriate Cairenes add fresh research and published the book as *Cairo: A Practical Guide*. Its first printing of six thousand copies immediately sold out. Over the next thirty- »

▲ The AUC Press is the largest English-language book publisher in the Middle East. Its books regularly win international publishing and translation awards. "Clearly, we're doing something right," says editor Jody Baboukis

> "When I wrote *The Yacoubian Building*, the AUC Press published it in English. That was the beginning of my international success."
>
> Novelist Alaa Al Aswany, *above*, with Omar Sharif

seven years it was consistently revised and reprinted in new editions, reaching a seventeenth in 2011. Fewer expatriates in Cairo since the Revolution and the fact that the sort of practical information in which the guide deals is now easily obtainable online mean that there are no plans currently for an eighteenth edition.

Rodenbeck also secured the rights to publish English-language editions of the works of Naguib Mahfouz, beginning with *Miramar* in 1978. When, ten years later, Mahfouz was awarded the Nobel prize for literature it was a massive boost for the Press, not only in terms of revenue but in international profile—a story taken up elsewhere in this book (see pp240–42). By this time, Rodenbeck, a professor in the Department of English and Comparative Literature, had decided to return to teaching. He was replaced as director of the Press by Mark Linz, who had previously headed several publishing companies in New York. During his tenure, Linz significantly expanded the publishing program, adding full-color books, guidebooks to Egypt, co-edition deals with major international publishers, and more Mahfouz. The Press also increased its commitment to the translation of Arabic literature into English, beginning with classic authors of the likes of Yusuf Idris, Taha Hussein, and Ghassan Kanafani, but increasingly taking chances on little-known and first-time writers. This policy paid off spectacularly when, in 2004, AUC Press published the English-language edition of Alaa Al Aswany's debut novel *The Yacoubian Building*, which became an international, Dan Brown-sized bestseller.

"One peculiar feature of AUC Press," says current director Nigel Fletcher-Jones, "is that it's often the first point of contact that people in other parts of the world have with AUC." Better known internationally than its parent institution, the Press is thus a major marketing tool for AUC outside Egypt. That exposure in foreign markets has become even more valuable since the events of 2011, after which the revenue raised from the sales of AUC Press titles overseas began outstripping that made in Cairo and Egypt.

The Press currently costs the university a substantial amount a year, but Fletcher-Jones believes that once the tourists return to Egypt there is a good chance of edging into profit. Not that profit should be the defining criterion on which a university press is judged. As American newsman Dan Rather stated in a speech given to the Association of University Presses in June 2017, in an era of gossip, disinformation, and fake news, university presses, with their focus on research, stand as a "bulwark of truth"—and what price on that? ◈

▶ Some of the Press's all-time best-selling titles

11

SETTING THE PROTOCOL

As late as 1970, AUC still had an undefined academic and legal status within Egypt

▲ Vice President Ahmed Abdel Ghaffar Saleh, with daughter and prima ballerina Magda Saleh

By the end of the 1960s, two questions of long-standing concern had come to a head. One was the recognition of the university's degrees within Egypt. The second, larger question concerned AUC's legal status in Egypt. The government was planning to enact what was known as Law 52 for "organizing higher private institutes." This would put operations like AUC under the strict supervision of the Ministry of Higher Education—unless some good reason for exemption could be found.

On the matter of the recognition of degrees, most people understood that AUC offered a good education and that was sufficient to keep students enrolling. But the simple fact was that the diploma offered by AUC was not recognized by the Egyptian government, which meant that AUC graduates could not get governmental jobs.

In order for AUC's degrees to have equal standing with those of Egypt's national universities, the People's Assembly and new president Anwar Sadat would have to give their approval.

Before this could happen, it was necessary for every department at AUC to extensively detail their courses and curricula, and prove that they were the equal of, if not better than comparative courses taught at other Egyptian universities. While this was going on, Vice President Ahmed Abdel Ghaffer Saleh opened discussions with Egypt's Supreme Council of National Universities to ensure that AUC's case was heard.

When it came to Law 52, it was discovered that there was an "escape clause" that exempted institutions established "within the framework of cultural agreements by foreign countries." The only problem was that at this time the United States was out of favor and its embassy had been closed after America supported Israel in the 1967 War (see pp58–59). Nevertheless, in summer 1971, just prior to the implementation of Law 52, the United States informed Egypt's Ministry of Foreign Affairs that it considered AUC to be a cultural institute within the framework of an existing 1962 US–Egyptian cultural agreement. The Egyptian government responded that it accepted this view and

14

PROTOCOL

PROTOCOL

Between the Government of the Arab Republic of Egypt and Board of Trustees of the American University in Cairo, Incorporated in Washington, D. C. in the United States of America, concerning the Status and Organization of the American University in Cairo.

Whereas the cultural agreement concluded between the Government of Egypt and the Government of the United States of America on 21st May 1962 provided in its first Article for the establishment of cultural centers and institutes in the country of the other party, and lays down in its fourth Article that both Governments shall encourage close cooperation between the cultural and professional organization and the educational, scientific and cultural institutes existing in their respective countries;

And whereas the United States Government considers the American University in Cairo to be a cultural institute falling within the scope of Article 1, Paragraph (d) of said cultural agreement and within the provisions of Article 1, Paragraph (a) of Law no. 52 of 1970;

And whereas it is the intent of the Board of Trustees of the American University in Cairo, being the ultimate authority in all matters affecting the institution, to cooperate constructively with competent authorities in the Arab Republic of Egypt in order that said University may perform its educational activities in the best possible manner;

AFT

Cecil K. Byrd

◄ Among other things, the 1975 Protocol sets the target ratio for American vs Egyptian faculty members (50/50) and for the make up of the student body (not less than 75% Egyptian) at AUC

PRESIDENT #6
CECIL BYRD
(1974–77)
Byrd came to AUC from Indiana University to serve as a consultant on the construction of AUC's new library building. In 1973, he was appointed dean of the faculties. When President Thoron became seriously ill, Byrd was named acting president. His position was made permanent upon Thoron's death in 1974. Under Byrd the final protocol with the Egyptian government was signed in 1975. On leaving AUC he returned to Indiana University as a professor and librarian at the Lilly Library.

would exempt AUC from the law. "It gives the university a firm and specific legal basis for its existence for the first time," said President Christopher Thoron.

However, clearly at this time the political climate was unfavorable for approval. It took a further four years, until diplomatic relations were resumed between the United States and Egypt, before on 13 November 1975 a protocol was finally signed.

The protocol (which included recognition of AUC degrees) brought the university into the educational mainstream, stamping it with a respectability that now made it acceptable for parents to send their children to AUC in far greater numbers than ever before. ⊛

12

THE STORM CENTER OF WAR

The 1939–45 global conflict had little real impact on AUC, but the university lost its founder and president

---

At the end of each academic year the president prepares a written summary of the past twelve months at AUC and submits it to the Board of Trustees. President Charles Watson's report for the year 1941–42 was a little more dramatic than usual.

Gentlemen—

This Report has been prepared under circumstances of exceptional difficulty. With the entire American staff and their families scattered by military evacuation, some to the Anglo-Egyptian Sudan and some to Eritrea, far removed from Cairo and its official records, it may well be imagined that in some respects this record of the year 1941–42 will leave something to be desired. Furthermore, under such circumstances, it is difficult to carry oneself back to the peaceful atmosphere and sense of security belonging to the first eleven months of the year, following which the storm of war swept upon us with startling suddenness, threatening to engulf us and our work with total disaster.

The war that broke out in Europe in September 1939, and gradually seeped around the globe, took a year to reach Egypt. In September 1940, the Italian army in Libya advanced across the border toward Marsa Matruh. Allied forces in Egypt put them to flight, gave chase, and captured Tobruk. Far removed from the fighting though it was, seen from AUC, Cairo nevertheless had the appearance of a warzone city: British military headquarters were in Garden City, a short distance from the university, while across the square Allied troops filed in and out of Qasr al-Nil barracks. On campus, windows were boarded against possible air raids, and walls and fences were topped with barbed wire in case of street riots. Otherwise, university life progressed as normal.

By January 1942, the situation had changed. Germany had dispatched a large, well-equipped army to North Africa. It drove the British and their allies back out of Libya and sent them into retreat along

the Mediterranean coast. By 30 June the Germans had reached Alamein, just sixty miles from Alexandria. The port city suffered heavy air raids, but in Cairo many believed the Germans planned to by-pass Alexandria altogether and occupy the capital within the next twenty-four hours. On 1 July the British Embassy and military headquarters in Cairo began burning documents, and the air over Qasr al-Aini was thick with smoke and charred bits of paper floating down like black snow.

Not that many of the American faculty of AUC were around to witness what became known as Ash or Black Wednesday. Just the previous evening, thirteen of them had been evacuated by train to Aswan. On arrival, they transferred to a stern-wheeled steamer that took them to Wadi Halfa on the border with Sudan. Another train then bore the party across the Nubian desert to Khartoum. Back in Cairo, the last three American AUCians evacuated themselves to Suez to find passage aboard a ship.

The American party in Sudan, which included the seventy-one-year-old Charles Watson, stayed just outside Khartoum at a mission school. Conditions were primitive. They shared a three-room shack, ≫

▲ Photographs from an album kept by one of the AUCians evacuated to Khartoum in 1942 show the mission school compound where they stayed, a lunch scene, and the laundry room

"Doubtless your thought of us is that we are at the storm center of war."

Charles Watson, in a letter, 4 November 1940

men in one room, women in another, and women with children in the third. It rained nearly every day and when it didn't there were dust storms. The three AUC faculty who sailed from Suez, meanwhile, were landed at Massawa in Eritrea.

In Khartoum, Watson was in a contemplative mood as he compiled his annual report to the trustees. "As to the future, many are the questionings that can be listed," he wrote. "Will Egypt, even yet, come under the blighting influences of Nazi occupation? Will this world war continue across 1943 and 1944 or even longer? Will Egyptian nationalism restrict or even shackle the University's freedom of action in coming years? Will American philanthropy be equal to the maintenance and development of the American University at Cairo? To these and many other questionings the only answer is in patient waiting upon God."

The answer to the first of those questions came sooner rather than later. The Allied armies defeated the Germans at Alamein and the Americans began leaving Sudan to return to Cairo. Classes for the new year began at AUC on 21 September. An unexpected consequence of the war was a spike in student numbers. Travel restrictions prevented many who might have done so from traveling to Europe for a university education and they enrolled at AUC instead. Many of these new students came from the Greek, Syrian, Armenian, Palestinian, and Jewish communities. Meanwhile, AUC diverted resources to the war effort. It invited the American Red Cross to set up a forces' canteen on the university athletic field, and offered the soldiers special courses in Arab and Egyptian culture.

Answers to some of Watson's other questions would come eventually but the president would not be around to receive them. Not long after returning from Sudan he became seriously ill. Doctors gave him little chance of survival. In fact, he recovered, but age and overwork were clearly taking their toll and his retirement was imminent. The selection of his successor was relatively straightforward: Watson favored the man who had been dean since 1938, John Badeau (see p35). The trustees agreed unanimously.

In late July 1945, Watson and family boarded a ship at Port Said for their journey back to America. "This, my last report as president, is being written under considerable limitations," he wrote. "At the moment I am on board the SS *Fernplant* on my way to USA, but taking cargo at Mersin, Turkey." It would be his final voyage. Back in the United States, Watson set to fundraising but he suffered a cerebral hemorrhage and, on 10 January 1948, AUC's founder and president for its first twenty-five years, died at Bryn Mawr, Pennsylvania. ✣

▶ A letter sent by AUC president Charles Watson to Friends of the American University in Cairo in which he describes the effects of war on the life of the city

PRIVATE AND CONFIDENTIAL

Dated in Cairo March 22, 1941 this letter came by air mail across the Pacific via Sydney, Auckland and San Francisco arriving in Philadelphia on April 25th. It has been printed in America and is being mailed immediately to the University's friends.

113, Sharia Kasr-el-Aini,
Cairo, Egypt.
March 22, 1941.

To the Friends of The American University at Cairo:

My mind naturally goes back to November when I wrote you last. After a summer of anxiety over the possibility of an Italian invasion on the West and frequent air-raid alarms that sent us scurrying at all hours of the night down to our shelters in the basement, there came the organization and steady advance of General Wavell's expeditionary forces westward. Air raid alarms became more and more rare as the Italians had quite enough to do at the front not to trouble us innocent people in the rear. To be sure an occasional alarm was sounded in Cairo, as planes flew high overhead with the Suez Canal as their objective, so we have been kept in practise, but without much real anxiety. Now the Germans are coming into the picture of this Middle Near East and our sense of peace is once again disturbed, not in the least with any fear of invasion, but solely in respect to possible bombing. One felt that the Italians were mindful of their 65,000 countrymen in Egypt's great cities and were also disinclined to work destruction on territory they hoped to possess. But no such reassurances are ours as to the Germans in case they establish air bases to the north of us in Greece.

Cairo has all the ear-marks of a war zone city. The streets are crowded with soldiers on leave. What a variety of uniforms, mostly Australians and New Zealanders, but also Scotch Highlanders, Free French and others, not to overlook the nurses with their bright red capes. Our Cairo streets were never meant to carry the heavy traffic of local life plus military trucks, whether Egyptian or British. The noise of this traffic reaches into the midnight watches and with our all but total blackout, night driving is hazardous. My car has just had its fenders painted white, with a white band across the back, to impart to it some additional visibility for night trips.

Almost everybody is engaged in some form of war work, at least for such time or strength as can be spared from one's regular occupation. Clubs are being opened for the soldiers. Sewing groups seem to be at work everywhere. There is also much personal service rendered. For example, Mrs. Watson and I have set aside Sunday night for soldiers we can bring home with us from church, just to give them a glimpse of a home and a taste of a home dinner and a chance for some hymn singing around the piano. How they can sing and how they can eat too! The trouble is to know how many to provide for. Last Sunday I was instructed to bring home eight, but I made a catch of thirteen, making us seventeen in all. So it was a case of F. H. B. (family hold back). It opens up so many human relationships. We learn of this boy's mother and sweetheart, or the other's wife and children. After weeks comes a letter from the mother in New Zealand, who writes to thank us for a kindness to her boy. Others, too, are rendering similar services. But how we wish it could be done for all, as we see them by the hundreds in the streets.

13

MAKING FRIENDS IN THE NEW EGYPT

When the Free Officers took control of Egypt in 1952, no one knew how, but it was sure to affect AUC in some way

When, after twenty-five years, Charles Watson resigned from the AUC presidency in 1944 it was the end of an era. Nobody knew it yet, but the end of an era was fast approaching for Egypt, too. Its arrival was announced early in the morning of 23 July 1952, when a young army officer named Anwar al-Sadat broadcast on Cairo Radio that there had been a revolution. Within a matter of days, King Farouk was sent into exile and the military men were in charge. Sweeping political, social, and economic changes followed. Watson's successor, President Badeau, greeted these developments as a "fresh sea breeze"—one that "had blown across the dusty land carrying away its heat and haze." If there had been any worries that heightened nationalist fervor might have made life difficult for a high-profile, foreign-funded institution these fears were quickly allayed when newly installed president General Mohamed Naguib and revolutionary leader Colonel Gamal Abdel Nasser honored the university by appearing at its Arabic Language Day Convocation in early 1954.

Other foreign presences were less welcome in Egypt, and the new government demanded Britain remove its troops from the Suez Canal Zone. As the last foreign soldiers left Port Said, the dean of AUC sent a congratulatory letter to Nasser—now president of Egypt—on behalf of the university, and received a reply of "cordial gratitude." In July 1956, Nasser went a step further when he announced that Egypt was nationalizing the canal, which had been owned and operated by a joint British-French consortium since its construction in 1869. International tensions escalated until in October the British, French, and Israelis launched a joint invasion of Sinai and the Canal Zone.

Strategic sites around Cairo were bombed by enemy aircraft and as a precaution the Egyptian government required that all schools and universities be closed. Almost all AUC's American staff, along with most other Americans in Egypt, were evacuated by sea to Europe. A few stayed behind to assist the Egyptian staff who, of course, remained.

There were also twenty or thirty students who lived at the hostel on campus, mostly from Jordan and Palestine, and they were joined by a few university families, most of whom lived near the military airfields that were receiving attention from the enemy bombers. Many students enlisted, either as nurses or orderlies in the hospitals or as combatants in the Egyptian army. Meanwhile, the evacuated AUCians set up a university in exile in Geneva, where they held seminars to discuss academic issues and plan for their return.

As it happened, that return was quick in coming. The fighting was over in a matter of weeks, the aggressors forced by the United Nations to withdraw. Classes resumed on 26 December. To make up for the lost teaching time, ten minutes was added to each fifty-minute class through until the end of February. In this way, the university was able to finish its semester only one month behind schedule and students could finish their academic year without loss of credit. »

▲ American relief supplies for war victims are landed in Egypt, where the local reception committee includes AUC president Raymond McLain (left)

-2-

AMERICAN UNIVERSITY AT CAIRO

October 30, 1956

10:00 A.M.

The University Council has asked that the statement given below be circulated to all foreign staff.

"The position of the University Council in relation to the recent military movements of Israel is substantially that taken by the United States Embassy. All Western staff, particularly dependents, not performing essential functions are strongly encouraged to avail themselves of the evacuation facilties arranged by the Embassy. It is emphasized that the Embassy cannot order American non-government nationals to leave. The gravity of the situation, however, is also emphasized and any foreign staff member should feel completely free to leave Egypt should he or she wish to do so."

It is pointed out that this statement is as of the time indicated. All Western staff are requested to be available by telephone or to leave word how they may be reached quickly. Any person wishing to discuss their personal situation may call the President's Office (21830).

Raymond F. McLain
President

Meanwhile, the university council set up a blood bank on the campus, with President Raymond McLain, who succeeded Badeau in 1954, the first to donate. It solicited donations of clothing, and set up a sewing center to repair any damaged items before turning them over to the Ministry of Social Affairs for distribution. The university launched a fund-raising campaign, beginning with the faculty and students, and extending to supporters in America. Almost $50,000 was raised and used for the purchase of food and medicines, as well as a pump to reirrigate land around al-Arish and a jeep to help get aid to Bedouin tribes in Sinai.

Despite its brevity, repercussions arising from the Suez War created some serious long-term problems for AUC. Egyptian nationalism had hardened into a strong anti-foreign stance that saw the minority communities upon which AUC had depended for a substantial percentage of its students leave Egypt in great numbers. Meanwhile, Egyptians were less inclined to send their sons and daughters to an American college. The government introduced legislation that stipulated that every foreign school in Egypt should be owned and led by citizens of the newly formed United Arab Republic. AUC was faced with a dilemma: should it comply with the new law or should it liquidate itself and reopen elsewhere in the Middle East?

One hope was that the decades of good service AUC had provided the people of Egypt might be leveraged in the university's favor. "I believe it can be said . . . that the university proved itself to be a friend of Egypt and the Middle East in this particular period of crisis," wrote President McLain. "It is probably held in warmer regard right now by the Government, in spite of strained relations between Egypt and America, than at any time in its thirty-seven years of history." A personal appeal was made to President Nasser with the eventual result that AUC was exempted from the new law.

There are claims that as a young, unknown colonel, Nasser used to attend the public lectures at Ewart Hall, and there are those who speculate that one of the reasons that the Egyptian president was ultimately protective of AUC was because he recognized that it was not a colonial institution. Whatever the truth, AUC remained the only foreign educational facility in Egypt to continue operating substantially outside the government's control. At least for the moment. ❀

◀ A letter sent out by the administration advising all foreign faculty to leave the country as AUC closed, in line with all Cairo's other universities and schools

PRESIDENT #3
RAYMOND McLAIN (1954–63)
Ohio native McLain was president of Eureka College in Illinois at age thirty-one and later president of Transylvania College, Kentucky before AUC decided his experience might make him the right man to succeed John Badeau. When he arrived, AUC was still dependent on a very few donors, largely United Presbyterians, for its finances; McLain sourced new corporate donors and secured US government funding. He never learned Arabic (he believed it better to speak good English than poor Arabic) but became good friends with journalist Mohamed Hassanein Heikal, who he used as a conduit for messages to President Nasser.

14

SAVED BY THE INVENTORY

In the aftermath of the 1967 War, AUC came perilously close to being nationalized, renamed, and potentially dismembered

On Monday 5 June 1967 sirens wailed across Cairo. They had sounded in the weeks before but those were only drills. Now, puffs of anti-aircraft fire and the distant sound of explosions left city residents in no doubt that this time it was real. The conflict between Egypt and Israel that had been threatening for several weeks had erupted.

On Tuesday morning rumored reports of American and British assistance to Israel were widely and repeatedly circulated by all news media. At the suggestion of AUC Vice-President Dr. Ahmed Saleh, the university requested police protection as a precautionary measure and the government responded by placing guards around the grounds. At about midday, the university was informed that American staff should leave as soon as possible, since popular sentiment made protection of foreigners increasingly difficult. That evening American faculty and students boarded a blacked-out train for Alexandria, where they waited for a ship to take them over to Greece.

While in Alexandria AUC president Thomas Bartlett received a telephone call from Dr. Saleh to inform him that the Egyptian government had sequestered the university. This was not nationalization, but it put the university in the temporary custody of the government. In the days to come it was possibly the saving of AUC.

The government appointed Egyptian scientist Dr. Hussein Said as its special sequestrator. If the Egyptian government was going to take over AUC, it could not have picked a better man for the job. Said had served on the AUC University Council and, at one point, had been asked to serve as the university's vice-president, a role which he had only turned down because he had already been asked to serve as Egypt's minister of higher education.

On 9 June, President Nasser announced over the radio that he was resigning and immediately crowds streamed on to the streets demanding he remain. On Tahrir Square a crowd gathered outside AUC demanding it be razed. Said personally addressed the mob leaders, explaining the

▲ While Nasser's government closed the US Embassy in 1967, it was keen to preserve the American University

university now belonged to Egypt and if it were burned down it would be Egypt's loss, not America's. He reassured them that the name "The American University in Cairo" would be removed from the façade.

The name was covered rather than removed. Meanwhile, there were calls for full nationalization of AUC. Some called for it to be renamed as the "Palestine University" and for its assets to be shared between other Egyptian universities. In order to forestall any hasty action, Dr. Said insisted that before anything happened there needed to be a complete inventory. Teams were formed to meticulously record every item: every bit of property, every piece of furniture, every one of the tens of thousands of books in the library. The task took all summer, by which time cooler heads prevailed and the government was no longer so set on getting rid of the American University.

In fact, with the start of the academic year in October, Egypt began slowly to allow the return of some of the American staff—even though diplomatic relations with the United States had been severed and its embassy in Cairo closed. All this time, the American faculty, staff, and students were scattered worldwide. Temporary jobs had been found for some lecturers with US universities, others used the time for research; the Center for Arabic Study Abroad operated out of the University of California at Berkeley, staffed in part by faculty from AUC. Five ≫

"What happens in the next several months could determine the ultimate fate of the university."

Christopher Thoron,
17 August 1967

▶ Palestinian students started arriving at AUC in numbers in the mid 1940s. When anti-American protestors stoned the university in 1967, Palestinians offered to pay for the damages

PRESIDENT #4
THOMAS BARTLETT
(1963–69)
Stanford and Oxford graduate Thomas Bartlett was thirty-three at the time of his appointment but had already distinguished himself at the United Nations. During his time in office he was responsible for much of the expansion and construction of AUC's Downtown campus, including the purchase and remodeling of the Greek Campus, and he ably negotiated the university through the fallout of the 1967 War. Since stepping down, he has retained close ties to AUC, serving as a member of the Board of Trustees and, in 2002, briefly returning to serve as interim president.

American members of faculty, including the dean, Richard Crabbs, were allowed to return during the first semester. More were slowly permitted to come back during the second semester, by the end of which there were over fifty foreign faculty back at work at AUC, including thirty-six Americans. The only hiccup was the Egyptian authorities' refusal to grant AUC librarian James C. Van Luik a work permit, because they accused him of being pro-Copt and anti-Muslim.

Around this time, a journalist from CBS News asked President Thomas Bartlett why AUC had been allowed to open when anti-Americanism still prevailed in Egypt. "The reason," he replied, "is that these people have come to respect us and the institution as being what we say we are and that is no one's special pleader, but rather people who are genuinely interested in research, scholarship, education, and service."

The sequestration remained in effect, which was a matter of concern to the Board of Trustees and the US government, but the arrangement proved manageable. Thomas Bartlett and Hussein Said had worked together for years. While Said occupied what was the presidential office at the university, Bartlett created a new presidential office in a former conference room. In the words of Bartlett, the sequestration continued to be a formality rather than a matter of substance—although when pushed by a faculty member wanting to know who was really running things, he warned, "Don't try to find out which one of the nutshells has the nut under it."

The sequestration would continue through until 1975, when diplomatic relations between the United States and Egypt were finally resumed. It did not adversely affect the university. If anything, the careful Egyptian stewardship of this US-funded institution only served to underline the value of AUC to Egypt. For conclusive proof of this, Egyptians only had to note that among the students returning to AUC in October 1967 was President Nasser's younger daughter, Mona, who was beginning her senior year.

There is a story from around this time involving another of Nasser's children. President Bartlett's wife, Molly, used to drive around Cairo in a red Fiat sports car. It was not a particularly expensive car, but in a country that at the time had few imported foreign vehicles, it stood out. It certainly caught the eye of one of Mona's brothers, who made it known he would like to borrow the car for a weekend. There was no question of refusing. It was returned on the Monday all banged up. The Bartletts decided not to inform the boy's father for fear of creating an incident and had the car repaired. Both sides, the AUC and the Egyptian government, were prepared, quietly and, if necessary, behind the scenes, to do whatever was necessary to maintain a harmonious relationship. ✸

15

THE DEATH OF MANSOUR

The Islamic terror attacks of the late 1980s and 1990s came uncomfortably close to AUC

At around 11am on 18 August 1993, the peace of a summer campus was shattered by an explosion. It happened just off Tahrir Square, near the university's Sheikh Rihan gate. Explosives attached to a motorcycle were detonated as a car conveying the minister of the interior, Hassan al-Alfi, was passing by. This was not the first bomb attack to rattle the university. Six years earlier, in April 1987, a fanatic tossed two Molotov cocktails into the campus grounds. He claimed to be a member of Hizbullah who was protecting Egyptians from the corruption of American policy. No one was hurt. The 1993 attack was more deadly. The minister survived the assassination attempt, later confirmed to have been carried out by Islamic Jihad, but four others were killed, including the two suicide bombers and a ministerial bodyguard. The fourth fatality was Mansour Sheheta, a car-parking attendant on Sheikh Rihan Street, who was well known to staff and students at AUC.

AUCians have always had a love–hate relationship with the *menadis*, or parking attendants. AUC has never had any sort of designated parking facilities downtown, so students have always had to park on the surrounding streets, paying a small fee to the menadis for the privilege. Better than using the municipal car park in al-Bustan, which charges by the hour. Except over the years there have been incidents, like the student who left his car keys with the menadi, as is the custom, only to find on his return that ninety kilometers had been added to the odometer. There have been fights between students and menadis, complaints to the police, and even the occasional arrest.

Mansour, however, was a popular figure, nicknamed the "king of Sheikh Rihan." "Mansour was a wizard," remembers Samia Mehrez, who teaches modern Arabic literature at AUC. "He managed our cars and also our schedules on campus flawlessly. He used to wear a kind of military jacket with many pockets where he kept all our keys. He was a ball of energy. I don't know how he

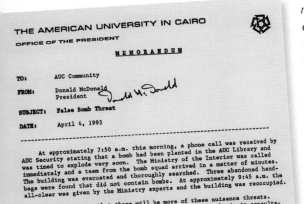

THE AMERICAN UNIVERSITY IN CAIRO

OFFICE OF THE PRESIDENT

MEMORANDUM

TO: AUC Community

FROM: Donald McDonald
         President

SUBJECT: False Bomb Threat

DATE: April 4, 1993

At approximately 7:50 a.m. this morning, a phone call was received by AUC Security stating that a bomb had been planted in the AUC Library and was timed to explode very soon. The Ministry of the Interior was called immediately and a team from the bomb squad arrived in a matter of minutes. The building was evacuated and thoroughly searched. Three abandoned handbags were found that did not contain bombs. At approximately 9:45 a.m. the all-clear was given by the Ministry experts and the building was reoccupied.

We fully expect that there will be more of these nuisance threats. Decisions will be made about each one on a case by case basis in consultation with the Ministry of the Interior.

▲ There was a time, not long ago, that bomb threats and terrorist attacks were a fact of life

▲ Finding somewhere to leave the car around AUC Downtown has never been easy, not in the 1990s when this photo was taken, and not now

did it." Car owners used to pay him one or two pounds a month—which, at the time, was a substantial amount of money—and rumors were that Mansour was a very rich man.

He is memorialized in Ahdaf Soueif's 1999 novel *The Map of Love*. One of the book's characters remembers how whenever she arrived at Sheikh Rihan Street Mansour would be there, waving and saying, "Leave it just. Leave it. Don't worry." She would hand over the keys and when she came back he would be there, with the keys, to point out where he had parked the car. "Mansour was famous. He acquired two assistants; but he was always the one who had the keys. He was the one who was always there, until one day, the bomb the Jama'at meant for al-Alfi, the minister of interior they hated, had found Mansour instead. And now all that was left of him was a pale brown stain on the wall of the university. A stain that would not scrub off."

In the chaotic aftermath of the bombing, the badly wounded Mansour was carried into the university and laid down in the corridor leading to Oriental Hall. This is where he died. Sheikh Rihan Street died with him, too, because after the assassination attempt the street—which leads to the Ministry of the Interior—was permanently closed to traffic and parking for security reasons.

The "two assistants" to which Soueif refers are Mansour's brothers, Ali and Reda. They still work parking cars around AUC. ❀

16

AND THEN THE REVOLUTION BROKE OUT

How does
a university
administration
respond to a
national uprising?

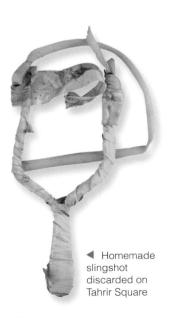

◄ Homemade
slingshot
discarded on
Tahrir Square

Lisa Anderson was less than a month into her AUC presidency when, on Tuesday 25 January 2011, around 15,000 protestors converged on Tahrir Square to begin the eighteen days of protest that would bring to an end the presidency of Hosni Mubarak. Anderson's immediate response was to convene an Emergency Management Team (EMT), composed of the university cabinet and the directors of security, communications, IT, and transportation, among others. The team met on Wednesday, Thursday, and again on Saturday, by which time the internet and mobile phone service had been out for around thirty-six hours, making communications all but impossible (AUC no longer kept a central list of landline numbers). On the Saturday the team learned that the Tahrir Campus had been broken into on the Friday night by both police and protestors, and had suffered damage as a result. It was decided that both the Tahrir and New Cairo campuses, where classes for the spring semester had been scheduled to start on the following day, should be officially closed.

Those members of the EMT who could, continued to meet daily throughout the following week, sometimes on the New Cairo Campus, at other times at the president's residence in Maadi. The latter was convenient given many EMT members were also living in Maadi. Here, as in much of Cairo, the streets were eerily quiet, with tanks and soldiers posted at main intersections. EMT meetings typically had three agenda items: what was going on with the two campuses; how were faculty and staff reacting; and what to anticipate next.

University security officers, drivers, and custodians were asked to work overtime to ensure the safety of AUC people and premises as the police abandoned the streets. Anderson and the vice-president, Brian MacDougall, regularly toured the two campuses, as well as faculty housing in Maadi and Rehab, and student residences in Zamalek. Meanwhile, payday arrived. The CIB bank agreed to give AUC a million Egyptian pounds in cash, which was used to provide an advance to any AUC employee who needed it. The EMT set up cashiers around Cairo,

one of whom was a twenty-two-year-old presidential intern living in Zamalek, Sarah Christian. She was told, "Sarah, a man is going to come and he's going to give you a large envelope containing 90,000 pounds."

Safety fears worsened as pro-regime forces provoked violent clashes on and around Tahrir Square. On Tuesday 1 February, the US Department of State ordered the evacuation of all non-essential US government personnel and family members from Egypt. Many American students were required by their home institutions to leave Egypt, and about »

▲ Revolutionary Monopoly. "Go to jail. Do not pass Go. Do not collect £200"

DOCUMENTING THE REVOLUTION

All the objects on these pages relating to the 2011 Revolution and its aftermath come from a collection entitled The University on the Square: Documenting Egypt's 21st Century Revolution, which is held by AUC's Rare Books and Special Collections Library. In addition to the sort of physical detritus shown here, gathered by activists, participants, and observers, many from AUC, the collection includes oral histories, photographs, video recordings, and visual art. Much of this can be accessed online.

▶ A cardboard flyer distributed in the months following the election of Mohamed Mursi to the presidency

220 of the approximately 480 US students did this. A smaller number of non-Egyptian students from elsewhere also left, as did about eighty faculty and staff—all of whom would return later in the month.

On 11 February Tahrir roared at the announcement that Hosni Mubarak was resigning as president. Two days later, on Sunday 13 February, AUC resumed classes. The first task would be to figure out who was still around to teach and how to get the evacuees back. AUC would be the only university operating in Egypt for most of the next month. The postponed February commencements for graduates and undergraduates were held in late March, with the keynote address delivered by President Anderson. She used a version of the speech she had intended for her inauguration, which had been canceled because of the revolution.

▶ A lanyard calling for
President Hosni Mubarak
to step down

In mid-April,
reflecting the mood of the
country, the Suzanne Mubarak
Conference Hall on the New Cairo Campus
now became room P071. In the months to come,
AUC faculty and alumni remained directly involved in the
unfolding national drama. University counselor Amr Salama
was approached to become minister of higher education
and scientific research by presidential candidate Ahmed Shafiq—
subsequently defeated in the 2012 elections by Mohamed Mursi. Trustee
Mohamed ElBaradei was also a presidential candidate until he withdrew
before the elections, while another trustee, Nabil Fahmy, served as
minister of foreign affairs in the short-lived government of Essam Sharaf.

There was no direct impact on AUC after Mohamed Mursi came
to power, other than the same problems that afflicted the rest of Cairo,
notably the electricity blackouts and disruptions caused by protests. But
the turbulence the country was experiencing did find an echo internally
in the form of worker strikes, and particularly acrimonious student
strikes that caused the closure of the New Cairo Campus, and increased
outspokenness within the faculty around issues of budget, tuition, and
working conditions (these stories are told elsewhere in this book, see
pp114–16). All of these challenged the institutional culture at AUC in a
way that had not happened before.

For a newly installed president it was an exciting, if trying, time
to run any institution in Egypt, not least one devoted to research
and learning. Looking back, seven or eight years after those events,
Lisa Anderson professes herself proud of AUC's ability to exhibit
flexibility, resilience, and enthusiasm under circumstances that did not
automatically elicit them. She remembers the humanity of her Ministry
of Interior bodyguards, one of whom took her to the pilgrimage site in
his hometown and another home to meet his wife; the open affection
the students had for each other when fellow student Omar Mohsen was
killed in the soccer riot at Port Said and the campus was completely
heartbroken; the resourcefulness of labor leaders who, without prior
experience in advocacy or negotiation, quickly learned on the job how
to manage their new-found responsibilities. "Hardly a day went by," she
recalls, "when I was not impressed by the ingenuity people displayed in
navigating the unwonted demands of life in a revolution." ⬡

PRESIDENT #11
LISA ANDERSON
(2011–2015)
A specialist on politics in
the Middle East and North
Africa, Anderson served as
AUC's provost from 2008
to 2010 before becoming
president in January 2011,
just in time for the uprising
against Hosni Mubarak's
regime. Fortunately, she
already had experience
overseeing a school at a
time of crisis: she was dean
at Columbia University's
School of International and
Public Affairs in New York
at the time of 9/11. When
the defiance of Tahrir
Square spread to campus,
Anderson also found herself
having to deal with disputes
with university support staff
demanding more rights and
striking students. One of her
notable achievements was
successfully steering AUC,
with calm and wisdom,
through turbulent times.

17

STUDENTS ON THE SQUARE

AUC students bear witness to the events on Tahrir Square, 25 January to 11 February 2011

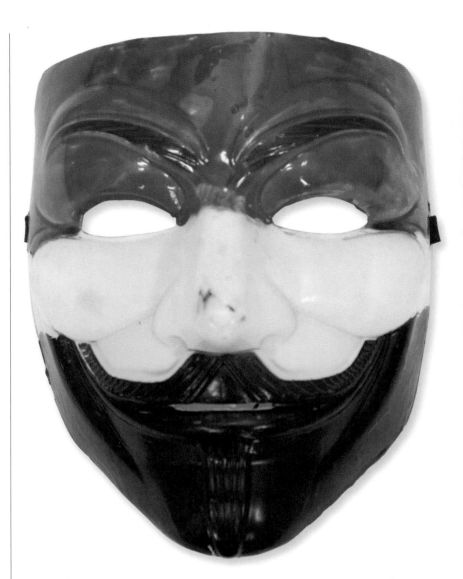

▶ The Guy Fawkes mask associated with the global Occupy movement made it to Tahrir Square, painted in the colors of the Egyptian flag

"I heard about it on Facebook, from the group 'We are all Khaled Said.' Everyone was talking about it. They gave fake venues on Facebook to keep it secret from the police but a friend of mine who's a journalist told me where to meet. It started in a place near Gamaat al-Duwal, a place called Nahya, a very poor area that's behind Sudan Street."
Sarah Abdel Rahman, double major in theatre and journalism

"I was living Downtown on Nubar Street, at the intersection with Mohamed Mahmoud, which is about a half block away from the interior ministry. I knew there were going to be demonstrations in Tahrir on that Tuesday, which was January twenty-fifth. I had gotten an invitation through a Facebook group."
Jordan Schreiber, an American study-abroad student

"We had to walk in twos because there were police everywhere. I got handed a paper with names and numbers of lawyers in case I got detained. It was my first demonstration, like ever, outside the walls of AUC. We started marching towards Gamaat al-Duwal, then Dokki, and then eventually to Tahrir."
Sarah Abdel Rahman

"I remember vividly going out on my balcony and looking down, and every intersection for as far as I could see down my street had police blockades with riot police in full gear. I remember thinking, 'Wow, they're really overreacting.' We went down to this café in Tahrir, two doors from KFC, and we were just drinking tea and smoking shisha, and we saw some protesters coming in from by the Egyptian Museum and we saw, I mean I'm not actually sure if I can claim this, but as far as I know, we saw the actual first clashes of the revolution between protesters and riot police, right there on the north side of the square."
Jordan Schreiber

"Once we got to the square, that's when the violence started—water cannons, which had chlorine, I think, and I ended up puking

everything I ate that morning because I swallowed some chlorine or something. And then the tear gas and then the bricks and then the fighting. I left when it got dark because at that point there was no signal on my phone and my battery was dead."
Sarah Abdel Rahman

"I was in the square on the twenty-fifth with some friends from about 3:30 or 4pm till about midnight. I was standing by the railings next to AUC campus, right next to the book store, just taking video of all clashes going on, and running when they would come, and then going back and filming again. So it was kind of like this back and forth of filming, then uploading it, you know. It was, like, kind of educating people back home, I guess."
Rosa Navarro, American graduate student

"I didn't go to Tahrir on the twenty-fifth because we were still discussing as a family whether or not I would be allowed to go to the demonstrations. But my dad made the point to mum that it was essential for me and my brother to be participants in this. I completely agreed. But we had to wait to see if it was going to be violent or not."
Omneya Mohammed Makhlouf, political science student

"I went to the square with a couple of friends and a tent. I stayed for the duration of the revolution. One of

the major events was the clashes on the third of February. There were some protestors organized by the Muslim Brotherhood. They had five groups of people. The first group picked up paving slabs from the ground, the second group broke them into four pieces, the third group handed them to the protesters on the front line, the fourth group were throwing, and the fifth group was pulling back the injured. The groups were always rotating, so no one got tired of a particular job."
Soliman al-Ashkar, economics undergraduate

"I was shot. Pellets, the small ones, thirteen in my legs. Everyone was saying, don't go to the hospitals because the regime is taking people to prison from the hospitals. So I refused to allow the ambulance to take me. I went to one of the »

field hospitals where medical students and doctors volunteered. Everyone there was injured in their heads and necks, and there was blood all over the place."
Roqaya Farouq Tbeileh, Palestinian student

"I remember a man came up to me and he asked if I was American. I said yes and he held up a tear gas canister and said 'Amrikiya,' and he held up a shot-gun casing and said 'Amrikiya,' and pointed at his head and there was this laceration that must have spanned you know, like, four or five inches and said 'Amrikiya.' And I've never felt that awful about anything in my life.

The fact that my tax dollars and my family's tax dollars went towards buying weapons that were used against a popular pro-democracy uprising was tough to swallow."
Jordan Schreiber

"I saw like a military tank that stopped. And I was wondering why it stopped and then I see that demonstrators are, like, dragging out the soldiers from inside and beating them up. It was a very, very bad scene. Some of us were angry at the demonstrators, so some people started protecting the soldiers. We made them change their clothes so that they'd blend in with the demonstrators. Then there's one guy

saying we should burn the tank and another guy says, like, 'Why would you want to do that? This is our tax money! We're not here to burn things.'"
Mohamed Ahmed al-Gindy, political science graduate

"The square became like my second home. It was like a music festival or a political festival where you get to meet people not from your economic background. Very different people and you are all equal. I have never learned as much as I learned in the square, like, just from interacting with people, especially not from my, you know, AUC bubble."
Sarah Abdel Rahman

▼ The scene on Tahrir Square on 25 February 2011. The AUC campus is marked by the two palms, just to the left of the hulking Mugamma building

"It was very difficult to get food into Tahrir Square, so this was my daily chore. I found a network of Egyptian women, who did the rounds, I didn't know them, I was given the number through a friend. I called and said, 'I hear that you have stuff.' Those people they would go around in the evening in Zamalek, collecting food and medicines, and all that and we would take the stuff. People from the NDP tried to, to you know, to grab the bags and to shout insults at everyone who was coming in with food. But, you know, if you were resilient enough you could get through."
Shahira Idriss, AUC alumna and journalist

"I got to talking with this guy, he was eighteen years old and he was a mechanic. What struck me was he didn't have a good high school education, he didn't go to college, yet he knew so much about the political scene in Egypt. And he knew so much about the revolution and why he was protesting and why he had camped out there for so many days. That was very admirable."
Omneya Mohammed Makhlouf

"On the eleventh, the night that Mubarak stepped down I remember being in the Square and everybody was hugging everybody. I had strangers hugging me. It was this euphoric amazing moment. Even though I wasn't Egyptian I was crying like everybody else, I was just happy to see everybody so excited."
Rosa Navarro

"Of course we all expected that after Mubarak stepped down the world would be perfect. Obviously, we were hit with a reality check. I think it will take at least five to ten years to have a truly democratic nation."
Sarah Abdel Rahman

All interviews took place in 2011 as part of The University on the Square project. ◈

18

IN THE MIDDLE OF IT

While the world's attention was on Tahrir Square, AUC faculty and staff were busy trying to get on with their jobs

———

When the revolution broke out, AUC had a ringside seat, whether anyone liked it or not. "We were not a target for the protestors but we were in the middle," says Mokhtar Shalaby, who was at that time AUC's assistant director of security. Not only does the Tahrir Campus face onto the square, but the streets either side—Mohamed Mahmoud and Sheikh Rihan—were the frequent sites of pitched battles throughout 2011, 2012, and into 2013.

Security guards had to distance themselves from the turmoil to safeguard the Downtown campus. "We didn't want to be associated with any faction in one way or the other," says Shalaby. "Our main aim was to protect AUC property."

The Downtown campus was closed, its gates locked, but that could not stop tear-gas canisters dropping into the university garden. "We didn't throw them back outside otherwise it would look like AUC was taking part in the uprising," says Shalaby. The guards just observed them until the tear gas dispersed.

On the twenty-eighth, the Day of Anger, events took a different turn. Anticipating that this was going to be a difficult day, AUC security guards organized themselves into twenty-four-hour shifts between the Tahrir, Greek, and Falaki campuses. At one point a fire broke out in the police booth just outside the Mohamed Mahmoud gate. The guards put it out using the university's water hoses, but protestors demanded the hoses to use against riot police. "We were afraid that if we said no they'd storm AUC," says Shalaby, "so we kept the water running for a little while before we were gradually able to turn it off."

A Molotov cocktail set fire to a tree near the AUC Bookstore. Worse, the campus was breached. Protestors broke through the old gate facing directly onto Tahrir Square. Some just wanted to escape the tear gas; others seized on stone ornaments and smashed them up to throw at the police. More scarily, riot police broke in through the Sheikh Rihan gate and threatened AUC security with guns. The intruders made their way up

to the roof where they remained for several hours.

The offices of the AUC Press were in this wing of the campus and early the following morning director of the Press Mark Linz went to inspect the damage. Interviewed in 2011 (Linz died in February 2013), he described the scene: "Many offices were completely ransacked, drawers pulled out, . . . computers smashed to the ground, and all the laptops were gone." He proceeded to the roof, which was scattered with spent shells and canisters, and rocks and stones. "There was blood on the roof, puddles of it, and one blood stain which sort of dragged down the stairs and then all of a sudden stopped at a window." **>>**

▲ On 28 January the Tahrir Campus was breached by both protestors and police. The AUC Press offices were ransacked and computers stolen. Among the wreckage the next day, staff found a pair of discarded police boots

▲ The Tahrir Campus wreathed in clouds of tear gas on 23 November 2012 during anti-Morsi protests. The photo was taken by Dillon Bowman, an American student in the Arabic-language program

The only other breach came on 11 November that year, during a period in which the violence around Tahrir was particularly intense and frequently lethal. Protestors broke into Hill House and the Science Building. As well as using the buildings as a vantage point from which to rain down missiles on the street below, they set about looting the buildings. Security managed to stop them with the help of other protestors.

While demonstrations and skirmishes continued in the aftermath of the revolution, some semblance of normality returned to the Tahrir Campus. But it was frequently interrupted. "The occasion that I will never forget," says Deena Boraie, then associate dean of the School of Continuing Education, "is the day the Salafis attacked the American Embassy [11 September 2012]. That was in the early afternoon and the tear gas was really heavy on the square. Our classes were in the palace, which is the most exposed to the tear gas, so I told my team to move them all up to the second floor. Then I got a phone call saying people

◄ Various types of cartridges, including CS gas, were recovered from around the AUC campus, including on the roof, after the events of 28 January

were gasping and dying—I forgot that tear gas rises. That was the dumbest decision I ever made."

Kevin O'Connell, professor of practice in the School of Business and associate dean for Executive Education, arrived in Cairo in fall 2011, during the months that Egypt was being ruled by the Supreme Council of the Armed Forces (SCAF). "I was told by three different people the same thing when I arrived in September—'What a shame you missed all the excitement.' Well they were wrong. I think the excitement had just started."

O'Connell's office is in the Falaki building, Downtown, close to the Interior Ministry. "The streets surrounding us were blocked off with concrete barricades. To get to work I had to go through barbed wire, past tanks, and by people with machines guns." Bizarrely, student enrolment actually increased. "I believe people were seeing that the country was unsettled and thought they'd better prepare themselves. What better thing than to get a postgraduate diploma from the American University?" Classes were occasionally canceled but they were always rescheduled, sometimes at alternative sites, and attendance was good—although the normal 75 percent attendance rule was relaxed. O'Connell remembers one student turning up twenty-five minutes late and on crutches, explaining that he had been the victim of an attempted car-jacking that morning. When he refused to hand over his keys the would-be thieves stabbed him in the thigh.

"It wasn't a very pleasant time," says Deena Boraie. "It lasted over a year and you don't realize it at the time, but the tension builds up. Sometimes with my staff, the husbands and family wouldn't let them come to work. We had to be flexible. But we got through and it didn't harm our reputation." ⬡

> "People were trying to find any place to flee. They broke into the campus, and the police broke in right after them."
>
> Osama Talaat, AUC security guard

19

MOHAMED MAHMOUD STREET

As battles raged on the streets during the Revolution, they were also fought on AUC walls with brushes and paint

The main entrance to the Tahrir Campus was on Mohamed Mahmoud Street, scene of some of the most violent clashes of 2011 to 2013. Many of these were memorialized in murals on Mohamed Mahmoud. The biggest canvas, and a prime site for the graffiti artists, was the wall around AUC. Like a cassette tape, it was recorded on, erased, recorded over again, erased again, in a battle of wills between the furiously prolific artists and the whitewash-teams of the security forces.

As a constantly updated documentation of the events unfolding around Tahrir Square, the AUC wall became an object of fascination for the world's media. Its temporary works included portraits of Mina Danial—a Coptic activist killed in front of Maspero—and Sheikh Emad Eddin Effat, an Azhar cleric allegedly shot to death while protesting in front of the Cabinet building. In late 2011, portraits of men and women with a bandaged eye bore witness to the numerous protestors who had been shot in the face by riot police.

After 2 February 2012, the wall became a public memorial to the seventy-four young men stabbed, beaten, and trampled to death during what should have been a football game in Port Said. During this time, the street was the site of pitched battles, and the air was thick with tear gas, but the artists continued to paint. A new mural depicted portraits of the 'martyrs' with angel wings, mourned by processions of wailing women done in a style that referenced ancient Egyptian tomb paintings.

For nine months, AUC instructed university guards to stop municipal workers from painting over the murals. Eventually the governorate prevailed and the whitewash went on. New paintings, of course, appeared. In 2015 part of the wall itself went. It was pulled down to give workmen and their bulldozers access in their job of demolishing the AUC Science Building, which lay on the other side of the wall. Thankfully, the work was well documented online and in numerous books, including Mia Gröndahl's *Revolution Graffiti* published by the AUC Press. 🏵

▲ In May 2012, the graffiti artists painted the Mohamed Mahmoud wall with a mural of mothers holding portraits of the sons they lost in the Port Said football massacre

20

THE KEEPERS OF CONTINUITY

The Board of Trustees is key to AUC, but who are its members and what do they do?

There was a Board of Trustees even before there was an American University in Cairo. AUC was incorporated in July 1919, but the board came together over four-and-a-half years earlier in November 1914. The first board was formed of representatives of all the American groups involved in sponsoring Charles Watson's proposed new university. From day one, it was decided that this guiding organization should be largely autonomous and self-perpetuating—in other words, it was beholden to no outside agencies and it selected its own members. This remains the case until today. The first and greatest task of the trustees back then was fundraising, which also remains key today.

However, when asked to define the role of the board, current chair Richard Bartlett offers the following: "I like to think of the board as being responsible for intergenerational equity. That is, recognizing that the university was built by prior generations and needs to serve future generations." Bartlett describes the board as the stewards of a perpetual project, balancing the current generation's claims on AUC's programs, resources, and funds with the claim of future generations. "The board is not in charge because it is infallible," says Bartlett, "it is in charge because it has no direct interests. The hope is that it can put itself in a place that it will make hard decisions rather than convenient ones."

In practice, the board meets three times a year, twice in the United States and once in Cairo. They are joined in this by the university's president—who serves at the board's request. At the meetings they consider reports from the university administrators, deans, and financial officers. The aim is not to micromanage the institution but to set policy and safeguard long-term interests. In theory the board does not get involved in the day-to-day finances or academic protocols, it is there to focus on big-picture issues: for example, it was the board's decision to build a new campus. It was then the board's job to raise the funds.

Board members are drawn from the fields of business, academia, diplomacy, and, increasingly, the ranks of AUC alumni. Notable trustees

in recent times have included Ahmed Zuweil and Mohamed ElBaradei. Of the current thirty-one trustees, just over half are American, with eleven Egyptians, which is a substantial advance on the five Egyptian members on the board throughout much of the 2000s. (The majority of the rest of the members come from the Gulf and Saudi Arabia.) Eleven of the trustees are alumni, nine are women, both numbers that have seen a steady rise in the last decade. The average age of the board is also coming down, with recent additions like the AI pioneer Rana El Kaliouby ('98), who at the time of her appointment was still in her thirties. "I think I brought down the average age of the board by quite a bit," she says.

Although the word "job" is used above, it is perhaps inappropriate as job implies a salary. "A lot of students have misconceptions. They think we're paid, which is ridiculous," says Teresa C. Barger, co-founder and managing director of Cartica Capital, a graduate of the CASA program, and a trustee since 2015. "Actually *we* pay. We are of ranging financial means but everyone gives as much as they can." Usually every member of the board makes a personal financial contribution to AUC every year, in addition to the work they do.

On a more unofficial level, it is also expected that trustees will promote AUC in America and elsewhere, spreading the word about the university, raising awareness and interest. "We should be shot if we don't. It's our duty," says Barger. ✿

"I love it.
You get these
amazingly
experienced
people on the
board."

Trustee Rana El Kaliouby

21

CHOOSING A PRESIDENT

What qualifies a person for the top job at AUC and how do they get there?

"The first topic at every board meeting should be, should we fire the president," says chairman of AUC's Board of Trustees Richard Bartlett. "And if the answer is no, then the next question is how can we best support the president?" Obviously, he adds, nobody actually asks the questions out loud, it's purely an intellectual exercise, but so critical is the role of the president that the essential responsibility of the board is to reassure themselves that the office is in good hands.

At the time of writing AUC is on its twelfth president and, reassuringly, none of them have ever been fired, although one was asked to prepare a letter of resignation and a couple did not have their contracts renewed. Just twelve presidents in one hundred years suggests a reassuring soundness of governance. It averages out at roughly eight years in office for each incumbent, except that first president Charles Watson held the reins for a full twenty-five years. Still, even adjusted for Watson, AUC presidents have averaged six or seven years in office, an indication that the board has consistently succeeded in landing the right person for the job (eleven times a man, only once a woman).

When it comes to selecting a new president, AUC's protocol with the Egyptian government requires that it be an American. In the case of the first president, the matter was simple: it was the man who founded AUC, Charles Watson. When he stepped down he nominated his own successor, Dean John Badeau. It was only when Badeau resigned that the university had to undertake its first proper presidential search.

The first two persons approached turned down the job. The third came to Cairo to look around, where he met Gamal Abdel Nasser and the American ambassador before he was sufficiently reassured to accept the position. That was Raymond McLain; on his retirement, the board came up with a few names, one of which was Thomas Bartlett. He was considered by an appointed presidential committee and duly approved.

Christopher Thoron, was already impressing as executive secretary to the board in New York when he was added to the shortlist of potential candidates to succeed Bartlett and soon found himself installed in the presidential office of the Khairy Palace. Since then, the presidential search process has evolved. Former AUC provost Tim Sullivan was on every presidential search committee from the 1970s until 1998, chairing two of them, and playing a role in the selection of four AUC presidents. "The job description was established by the Board of Trustees, as were the basic rules of the game. The Presidential Committee, consisting of faculty and staff, reviewed CVs, participated in the process of setting the short list, and interviewed finalists in Cairo." The Committee made its recommendations, but the board made the final decision.

Sullivan laid out the requirements of the job. "We were always looking for a president who would be a good chief executive officer, and able to function as the chief strategist as well as the chief representative of the university." On strategy he says, "The president of AUC needs to have the ability to deal with policy issues at a strategic level, not merely at the more granular level of day-to-day management." On those executive management skills: "Once strategy is set, the president needs to insure that it is executed." And regarding representation: "AUC's president needs to be able to deal with all of the university's major stakeholders in a manner that advances the interests of AUC."

Examining the backgrounds of past presidents, diplomatic connections are an asset (Bartlett, Thoron, Pedersen, Ricciardone), as is experience with the Ford Foundation (Gerhart, Arnold). Excelling in a key administration post can also pave the way to the top (Badeau, a former dean; Anderson, a former provost).

In addition, Sullivan believes that one of the most important attributes of a good leader is that they are good listeners. "I was always trying to figure out if a candidate would listen to us and engage in a constructive dialogue with faculty, staff, and others. AUC works best when there is a high degree of collegiality." ⬡

PRESIDENT #5
CHRISTOPHER THORON
(1969–74)
A tall, athletic New Englander with a diplomatic background, Thoron came to AUC from the United Nations. What the board did not know when they confirmed him as president was that while working for the US government, Thoron had also represented the CIA. While he was certainly no longer on the books of the intelligence agency during his time with AUC, the revelation had the potential to jeopardize the relationship with the Egyptian government. The board voted to request Thoron's resignation, but the decision was subsequently reversed, leading to several board members quitting. Thoron was president for five years with seemingly no adverse political consequences. He stepped down because of illness and died of cancer soon after.

22

THE HALF-CENTURY CLUB

Honoring the university's longest-serving faculty and staff

In spring 2014 a ceremony took place honoring the three longest-serving members of AUC. Shahira El Sawy, then dean of libraries and learning technologies, Pakinam Askalani, chemistry professor, and Abdel Messih Abdalla Meawad of the travel office, were all bestowed with Legacy of Service medals for their decades of commitment, which at the time were fifty years, fifty years, and sixty-four years respectively.

Shahira El Sawy came to AUC in 1962 to pursue a master's in anthropology. She was invited to fill a temporary vacancy in the social sciences department at the library. She said, "Yes, but only for six months"—that was fifty-seven years ago and she is still at AUC ("I don't know how it happened"). Pakinam Askalani was appointed in September 1964 as an assistant instructor in the chemistry department, although her relationship with AUC goes back even further, to 1958 when she enrolled as an undergraduate. She was one of the first two graduates of the masters of science program. Abdel Messih joined AUC in 1940, during the tenure of the university's second president John Badeau, so when he retired in 2016 he had served under ten of the eleven full presidents AUC had had until that point. He started in the post room but found greatest satisfaction in the 1960s when, alongside Molly Bartlett, wife of President Bartlett, he worked on acquiring and managing faculty housing in Maadi. His last role was to meet and assist new faculty and staff on their first arrival in Egypt. Because of this he was known and held in great affection by many at the university.

Missing from that ceremony in 2014 was Farkhonda Hassan, who also began teaching in 1964 but left the university in 2012, two years shy of her half-century. However, she remains close ties as a professor emerita in the School of Sciences and Engineering. Sohair Mehnna joined AUC's Social Research Center in 1963, where she still directs fieldwork operations. Since 2014, more faculty have joined the half-century club. Two professors of physics, Hosny Omar and Salah Arafa, both began their teaching careers at AUC in 1968. It is no coincidence that all these

scientists should arrive around the same time given that in 1966 the university had just opened a new science building, massively expanding its number of test tubes, Bunsen burners, and white lab coats, as well as the intake of science students, all requiring more teaching staff.

We should also mention others who are no longer working at AUC but who, before they retired, qualified for membership of the half-century club. That list would include Doris Shoukri, who began teaching in 1955 and was for decades the chair of the English and Comparative Literature department. She retired in 2002 but continued to teach classes part-time for many years afterwards. There would also be Adel Beshai, who came to AUC as a student in 1959, then joined the academic staff in 1965 and was a longtime chair of the Economics department until he retired fifty-three years later in 2018. Daisy Fleita also joined AUC's faculty in 1965 and taught chemistry for fifty-one years until she retired in 2016.

Back to those who are still with the university. Professor of mechanical engineering Mahmoud Farag became a full-time member of faculty in 1971; however, he had been tutoring AUC science students part-time since 1969—which means as AUC celebrates its centenary in 2019, Mahmoud has been with the university for precisely half its existence. When he began, there was no engineering department; he helped found it and became its first chair.

Farkhonda Hassan, who remembers clearly the university's seventy-fifth anniversary in 1994, said she can't believe the centennial is this year. "I have been at AUC for more than half a century. I never imagined that I would make it to the centennial, but I really feel happy to be here," Hassan said. "I feel like I am part of AUC and AUC is part of me." ❀

▲ From left to right, Pakinam Askalani, Shahira El Sawy, and Abdel Messih Abdalla Meawad, photographed in 2014 receiving their long-service awards

23

THE SECRET LIVES OF FACULTY

As well as being learned in their subjects, AUC professors and instructors nurture hidden talents

▲ Heavy metal guitarist and sometime professor of journalism, Firas al-Atraqchi

When not advising the budding newshounds of *Caravan*, professor in the Department of Journalism and Mass Communication Firas al-Atraqchi plugs in and shreds heavy metal classics. He used to play rhythm guitar in a band called Masque, whose claim to fame is that they once performed in a Monsters of Rock concert at Cairo Stadium. These days al-Atraqchi jams with students. His colleague in teaching journalism (and a former chair of the department) Mervat Abu Oaf was, along with her sisters Maha, Manal, and Mona (all AUC alumni), and actor brother Ezzat, part of the 4M Band, which took Egypt by storm in the 1980s. They released eight albums and toured the Arab world. Yet another journalism professor, Rasha Abdulla, is both a professional singer and a guitar player, and has performed as both solo artist and part of a band at the Cairo Opera House and Citadel Music Festival. She is also the official voice of Daisy Duck for Arabic-language Disney productions, and records songs and voice-overs for the Arabic version of *Sesame Street*.

No less than three AUC faculty are involved with jazz group MAD*bossa*. Arthur Bos, chair of the Department of Biology and associate professor of marine biology is on guitar and vocals, Carie Forden, professor of psychology is on drums, and Jillian Campana, professor and director of the Theatre program is also on vocals. The group does its own take on jazz standards, many of them Brazilian bossa novas and sambas, and gigs around Cairo.

In the Department of Rhetoric and Composition senior instructor Kathleen Saville is a record-breaking long-distance rower. In 1981, she and her husband rowed across the North Atlantic Ocean from Morocco to Antigua in a twenty-five-foot boat of their own making. In 1984–85, they rowed the South Pacific from Peru to Australia in the same vessel. Saville earned two Guinness world records as the first woman to make these crossings in a rowboat—adventures recounted in her memoir *Rowing for My Life: Two Oceans, Two Lives, One Journey*. Richard Hoath, her colleague in Rhetoric and Composition, is an internationally

▲ The fruits of creativity
from professor of mechanical
engineering Mahmoud Farag

◀ World record-breaking rower
Kathleen Saville and her partner
in American Samoa in 1985

recognized naturalist, who has published extensively on the fauna of
Egypt in scientific journals, popular magazines, and as a columnist for
Egypt Today. His *Field Guide to the Mammals of Egypt* (AUC Press) went
into a second edition in 2009. Fikry Boutros, another senior instructor
in the same department, practices apiculture—keeping bees to produce
honey and royal jelly. He's also a passionate pistol shooter. The two
pastimes are kept quite separate.

Professor emerita in the Department of History Huda Lutfi is well
known these days as one of Egypt's leading artists, but professor of
mechanical engineering Mahmoud Farag also spends his spare time
painting, printing, and sculpting. He has a book on contemporary
sculpture forthcoming from Cambridge Scholars Publishing. Hassan al-
Fawal, professor and dean of the School of Sciences and Engineering, is
also an accomplished artist and his office is decorated with his drawings.
Bahia Shehab, associate professor of practice in the Department of the
Arts, is an internationally recognized street artist. She began during the
revolution in Cairo and has since painted walls in fifteen different cities
so far. She has a book on her work entitled *At the Corner of a Dream*
forthcoming from the UK's Gingko Press. Assistant professor teaching
on public health and scientific thinking Mahmoud Shaltout juggles an
alternative career as a comic artist. Under the name MacToot his work
has featured in publications including *Caravan* and *AUC Times*. He's
currently working on a book project with Lisa White of AUC's Arabic
department, which will be published by the AUC Press in 2020.

Back in the Department of History, assistant professor Mark
Deets is a former helicopter pilot. Not just any helicopter pilot: from ≫

▲ Mark Deets at the controls of a US Marine helicopter as President Bush disembarks

▶ "Those who have no land have no sea"—a quote from Mahmoud Darwish, painted by Bahia Shehab in Kefalonia, Greece, August 2016

May 1999 to December 2002 he was assigned to Marine Helicopter Squadron One (HMX-1) in Quantico, Virginia, the squadron that provides executive rotary-wing transportation for the president, vice president, and cabinet members of the United States. He flew President Clinton from Dublin to Belfast in December 2000 after he had helped secure a peace agreement in Northern Ireland. He flew President Bush back to the White House from Andrews Airbase after his vacation at his Texas ranch in 2001. The following month he flew at 50 meters over the Pentagon as the fires still burned following the attacks of 9/11. He doesn't just teach history, he lived it.

Professor of applied linguistics Reem Bassiouney is also an award-winning novelist, having received the King Fahd Prize for translation for her novel *The Pistachio Seller* in 2009 and the Sawiris Prize in 2010 for best novel. Physics professor Amr Shaarawi also had his first novel *Tokar* published in 2016. It received an award from the Academy of Arabic Language in Cairo as the best historical novel printed in the previous five years. Omid Tofighian, an assistant professor in the Department of Philosophy recently translated the work of Behrouz Boochani, a journalist–refugee who was imprisoned on Australia's Manus island, from Farsi to English; it was published under the title *No Friend but the Mountains: Writing from Manus Prison* and won the Victorian Prize for Literature 2019.

Emeritus professor of English John Rodenbeck has not—to our knowledge—written a novel but while at AUC he acted in both English-

language theatre and as an extra in Egyptian movies. One colleague went to see him play King Henry II in James Goldman's *The Lion in Winter* and afterwards congratulated him on his performance. "Yes, I think I missed my calling," agreed Rodenbeck.

"You wish you'd been an actor?"

"No, a king!"

Associate dean for the Rare Books and Special Collections Library Philip Croom collects houses, specifically nineteenth-century architectural treasures in need of restoration. He has three in the United States; the most recent acquisition is an 1834 mansion with two spiral staircases and walls five bricks thick. Associate dean in the School of Business Kevin O'Connell has a similar interest in historic preservation. He has spent several years renovating a seaside mansion in Massachusetts built by the celebrated nineteenth-century American architect Richard Morris Hunt.

Sherif Abdel Azeem, professor of electronics and communications, founded a charity, Resala, which, among other activities, cares for orphans, provides assistance to the blind, deaf, and others with special needs, offers free tutoring for needy students, collects and distributes used clothes, and offers shelter to street kids. It is now one of the largest such organizations in Egypt. Abdel Azeem was selected by the Egyptian Parliament to be among the committee of fifty Egyptians responsible for writing the Egyptian Constitution in 2012 and he received Egypt's Medal of Excellence in 2013. ⬡

24

MAKING RESEARCH PAY

Scientific research at AUC is resulting in innovation with added commercial potential

A UC has long supported pioneering research across a variety of disciplines. There have been early experiments at introducing sustainable energies into rural communities (Basaisa, see pp196–97), documenting disappearing ways of life (Nubia, see pp188–91), and greening the desert (the Desert Development Center, see pp202–05). More recently, departments at the university have variously been investigating possibilities for green architecture and soilless farming in Egypt, programing traffic lights to avoid accidents, looking at ways of manufacturing more durable cars, and using technology to uncover ancient Egyptian tombs.

Missing from this list are projects involving pure science. Traditionally, applied scientific research took a backseat to teaching science at AUC, but this is changing, particularly since the creation of the New Cairo Campus with its state-of-the-art science facilities. As a result, AUC science departments have been engaged in research that has the potential to bring benefits not just to Egypt but the whole world.

MAKING THE MOST OF EXTREMOPHILES

Where others dive the Red Sea to marvel at the coral and colourful fish, Rania Siam is more interested in the type of marine life that cannot be seen by the naked eye. She studies microorganisms. Siam, who holds a PhD in microbiology and immunology, and is professor of microbiology at AUC's School of Science and Engineering, researches microbes that live in the Red Sea's Central Rift around deepwater hydrothermal vents, where temperatures can reach up to seventy degrees Celsius. In addition to the high pressures and temperatures, the water has high salinity and is toxic with heavy metals. But the organisms Siam studies are highly resilient and have a genetic makeup that allows them to survive conditions that would kill anything else. Some researchers believe that life may even have begun with such organisms. Siam's research involves decoding the genetic makeup of these extremophiles (the wonderful

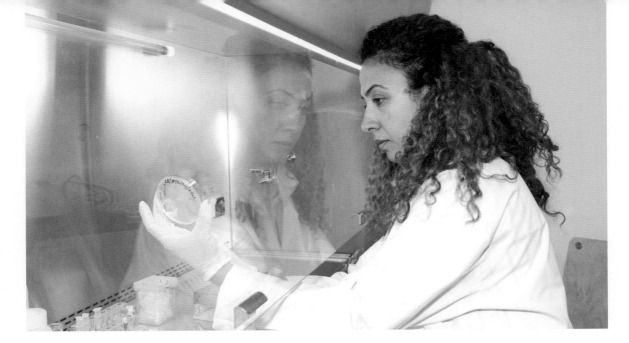

▲ Professor of microbiology Rania Siam, whose research into extremophiles collected from the depths of the Red Sea investigates the very boundaries of life itself

term for organisms that thrive in physically or geochemically extreme conditions) to gain an understanding of the evolution of biological life.

At the same time, Siam and her team are particularly interested in how extremophile genes can be utilized in practical applications. "We are looking for enzymes with biotechnological and pharmaceutical applications. That's the work I and the students on my team are currently focusing on." They have identified an enzyme—or, rather, an extremozyme—that could have multiple applications in different industries. "One enzyme could be used in the detergent industry," explains Siam. "When we wash things we sometimes wash at high temperatures and some enzymes do not function at those temperatures, but this one does." The team has also identified another enzyme that can detoxify very high concentrations of mercury and they are looking at the unique properties of enzymes that could target different cancer cell lines.

THE FIGHT AGAINST HEPATITIS C

The disease being targeted by Hassan Azzazy, professor and chair of AUC's chemistry department, is hepatitis C. With an estimated fifteen to twenty percent of the Egyptian population affected by hepatitis C, the infection rate is the highest in the world. Infected people may carry the virus for as long as twenty years before facing liver failure but because they do not show profound symptoms it often goes undetected. Part of the problem is the high cost of the current two-step testing. Azzazy and his team may have come up with the solution.

They have developed a fully automated, robotic machine for hepatitis C diagnosis. "Our machine automatically performs all the functions that any lab might need to test a patient's blood," says Azzazy. "The »

▶ Chemistry professor Hassan Azzazy, who leads a team that has developed a fully automated, cost-effective, robotic machine for diagnosing hepatitis C

> "At D-Kimia, we are using bio- and nanotechnology to address a medical problem with robotics."

Professor of chemistry
Dr. Hassan Azzazy

machine is controlled by a computer, so no human hands are required to handle the highly infectious materials and, at the end of the process, the machine can self-sterilize." The new test, which relies on gold nanoparticles that change color on contact with the virus, should cost about one tenth of the cost of the test currently available.

This new technology has been developed by D-Kimia, which is AUC's first spin-off company. Spin-offs are commonplace at top-tier research institutions in the United States and are now being embraced by AUC. The spin-off model begins with technology, innovation, and patents developed by faculty members using the university's resources, which are then given to a company to develop into a fully formed product. It's a mutually beneficial partnership between faculty members and the university, and is an indicator that important research is being manifested into a product that contributes to society. "This is actually one of the most stringent criteria by which you evaluate a university," says Azzazy. "With AUC, we have to ask, where is the output? What is our contribution to alleviate the pains of society? Where is our contribution to the economy and to unemployment? The success of spin-off companies is a way to assess those questions."

Since 2010 AUC has had a Technology Transfer Office (TTO), the specific role of which is to work with the university's researchers and inventors to accelerate the process of bringing their developed technologies to the community. So far the TTO has filed eight patents based on Azzazy's work. Other AUC research projects with which the office is involved include nanocapsules for the slow release of drugs or scents, a solar-powered ice-making machine for small fishing boats,

◀ Dr. Nageh Allam and his PhD student Bassant Aly, who, together, are investigating the many possibilities of electrically conductive silk

3D printers that print metals, and a bulletproof vest that causes bullets to disintegrate.

GLOW WORMS

In mid-May 2019, the TTO filed for its latest patent, and it is one that Technology Transfer director Ahmed Ellaithy is particularly excited about. It involves supercapacitors, which are the batteries of the future, and the humble silkworm. PhD student Bassant Aly, who has kept silkworms as a hobby since she was six years old, has been experimenting with introducing chemicals into the worms' diet that result in them producing silk that can carry an electrical charge. She is now working with a team headed by associate professor of physics Nageh Allam to explore the possibilities of such a material. Dr. Allam, who specializes in the interface between nanoscience, physics, and chemistry, sees multiple applications for the technology, including for use in supercapacitors (materials that store and release electrical charges) and in biosensors (devices that convert a biological response into an electrical signal), and in creating hydrogen (a potential fuel of the future) from water. Conductive silk could also be developed into "flexible electronics," woven into clothing for example, or used as a replacement for wires in computers – unlike metal wires, silk will not overheat.

While Dr. Allam's team continues to experiment in this potentially groundbreaking new area, Ahmed Ellaithy and AUC's TTO is actively looking for companies to partner in developing the commercial potential. "The TTO helps the community gain access to these cutting-edge technologies quickly and conveniently," says Ellaithy. "It follows suit with the university's strategic vision." ⊛

25

ONE OF THE STRONGEST

AUC and its
relationship with
Nobel laureate
Ahmed Zewail

From humble beginnings in Damanhour, Desouk, and Alexandria, Ahmed Zewail went on to be awarded a Nobel Prize for chemistry in 1999. He won it for developing a sort of "flashlight" of ultrashort laser pulses, which enabled him to watch chemical reactions unfold on timescales of "femtoseconds"—millionths of a billionth of a second. He was the first Egyptian, or Arab, to win a Nobel in any of the sciences and, despite living most of his life in the United States (where he served as a member of President Obama's science and technology advisory panel, from 2009 to 2013), he used that stature to champion science education and research in Egypt and the Middle East.

Until Zewail died in 2016, at the age of seventy, he enjoyed a close relationship with AUC. He was a distinguished visiting professor in 1988–89 and AUC became the first university in Egypt to award Zewail an honorary degree, in 1993. He was elected to AUC's Board of Trustees in 1999 (a few months *before* he became a Nobel laureate). In 2011, he established the Ahmed Zewail Prize for Excellence in the Sciences and Humanities. The following year, AUC Press published his autobiography, *Voyage through Time: Walks of Life to the Nobel Prize*. Speaking to *AUC Today* in 2000, Zewail referred to his relationship with AUC as "one of the strongest" he had with any institution in the Middle East.

Zewail also spoke at AUC on a number of occasions. His appearances were always greeted by the sort of thunderous applause more commonly associated with a movie or soccer star than a scientist. At AUC in 2004 he relayed his vision of the Arab and Islamic world: "In order for any nation to be put on the twenty-first-century map, it has to have a clear vision for the role of science and technology," he said. On 5 June 2011 he delivered the inaugural lecture of the Zewail Foundation Public Lecture Series in Science and Culture. Titled "Egypt is the Hope," in it he discussed Egypt's future in the post-revolutionary period. Addressing a packed Ewart Hall, Zewail said, "The January 25th revolution was a model revolution as it represented the unity of a

▲ The Nobel medal for outstanding contributions in chemistry, as awarded to Ahmed Zewail in 1999

whole nation with all segments of the society." He added that he never imagined how much corruption existed in Egypt until the revolution brought it to light. He continued his remarks, discussing opportunities for economic development in Egypt including the expansion of the country's agriculture and tourism industries, and a focused effort to improve education. "There will never be a revival without focusing on education," he noted, before making the first public announcement of his own contribution to the cause, with the revival of a stalled national project that now would be known as the Zewail City of Science and Technology.

▲ Nobel laureate Ahmed Zewail was a distinguished visiting professor at AUC, a guest speaker, and with the university he established the Ahmed Zewail Prize for Excellence in the Sciences and Humanities

"Ahmed Zewail leaves behind a legacy of extraordinary achievements; he was an icon in the world of science," said Richard Bartlett, chair of AUC's Board of Trustees. "He was also an AUC trustee for seventeen years, deeply committed to the university's mission of education and service in Egypt. We will miss his companionship, enthusiasm, and devotion for science and scientific progress, and unwavering support of AUC." ❀

> **"I have complete confidence in Egyptians, who have always made history."**
>
> Ahmed Zewail, speaking at Ewart Hall, 5 June 2011

26

WELCOME TO CYBER-SPACE

In the mid 1990s AUC took its first bold steps onto the World Wide Web

Ask long-serving members of faculty what the greatest change has been to AUC and they will typically cite one of two things: the move to the New Cairo Campus or the arrival of the internet. Hard to believe, but there are people alive who remember a time before Twitter, Instagram, Tumblr, and taking photos of your food before eating it.

Here is a time line charting how and when AUC went online.

1990 AUC develops its own internal administrative network operating university-wide, connecting computers in different departments and buildings.

FEB 1991 AUC joins the electronic communication networks of EARN/BITNET via the computer center on the third floor of Hill House. EARN stands for European Academic Research Network and BITNET for "Because It's Time" Network (really) and these link 1,300 universities and research centers in thirty-eight countries around the world, allowing them to exchange information. Most activity takes place in dedicated user groups.

SEPT 1991 Dr. Mohamed Hisham El Sherif fills the new position of associate vice-president for computing. He is to coordinate the campus-wide planning for computing and prepare for the future day when AUC will link up with an international network. (El Sherif, who graduated in 1979 with a diploma from AUC, became Egypt's minister of local development in 2018.)

1991/92 The Academic Computer Center introduces email services. It begins on a humble scale with around 300 users, mostly faculty and administration.

FEB 1993 *AUC Today* introduces readers to the concept of email: "Electronic mail is received by a user when he or she types in the correct username and password. On the terminal screen information appears that tells the user whether new mail has been received. Once the new message has been read, the user has the option of either responding to that message, forwarding that message to another user, or reading the next one." It'll never catch on.

1993 AUC is officially connected to the Egyptian University Network (EUN) via a leased line to the sinisterly named Foreign Relations Collaboration Unit (FRCU) at Cairo University.

1994 AUC launches a very basic on-line, campus-wide information service

information freely available. Not everybody has entered this brave new online world: a Board of Trustees memo reveals that of the eleven members of its Century Committee, formed to explore the *future* of AUC, only four have email.

SEPT 1996 *AUC Today* runs a story about "surfing the net." Charmingly, the medium is referred to as the "Webs," as in, "Who will access AUC's Webs?"

MAR 1997 On 24 March AUC receives a bomb threat by email: "I will Fuck Auc on Thursday march 27th with a bomb that Auc students will re gret bye."

NOV 1997 A new server and internet line is acquired to speed up access to Saqqarah Web.

MAR 1999 At 11.45am on 7 March a new AUC website is publicly launched at the ACS Technology Fair, with the now familiar address www.aucegypt.edu

2000 By this time, as the use of laptops is becoming more common, there is blanket wireless coverage on all parts of the Tahrir Campus, including the Greek Campus and Falaki buildings, but not the villa housing the Rare Books Library, which is not permitted to have wifi because of security concerns from the interior ministry next door.

2008 On 21 April, AUC makes its first post on Facebook, an album of nine photos of the Tahrir Campus. Meanwhile, coinciding with the move to the New Cairo Campus, the university establishes a new email service powered by Google and based on gmail. ⊛

called NetNews. Use of email within the university is growing. Faculty and administration automatically qualify for accounts but students have to present a written memo from a supervising professor to the director of Academic Computing Services (ACS). The problem is the university has only five dial-up lines, which means connecting to the internet is slower than the Sixth of October Bridge at 5pm on a Thursday.

1995 Work begins on a new AUC "On-Line Information/Worldwide Web Project" to be called Ramses, Nile, Horus, Citadel, Saqqarah Web. The public relations department says, "Why can't we just call it the American University in Cairo website?" but nobody listens. In

September, Mohamed Hisham El Sherif steps down as vice president for computing to be replaced by Sami Akabawi.

JAN 1996 A first documented instance of email harassment of a female member of faculty by a student. Seemingly, the student has not realized that email accounts are not anonymous, and he is quickly identified and apologizes.

MAR 1996 Saqqarah Web becomes operational. The website contains statistics on AUC, the university catalog and telephone directory, various manuals and handbooks, as well as policies and procedures of the university. Some question the wisdom of making all this

27

FOR THE RECORD

AUC has its own recording studio where artists of tomorrow can cut their first tracks

Henry Panion III is a composer, arranger, conductor, and educator. His musical career has seen him collaborate with Stevie Wonder, Aretha Franklin, The Blind Boys of Alabama, Chaka Khan, and Coolio. He has worked across genres, from classical to gospel, hymns to hip-hop. He has won two Grammys. He also helped design AUC's music technology studio and program.

Panion was invited to AUC back around 2007 by the director of the Music department, John Baboukis. Panion came as a visiting distinguished professor, staying for about two weeks, of which he spent one week teaching courses and giving workshops. He also consulted on an idea Baboukis had for a new program in music technology. Together, Baboukis and Panion visited the site of the New Cairo Campus, then under construction, and took a look at the spaces allotted to the music program. Noting two small rooms, one earmarked for storage and another a listening room, Panion suggested if they were knocked together the department could kit the new space out as a recording studio. "That would never in a million years have occurred to me," says Baboukis. That night over dinner at his hotel, Panion took a placemat and sketched on it a plan for the studio. The next day Baboukis sent it to the architect. "This whole concept came out of the head of Henry Panion and he is the reason we have a music technology program at AUC," adds Baboukis.

The music technology major was introduced in 2011, joined the following year by a major in music performance. The studio is a key component of the music technology major, which is the only one of its kind in Egypt. On this course, students learn how to record, edit, mix, and master music for any medium—songs, film scores, game soundtracks, advertising jingles. In this they are guided by director of the music technology program Wael al-Mahallawy, a professional sound engineer who has produced innumerable movie soundtracks. He enthuses about the resources available at AUC. "We have more than sixty microphones—dynamic microphones, condenser microphones, ribbon

◀ Music technology and
performance student Joudi Abou
Ayed (Joudi Nox), mixing down
tracks for her graduation project
in the AUC studio

microphones. We even have vintage stuff from the sixties." The studio,
he says, offers two types of sound recording: old analog-style, as well as
digital. "Normally, if you build a new studio it is only digital. Our studio
is different, we offer different flavors!"

The music tech major also includes music theory, and the students
also have to choose an instrument, which they learn how to play over
the four years. "In Egypt you can find a lot of sound engineers but
without any background in music," says al-Mahallawy. "We produce
professionals who know how to record but also can perform."

Joudi Abou Ayed is a half-Lebanese, half-Palestinian scholarship
student doing a double major in music technology and performance.
Back in El Koura in north Lebanon, her parents were expecting her to
study medicine until Joudi gave them a formal presentation on music
technology and how it could lead to a good job. They relented and she
came to Cairo. "To be honest, I didn't even really know what music
technology was, then I got here and saw the studio and I thought, 'Yes!
I'm going to learn something here!'" When we meet she is working on
her capstone project, an album of twenty-five minutes of self-written,
self-produced songs. "It's like a real-life experience," says Abou Ayed,
who posts performances online under the name Joudi Nox. The intention
going forward is to do a degree in business then start her own record
label. "All my friends who graduated a year or two ago are working." ⚛

28

DESIGNING FOR LIFE

One of AUC's most recently added programs is proving to be one of its most popular

B ahia Shehab recalls feeling "liberated" the first time she spray-painted a wall in Cairo. "It was a beautiful moment," she says. She first took to the streets during the Egyptian uprisings and began spray painting ﻻ ("No") in response to the violence around her. "I wanted to get across how people were feeling in the square and what it felt like to be part of that event," she says.

After the revolution, she took her graffiti to other cities around the world: in Madison, Wisconsin she painted "No to the impossible;" in Vancouver, she painted "Stand at the corner of a dream and fight;" in Paris it was, "I will dream." In Cairo she really stepped it up—she founded a graphic design program at AUC.

Shehab graduated in graphic design at the American University of Beirut and then worked in advertising in Dubai. Subsequently she moved to Cairo and enrolled at AUC where she did an MA in Islamic Art and Architecture. "I was looking for answers as to why Arab visual culture and specifically our script has regressed." Afterwards, she was invited to teach and design courses, which is when the plans for a graphic design major came together.

"I saw the need for skilled creative thinkers. Design is about problem-solving and we live in a country and region that badly needs creative minds to solve our problems. AUC can be a great platform to foster the leaders who will drive social change."

The major was launched in 2011 with Shehab as the only full-time faculty and with thirteen enrolled students. Just eight years later, there are five full-time and more than seventeen adjunct faculty, with an intake of over 120 major and eighty minor students—which is extraordinary growth by any standards. In fact, graphic design is the fastest growing major at AUC after architecture.

Haytham Nawar, who studied design in Switzerland and who joined the program as assistant professor in 2014, says that the course is about far more than just graphics. "We want the students to think in ≫

▶ Recognizing female Egyptian pioneers through postage stamps, a final-year graduation project by Maha Hesham ('18). Maha also designed a booklet in which the stamps are packaged with text that pays tribute to the life and achievements of her chosen subjects

▲ Ahmad Khalil's project, CHAIROS (a mash-up of the words "Cairo" and "chaos"), takes inspiration from the detritus of the Egyptian streets. He created patterns of objects including air-conditioning units, loaves of bread, and car licence plates, which he then then printed on fabrics and incorporated into two haute-couture fashion pieces, a coat and a dress

◄ Mariam Ibrahim's redesigned hospital gown not only covers a patient's dignity but works to aid recovery. The gown incorporates sensors that measure blood oxygen levels, pulse, temperature, and posture. The data can be viewed on a web app that updates every thirty seconds, providing healthcare professionals with at-a-glance vital patient-care information

"Our students know that they can create the change they want to see in the world."

Bahia Shehab, associate professor of design

3D, so they can interact with architecture and product design, and think about space or interior design, or visual art, like installations. We want them to use technology and to be completely interdisciplinary."

The students' final graduating projects, which are displayed annually at the Sharjah gallery on the New Cairo Campus, are a reflection of this approach. In the four final shows that have been held since the program began, the work (most of which tackles major social issues, including women's rights, economic disparity, and the preservation of cultural heritage) has embraced fashion design, video, board games, online technologies, and phone apps. Take, for example, the final project by Ahd Sherif, who graduated in 2014. She designed a sexual education kit, focusing on presenting the material in a way that is accessible and appropriate for students. "I created something that, in my opinion, can change someone's life," she explained.

"This is why the program is popular," says Shehab, "design empowers. And when the students have the freedom to choose to work on a subject

◄ Farida Khaled's "Bananatopia" highlights social disparities across Cairo using the banana as an index. Why bananas? Because they are commonly available year round, and consumed by all. But not all bananas are equal. Farida analyses which types are consumed where and how much they cost. She maps the results to show the invisible banana borders separating the city's rich and poor

▲ Youssef Zaki was out on the streets during the revolution, spray-paint in hand. Inspired by those events, he has created an app that uses augmented reality to allow users to create their own virtual, geo-located graffiti all over the streets of Egypt

▲ Sarah Osman's project looks at the history of Egyptian animation and demonstrates how it was influenced by the politics of the time. She matches archive news footage to archive cartoons, in the process excavating the work of forgotten artists and film-makers

that they are passionate about the results are always fascinating."

For Nawar, there is another, more practical appeal to the program. "It is creative but it is connected to the market. If you say, 'My son is an artist,' the response is going to be, 'Yeah, but what does he do for a living?' But if you say, 'My son is a designer,' then it's more like, 'He must be making good money.'"

Shehab and her colleagues are currently in the process of developing a new fashion major, and hope to establish majors in media, industrial, and, possibly, interior design in collaboration with the department of architecture. As a spin-off from her teaching researches, Shehab, who is the first Arab woman to receive the UNESCO-Sharjah Prize for Arab Culture, also recently wrote the ground-breaking *A History of Arabic Graphic Design* (co-authored with Haytham Nawar and published by AUC Press). However, of everything she has accomplished to date, the thing she is most proud of, she says, is her students. "They can bring about the change I want to see in the world," she says. ❦

29

NOT A SOFTER OPTION

Architecture
at AUC is
challenging gender
assumptions

The Wikipedia page for Egyptian women architects has just one entry—Shahira Fahmy, and she is probably better known these days as an actress. So it might come as some surprise to learn that at AUC around eighty percent of students studying architecture are women. "It may be more," says Professor Ahmed Sherif, chair of the architecture department. The other possibly surprising fact about architecture at AUC is its popularity. When it was introduced as an independent major in 2008 (previously it was part of construction engineering), architecture became the fastest growing program in the university's history. The number of students on the program has now been capped, but architecture is still the third-highest in demand of all AUC courses.

Sherif has a theory. "Architecture is multidisciplinary by nature and it caters to students of different interests. It allows them to explore their creativity." But at the same time, he adds, it is a professionally oriented program. "Just this morning," says Sherif, "I was with some students who were presenting to the CEO of a major real estate company. The company came to us and said, 'We have this piece of land and we have these objectives, design something for us.' So the students have a real client, they are not just designing in a vacuum. They start to understand market needs and get a feel for how it is to be in a real practice."

Architecture students at AUC are doubly fortunate, he adds, because they don't have far to go to find inspiration. "We use our campus as a teaching resource. When I want to give an example to the students of how to do something, I tell them, 'Go to the library building and take a look at what they did there.'"

Mirette Khorshed ('11), who graduated as part of the first intake of AUC architecture majors and has since come back to teach, also credits the physical aspect of the New Cairo Campus with shaping the way she thinks about the built environment. "AUC is always somewhere that I walk around and actively think about the buildings. Maybe it's because I can't find my office, but maybe also by being a little bit lost you actually

start noticing what's going on, how every building is a little bit different, how every building has its own identity."

She remembers that her graduating class was sixteen women and four men. "It's a cultural thing," says associate professor Magda Mostafa, who helped set up the first architecture program, and who has a special interest in designing for children with special needs and sensory challenges. "The majority of boys get into construction engineering and girls go into architecture, which is seen as the softer of the built-environment degrees—although I don't support that stereotype."

So why is there only one Egyptian woman architect on Wikipedia? "There are very, very few female architects who go on to head their own firms. I can think of only a handful," says Magda Mostafa. "A lot of them go into academia, or they may go into architectural practices but they don't take the lead."

"Women are poorly represented in architectural practices because there is little consideration of what they have to go through to balance career and family," says Nada Nafeh ('11). "And female architects also generally earn less than their male peers." After AUC, Nafeh worked for Cairo-based practice The Design Avenue before gaining a master's in Canada. "In the construction field in Egypt, there's also a tendency to question women's abilities to lead jobs on site. Women have to work really hard to be taken seriously and their chances of being hired are less." Nafeh currently works for a German development agency.

But Ahmed Sherif believes that the situation is changing. "Ten, twenty years from today the whole profession will have changed. In my office we have twenty architects, sixteen are women and only four are men." ⬡

▲ Students of architecture at AUC are overwhelmingly women, although this gender breakdown is not reflected in the workplace

30

SONS OF PASHAS, BEYS, AND EFFENDIS

A brief note on the background of the early student body

For an insight into the make-up of the early (all-male) student body, we have this from Charles Watson's report to the trustees in October 1922: "We are in the midst of enrolment for the College for the new year. Already 182 students have signed up. A questionnaire filled out by 171 of our students yielded some most interesting generalizations as to our student body. The fathers of five bear the title of Pasha, 49 the title of Bey, 67 the title of Effendi (meaning a modern Egyptian, with Western dress),

two the title of Monsieur (probably Armenian or foreign), 20 the title of Sheikh (Oriéntal Moslem type), two the title of Is Sayad (descendant of the Prophet), one the title of Priest (a Copt). As to the chief occupations of the fathers, the replies show 62 landowners, 26 government officials, 19 merchants, 12 doctors, eight army officers, eight engineers, while the rest are widely distributed. This is most suggestive as to the type of education we should provide." ❁

▲ The student body for much of the 1920s was entirely male, generally from well-off families, and totally at home in a tarboosh

31

THE FIRST COED

In 1928,
Eva Habib al-Masri
became the first
female student to
enroll at AUC

▼ Extract from a letter home
written by faculty member,
John Larimer (1928–30)

It was the ninth intake before AUC accepted its first female student. Coed colleges were common in other parts of the world but, still, President Charles Watson took some persuading that this was a good idea in Egypt, where no woman had ever gone to university. It helped that Eva Habib al-Masri was a star pupil, who had excelled at the American Mission College for Girls in Cairo, attaining the highest average grade in her class for the final three years. Eva's father fully backed her wish to attend AUC. "I am giving her the joy and the pride of being a pioneer in the field of coeducation, which is coming to Egypt as certainly as the rising sun comes every morning," he said.

On her first day she was the only female among 350 students. For the second year she was joined by three American girls, while in her third year the number of coeds grew to ten. She studied social sciences, natural sciences (organic chemistry, physics, geology, and astronomy), as well as English and French literature. She also took a course in journalism in her first year, which led her to join the team producing *The AUC Review*, and eventually becoming its editor.

She won the annual spelling contest *(see below)* and received the highest grades in all her classes. "My commencement day was a memorable day," she wrote in her memoirs. "As long as I live, I will remember it with a feeling of great joy. [Feminist leader] Madame Hoda Shaarawi was present, and a few days later called me up to tell me that

February 26, 1929

Dear Betty,

I have a few minutes this quiet Sunday afternoon in which to write to you. It is the end of a very busy week, and the beginning of still another one I fear. The weather has taken a turn for the worse, and has become a little cold. Ideal football weather, but out of place in Cairo. Somehow this kind of weather always makes me miserable. I'm looking forward to the hot season - it will be an experience at least, though all my companions are not anxious for it to come. Well, they've gone thru it.

This past week has been particularly full. On Friday we had the school spelling match, which was closely contested. It was quite interesting. The only girl student in the entire school won the cup and the money. American vice-consul was here to present it. The girl had a lot of courage - in this land of retarded womanhood - to get up before a big hall filled with boys and compete against them in a any respect. Well, she believe a girl can't hold a candle to them in a any respect. Well, she showed them.

Friday afternoon was the pleasant little tea at the home of the American Minister and his wife. A lot of formality of course, and difficult for me to fall in with. I wish I could feel more at home in society circles. I was supposed to leave two cards, but forgot to even take them along. If I can muster up courage I'll make a call on them next week and then leave my cards. That I'm afraid of though is that they will be home - to me that would be a real catastrophe.

On Saturday night - last night - the University held its annual mid-winter dinner

> This past week has been particularly full. On Friday we had the school spelling match, which was closely contested. It was quite interesting. The only girl student in the entire school won the cup and the money. American vice-consul was here to present it. The girl had a lot of courage - in this land of retarded womanhood - to get up before a big hall filled with boys and compete against them. And the boys over here believe a girl can't hold a candle to them in a any respect. Well, she showed them.

"It's different today when AUC is fifty percent girls, fifty percent boys. I would never have dreamed the day would come when this could be the case."

Eva Habib al-Masri, speaking in 1969

she was exceedingly glad to see me graduate because I represented the beginning of the realization of her dream, which was that higher education would be made accessible to Egypt's young women."

Her first job after graduating was editor-in-chief of *al-Misriya*, a feminist magazine founded by Shaarawi. In the 1940s, Eva and her husband emigrated to the United States, where she became an American citizen and a librarian in the New York University Libraries. ⊛

32

FOUR FEMALES FOR EVERY MAN

In the late 1970s the university had a chronic gender imbalance

The university has faced countless challenges over its one-hundred-year history, typically involving raising funds, but toward the end of the 1970s it faced a more unusual problem: too many women and not enough men. The issue was highlighted in a 1979 article in *The Caravan* under the headline "Four Females for Every Man." Analysis showed, it said, that eighty percent of the recent freshman class was made up of girls, with just twenty percent male. One sociology professor reported that in one of his classes containing forty students only one was male. The professor claimed he spent the whole semester persuading the boy not to drop out.

Since female students were first admitted in 1928, they had always been in the minority, right up until around 1960, when, for the first time, the girls slightly outnumbered the boys. The two remained roughly in balance for the next fifteen years or so until in the mid 1970s the intake of girls shot ahead of the boys. By the end of the decade AUC was increasingly being seen almost as an elite girls' finishing school.

The university considered this an unhealthy situation. The Board of Trustees formed an action committee to look into the issue. It reported back that there were two main reasons for girls enrolling at AUC rather than boys. First was that the girls scored better than boys in the *thanaweya amma*, which meant the boys were not meeting AUC's academic entrance requirements. The other reason was that boys favored more career-oriented programs, such as engineering and medicine, which AUC did not offer at the time.

In light of this, the committee offered two suggestions: to expand the number of majors in professional subjects and to lower admission standards for boys. These ideas did not go down well with everybody. "Dear editor," wrote one female AUC student to the *Caravan* newspaper, "I was shocked and horrified upon reading the article 'Boy/Girl Ratio at AUC Surveyed.' [AUC] is ready to jeopardize the educational standard of the university just to raise the number of male students! This is a

1930	4	74	5%	95%
1934	13	67	16%	84%
1939	19	38	33.3%	66.6%
1945	29	105	22%	78%
1949	66	169	28%	72%
1955	185	240	44%	56%
1961	174	160	52%	48%
1965	388	398	49%	51%
1970	625	578	52%	48%
1975	717	643	53%	47%
1981	1,337	661	67%	33%
1985	1,450	989	59%	41%
1990	1,802	1,696	52%	48%
1995	2,167	2,009	52%	48%
2000	2,509	2,137	54%	46%
2005	2,584	2,319	53%	47%
2010	3,499	3,054	53%	47%
2015	3,701	2,958	56%	44%

▲ The perception of AUC as some sort of "young ladies' finishing school" was common until well into the 1980s

◄ The figures for 1979, when the student ratio of women to men was reported to be 4:1, are not available but clearly there was a peak around that time

university not a lonely hearts club. You should be interested in the ratio of professors to students, not males to females."

In the event, admission standards were not lowered, but the university did introduce new undergraduate programs in business administration, mechanical engineering, and computer science. This paid almost immediate dividends. As soon as 1982, the administration was noting that the male/female ratio had already moved toward more equality, with the new freshman class consisting of sixty percent female and forty percent male. These days the ratio is almost fifty/ fifty. As for the fears about AUC turning into a lonely hearts club, well, the correspondent of 1979 may have had a point—just google "AUC crushes" or "AUC blind dating." ❀

33

DON'T CALL ME "MUZZA"

Until it was discontinued in the 1970s, the crowning of Miss AUC was one of the oldest, most celebrated, and occasionally most contentious university traditions

On Friday 20 March 1953, *Campus Caravan* ran the following news item: "Attiya Falaki, freshman, was crowned Miss AUC of 1953 before 500 excited spectators in a ceremony at 10 am today in Ewart Memorial Hall. Dr. Abdel Wehab Mooro, President of Cairo University, placed the Miss AUC crown on Tati's head as the symbol of her newly-won title. Dr. Doria Shafik, president of Bint El Nil organization, presented her with the Miss AUC ribbon."

If you just skimmed those brief three sentences and thought, "So, AUC used to have some unfortunate beauty pageant," then go back and read them again. Note the venue. Ewart Hall was the university's grand auditorium, used for commencements and other ceremonies of high order. That the administration authorized its use for Miss AUC suggests this was a serious matter (serious enough to get five hundred students out of bed and into the hall for 10 am). Note that the person who crowned Ms Falaki was the president not of AUC but of Cairo University, suggesting that the Miss AUC contest had a fame that stretched far beyond the AUC campus. In fact, elsewhere the story claims the gentleman from Cairo University was there as a representative of General Naguib, no less a person than the president of Egypt. Note finally the identity of the person who presented Miss AUC with her ribbon: Doria Shafik was one of the principal leaders of the women's liberation movement in Egypt and a person whose endeavors led to Egyptian women getting the right to vote. Miss AUC had the feminist seal of approval.

Not that it started out that way. In the beginning it was just the usual beauty contest business of boys ogling girls. Back in 1930, in the 12 December edition of *The AUC Review*, editor Mustafa Amin Yusif (who went on to co-own *Akhbar al-Yom* and *Akher Sa'a*) asked his fellow students to write the name of the most beautiful coed (of which there were only seven at this early stage) and pass it on to him. The following two years, again under the auspices of *The Review*, elections were held

▲ Sonia Greiss, crowned Miss AUC 1963 in a special program at Ewart Hall. She received the crown from Dr. Laila al-Hamamsy, director of the Social Research Center and a former Miss AUC

"in order that the men of AUC might officially make known their choice of the most beautiful coed." The girls, quite rightly, viewed the affair with disdain and refused to have their photographs taken, and after 1932 the whole thing was dropped.

Miss AUC returned in 1941—preceded, it should be noted, by a "most eligible man of AUC" contest that ran in February 1940. By now, the number of female students at AUC was considerably higher, and as the girls were eligible to vote it became less about looks and more about popularity. Gulnar Djeddaoui, then a sophomore in social science, was voted Miss AUC for 1949. Interviewed in 1969 in Washington, where she was then working for the International Monetary Fund, Djeddaoui recalled being "terribly flattered and very, very happy to be Miss AUC." It wasn't a matter of beauty, she said, so much as how scholarly you were and how many social activities you took part in.

Djeddaoui received a certificate recognizing her title, which her mother told her to roll up and "not let go to her head." But by the time Attiya Falaki was crowned just a few years later, Miss AUC had become an altogether more elevated affair. In addition to the certificate, there were now the crown and ribbon, as well as host of gifts donated by local businesses eager to sponsor the proceedings. In 1953 ≫

MISS AUC SHOULD:

1. Typify what every AUC coed should look like
2. Have an all-round personality
3. Exemplify the AUC spirit
4. Participate in AUC activities
5. Have a good scholastic record

What it takes to be Miss AUC, as decreed by the organizing committee

MISS AUC WINNERS

1931	Baheya Farag
1932	Baheya Farag
1933	Harriet Barlow
1934–40	*No contest*
1941	Touny Setton
1942	Chrysanthe Mouski
1943–44	Yvette Azari
1945	Laila Meo
1947	Leila Shukri
1948	Marijane Behman
1949	Gulnar Djeddaoui
1950	Paule Khouri Haddad
1951	Nadia Haggag
1952	Dora Doss
1953	Attiya Falaki
1954	Lubna Abdel Aziz
1955	Olympia Carageorge
1956	Laila Rostom
1957–60	*No contest*
1961	Laila al-Chourbagui
1962	Mona Gibara
1963	Sonia Greiss
1964	Aziza Nouredin Ragai
1965	Jehan al-Abd
1966	Jehan Ragai
1967	Samia Farid
1968	Perihan Tewfik
1969	Zeinab Hashem
1970	Litsa Patsalis
1971	Salwa Morsi
1972	Nadia Hosni
1973	Ilham Khaliyl
1974	Nevine Loutfy
1975	Dara al-Tobgui
1977	Randa Dewey

this included a blouse from the Chemla department store, a handbag from Rivoli, material for a gown from Salon Vert, and a return flight to Lebanon, with hotel room.

Nineteen fifty-four saw the first awarding of the *Campus Caravan* Cup. Miss AUC that year was Lubna Abdel Aziz, better known to her friends as "Auntie Lulu," and soon to be known to all in Egypt through her leading roles in films including *al-Wisada al-khaliya* (1957) and *Ana hurra* (1959).

By now, as noted earlier, the Miss AUC election had gone far beyond being an AUCian affair. Almost every newspaper in Egypt published news of the event and pictures of the contestants. During election week reporters flocked to the university hoping to interview the participants. This was a contest with high stakes.

Accordingly, the contenders for the crown campaigned hard. They commanded teams of supporters. In 1954, *Campus Caravan* visited room 109 in the Hill House hostel: "Only a brief look into this room would immediately disclose that this was the headquarters of the Auntie Lulu supporters. Strewn all over the room were posters to people of whatever taste or manner. The slogans read 'Her voice brings joy to millions,' 'Green-eyed Lulu meteors to fame,' 'Lulu the pride and beauty of AUC,' and 'Be proud and logical: vote Lulu.'"

Two years later, the crown went to twenty-three-year-old journalism major Laila Rostom. No stranger to the spotlight, at the age of three she won the contest for "the most beautiful child on the beaches of Alexandria." Rostom would, of course, go on to achieve fame throughout the Arab world as a presenter of TV cultural affairs shows. Miss AUC may have been pretty but her defining characteristic was ambition.

By this time, the rules of the contest were also firmly established. All senior girls would go into a ballot, out of which would come a shortlist of three. These three could commence campaigning only five days before the second vote. The name of the winner would then be kept secret until the biggest social event of the year, the Miss AUC crowning ceremony and party.

However, contenders for the title would usually start campaigning months, if not years before, working hard to establish themselves as a public figure on campus. One useful step in achieving this would be a good showing in the talent contest, held each November. Over time, however, the determined qualities required to see off the competition, also began to put off voters. "The friendly spirit that characterized the Miss AUC contest a few years ago," reported *Caravan* in 1971, "seems to have disappeared." Three years later that spirit was apparently completely dead: "It was a typical Miss AUC, marred with hassling, quarrels, and

Paule Khouri Voted Miss AUC

Official Student Publication of the American University at Cairo

3 March 1950

Number 16

Volume XXV

CAMPUS CARAVAN

1950 Miss A.U.C. ...

Miss Paule Haddad Khouri

...And Very Close Competition

Miss Jacqueline Khoury

Miss Nadia Haggag

New Titleholder Dislikes Cliques, Happy at Winning

"It is hard for a newcomer to get acquainted in the various cliques that exist in the University," was the reaction of Miss Paule Haddad Khouri, newly elected Miss AUC for 1950 when questioned at her home earlier in the week by Campus Caravan reporters as to her impressions of University life.

Daughter of Mr. and Mrs. Edward Haddad Khouri, Miss Khouri has two sisters, Eyvette and René and one brother, Ralph. She studied until she was ten at home and continuing her education at the Pensionnat de la Mere de Dieu, she took honors in the second part of her French Baccalaurete majoring in Philosophy.

Elusive on many points in her youth, the new Miss AUC plied reporters with coffee as the interview continued to soften the barrage of questions. Regarding the male element at the University she would only reply, "there are a great variety of men on the campus".

She enjoys the relationship betweene members of the staff and students and considers the freindly envitoement very good.

A girl guide since 1944, Miss Khouri is now a Chief Guide and recently took a group of girls to Luxor and Aswan. Other interests include tennis and basketball, both of which she practices regularly.

"Home making is not a favorite pastime", acording to the new titleholder and her mother when questioned said, "the only trouble with my daughter is that she is very serious and likes to study too much".

"I am extremely confident of my daughter", continued the mother, "and it makes me very happy that we can rely on her for she can adjust to any environment".

Assembly is Held To Award Title

Brown eyed, soft spoken, twenty year old Miss Paule Haddad Khouri, sophomore social science and newcomer to the University, was today crowned Miss AUC for 1950 in a special general assembly held before 500 students following Monday's heatedly campaigned election in which male Faculty students voted for their choice in the annual contest sponsored by the Campus Caravan.

Miss Nadia Haggag, junior sociology, and Miss Jaqueline Khouri, senior journalism ran close seconds in what proved to be one of the most hotly contested elections in campus history.

Following a spirited pre-election campaign and four days of intensive speculation on the part of the male backers, the awarding of prizes in assembly by members of the staff, Campus Caravan editors and campus representatives came as a dramatic climax.

Miss Haddad Khouri came to the University this year after studying in French schools for ten years "to learn English and to continue her education". She is very interested in sports and is a member of the Tennis club and in charge of programs for the Student Christian association. She also likes basketball as well as classical music.

Tomorrow she will be guest of honor at a party given by members of the hostel, who earlier in the year she had given dancing lessons to along with other members of the Coeds club.

During the assembly she received a handbag given by the Campus Caravan staff, a scroll, a crown, flowers from the Coed's club and an inviation by the Hostel to attend their party.

Miss Haddad Khouri is the tenth coed to recieve the title and replaces Miss Gulnar Djeddaoui.

Runners up, Miss Haggag and Miss Jaqueline Khouri are also active in campus affairs. Miss Haggag took a lead in Captain Applejack, the Maskers production of last year and was president of the Coed's club. Miss Khouri is Editor in Chief of the Campus Caravan, president of the International Relations club and a former Student Council member.

> ### "Why not a Mr AUC? Or is it vain for a man to display his physical attributes?"
>
> Fatma Mashhour, *Caravan*, 30 Nov 1971

personal bickerings," reported the student newspaper of the 1974 contest. One contender put her rivals' noses out of joint by bringing in a Hasaballah-style, *baladi* brass band from outside to blast its horns on her behalf. "I have never seen such a thing in a university community," one foreign student told the reporter. "Such infights don't happen anywhere back home."

Spectating students began to take against the contest, labeling it "childish, sophomoric, frivolous, and a degradation to any establishment of learning." Another coed commented that it was "a shameful thing that girls at the university level should still want to prove themselves in such an elementary way." Many others would seem to have shared these views and the last Miss AUC took place in 1977. ✸

34

I PROTEST

The right to
freedom of
expression has long
been practiced
at AUC

AUC was born in a time of protest. In March 1919, Egypt's occupying British administration arrested and deported the leader of the Wafd movement Saad Zaghloul for the crime of working for national independence. This injustice galvanized the country into action, culminating in a general strike that brought Egypt to a standstill. By the time AUC opened the gates to its first intake of students the following year, the demonstrators had been mollified by promises extracted at the negotiating table, but the spirit of protest lodged around Tahrir Square.

When the British banished Zaghloul for a second time, in December 1921, AUCians took to the square. They were out again in 1946, joining other students and workers demanding complete British withdrawal from Egypt, and again in 1948, this time protesting the newly created state of Israel. Like motorcycle gang leader Marlon Brando in the movie *The Wild Ones*, who when asked what he was rebelling against replied "What've you got?" AUCians have never been short of things to protest. Food on campus, for example, which on at least two occasions, in 1945 and 1966, caused students to threaten strike action if it didn't improve.

AUCians gleefully embraced the student-led activism of the late 1960s and early seventies, adding their voices to protests against US bombing in Vietnam. In 1973 there were protests against the scapegoating of army officers for Egyptian military defeats. In October 1977, students contested an increase in dorm rent fees; in 1985 they protested the Israeli bombing of PLO headquarters in Tunis. In 1988 they were burning Israeli flags outside the administration offices; the following year they were inflamed by increases in photocopying prices. In 1991, they wielded placards opposing the presence of foreign troops on Arab soil; the following year they fulminated against alleged excessive profits made by the AUC bookstore.

In 2003, AUCians were in the vanguard of national protests against the American invasion of Iraq. On hearing that the United States air force had begun bombing Baghdad, AUC students spontaneously rushed

In the banner: كلية الآداب والعلوم / لجامعة الأميركية بالقاهرة

▲ In 1921 AUC students joined the masses in marching through the streets of Cairo carrying placards denouncing continued British rule in Egypt

onto Tahrir Square, occupying it before the security forces had time to react. It was only later that they were joined by students from Cairo University and other citizens. In 2008, after the move to New Cairo, the protests were against the unfinished state of the campus, with students demanding compensatory fee reductions.

But by far the biggest cause of student unrest over the one hundred years of the university's history has been tuition fees. If we look at just the recent era, there have been major protests against fee hikes in 1983, 1989, 1993, 2011, 2012, and 2016.

Responding to the student protests in 2011, President Lisa Anderson recognized the right of the student body to air its opinions—"The university is committed to a freedom of expression policy that recognizes the right of all members of the AUC community to express their views as they wish"—with the caveat, "as long as they do not do so in such a way as to disrupt university activities or damage university property." Just one year later the disruption could not have been greater.

In the spring of 2012, a Student Union president was elected ≫

▲ A student leader in the 2012 protests that shut down the campus argues with a member of faculty

on the platform that he would "bring the revolution to the university." Less than two weeks into the fall term a group of students brought the New Cairo Campus to a standstill when, with chains, locks, and parked cars, they closed all the university gates in protest at another tuition fee increase. As the days passed and the gates remained closed, hostility grew between those students, staff, and faculty who supported the protestors, and those who thought their methods overly aggressive and self-defeating. AUCians climbed fences to get onto campus, classes were canceled. Many students and faculty reported being intimidated by the protestors, and anger on both sides erupted into physical violence. Eventually, calmer heads prevailed and negotiations between student parties and the administration saw the protests end in return for a reduction in the proposed increase and a three-year cap on any future hikes. Needless to say, when that cap expired and the administration put up fees again, the action was met with organised student opposition.

Finding a voice and giving it expression is part of the student experience. Added to which, AUC prides itself on encouraging students to ask questions and think for themselves. Protests, then, are inevitable. How to resolve them in an intelligent, fair, and equitable manner is part of the educational experience. ❀

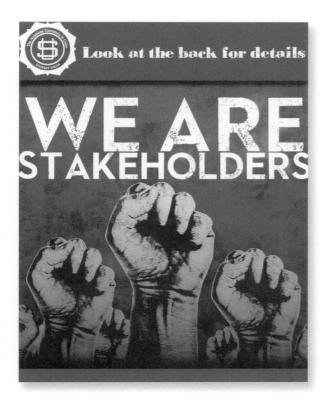

Look at the back for details

WE ARE STAKEHOLDERS

35

AUC'S OTHER PRESIDENTS

Student leaders talk about the importance of the Student Union in university life

W e interviewed seven former Student Union presidents to hear their thoughts on their time in office: Ahmed Ayoub, president 1975–76; Dahlia Khalifa, 1984–85; Ayman Ayad, 1985–86; Ahmed al-Bakry, 1986–87; Beethoven Tayel, 1993–94; Ahmed Alaa Fayed, 2011–12; Ahmed Atalla, 2013–14.

Why is the Student Union important?

Ahmed Ayoub: The Student Union expresses, speaks, and acts on behalf of the student body, which is the core of AUC.

Ayman Ayad: It introduces us as students to the importance of our voice, the concept of voting, and having a say in our own destiny. It is an avenue for students to get a glimpse of the real world before they join it.

What were the major issues that you had to deal with in your time as president?

Dahlia Khalifa: The issues back then are probably similar to those now: tuition fees, extracurricular activities, quality of education, quality of facilities, etc. The point is not necessarily what the issues are, but rather how you address them. In my time we approached issues in a very inclusive, participatory, and deliberative manner so that all voices

▲ Established in the earliest days of AUC, the Student Union has always fully played its part as a major stakeholder in the affairs of the university

"It's the electives you take that shape who you are, the people you meet, and the dreams you build."

Ahmed Atalla ('14), in office 2013–14

were heard, and constructive solutions were put forward. That is not to say that we didn't have a few strikes. What would campus life be without such expressions of political voice?

Ayman Ayad: During my time two critical events happened: the uprising of the security forces, which meant a complete evacuation of the campus for a few hours and a one-week curfew. Then there was the bombing of the PLO headquarters in Tunisia by Israeli forces, which prompted some students to stage a sit-in. It was a challenge dealing equally with those wanting to strike and those wanting to go to classes. There were eleven Israeli students studying at AUC and I was supposed to represent them, too.

Ahmed al-Bakry: We were engaged in a struggle to improve the professor-to-student ratio, which we upped by ten percent.

Beethoven Tayel: I had to deal with a wrecked Union, which came after a failed tuition fees strike that resulted in the resignation of the previous SU president and treasurer. Our image was tarnished and we had to win back the student body.

Ahmed Alaa Fayed: The 2012 strike. What began as a student strike over tuition fees escalated to a campus-wide movement taking in workers, staff, and security personnel.

Ahmed Atalla: The university shut-down and cancellation of classes after the events of 30 June. New declaration and attendance policies, a new student code of conduct, and transport cost increases for students.

"Enjoy every second of the AUC experience, since it will be engraved in your personality forever."

Ahmed al-Bakry ('87), in office 1986–87

Is there anything you are particular proud of having accomplished in your time as president?

Ahmed Ayoub: I was able to play a positive role in the readmission process of a few suspended students.

Dahlia Khalifa: I am proud of having participated in the drafting of the student constitution at the time. I also hope that I encouraged other fellow students to serve [in the Student Union], especially women.

Ahmed Alaa Fayed: Establishing and reviving the Egyptian Student Union, establishing the SU Information Desk, establishing the Student Government Cup, and for the first time the SU supported the travel of a delegation from the student government representatives to the annual American Student Government Association ASGA conference in the States.

Ahmed Atalla: We managed to negotiate a refund policy in the wake of the 2012 strike. We completely revamped the SU brand and outlets, and turned the SU from a subsidized service to a self-funding entity with a surplus of LE250,000 at end of the first year.

If you were to offer a piece of advice to the students of today what would that be?

Ahmed Ayoub: Be proud of being an AUCian.

Dahlia Khalifa: Exploit every minute of your time at AUC. Explore your interests and test your limits. Give more than you expect to receive, because what goes around always comes around.

Ahmed al-Bakry: These are the best years of your lives, so make the best use of them. Build friendships, learn how to research, and get involved in as many AUC events as possible.

Ahmed Alaa Fayed: Perseverance and hard work always pay off, but never forget to have fun along the way.

Ahmed Atalla: It's all about the experience, not your GPA, or the classes you take, or the courses. It's the electives you take that shape who you are, the people you meet, and the dreams you build.

Where did our former SU presidents end up? Ahmed Ayoub ('76) is now retired and handling personal and family interests after a forty-two-year career in the fields of satellite remote sensing and geographic information systems. Dahlia Khalifa ('86, '92) is a senior manager with the World Bank, working with governments around the world to encourage private-sector growth and job creation. Ayman Ayad ('86) is the managing partner in a consulting company specialized in training and development, based in the UAE, but with branches in Cairo, Toronto, and Riyadh. Ahmed al-Bakry ('87) is the chairman of Electrolux Egypt, the co-founder of the New Generation International School, and sits on the board of several organizations. Beethoven Tayel ('94) is the managing partner of a consulting company that specializes in strategy setting, optimization, and turnaround. He also manages a fund that invests in entrepreneurs working in Africa and the Middle East. Ahmed Alaa Fayed ('13) is an assistant professor of public policy at the Doha Institute for Graduate Studies. Ahmed Atalla ('14) is CEO of Raseedi Application, a telecom optimization app. ✤

"The point is not necessarily what the issues are, but rather how you address them."

Dahlia Khalifa ('86, '92), in office 1984–85

"Perseverance and hard work always pay off, but never forget to have fun along the way."

Ahmed Alaa Fayed ('13), in office 2011–12

36

A FAMILY AFFAIR

A three-generation alumni family shares memories with Tess Santorelli

For Farkhonda Hassan ('67), the phrase "mother knows best" takes on an entirely new meaning. Hassan, professor emerita in the School of Sciences and Engineering, has been teaching at AUC for fifty-five years. Her extensive roll call of students includes Nabil Fahmy ('74, '77), Egypt's former foreign minister and founding dean of the School of Global Affairs and Public Policy, and Her Majesty Queen Rania Al Abdullah of Jordan ('91). Yet she has some students she especially enjoyed having in her class—her children and grandchildren.

That particular list included her daughter, Wegdan Lotfi ('79, '91) and grandson Omar Khalifa ('08). Hassan recalls a time when Lotfi was one of her students. Her daughter had a problem with the marking on her exam paper. "She came up to the podium and asked me to explain to her why one of her answers was wrong," says Hassan. "I told her, 'You see this? I couldn't read it.' When she turned to sit down, she said something and the entire class laughed. Mother's Day was two days away and she'd mouthed to the class, 'I'm not getting her a Mother's Day gift.'"

Hassan, who is also co-chair of the Gender Advisory Board of the United Nations Commission on Science and Technology for Development, as well as secretary-general of Egypt's National Council for Women, and a former member of the Egyptian parliament from 1979 to 1984, still finds herself happiest when she is teaching. "I'm a little bit tired of walking across the new campus between classes," she says with a smile. "But still, I find myself in the classroom."

Hassan says having her grandchildren in class has taught her things she didn't previously know about them. "Like Omar, for example, he's very independent. I didn't know that before," Hassan said. "I learned that when he gets an idea, he will do it no matter what. He perseveres."

After graduating from AUC's Department of Chemistry in 1979 and having four children of her own, daughter Wegdan Lotfi earned her master's in solid-state physics in 1991. She became an adjunct faculty member in the Department of Chemistry where she also taught her own

◀ Professor emerita Farkhonda Hassan ('67), with her daughter Wegdan Lotfi ('79, '91), and grandson Omar Khalifa ('08)

children, including son Omar. "He got a B minus in my class," she says jokingly.

Khalifa may have followed his mother and grandmother to AUC but there the paths have diverged. He chose not to study science and he has, so far, not gone into teaching. After graduating with a bachelor's in political science, specializing in international relations, he founded his own publishing and advertising company, Omedia, in 2009. Inspired by the employment fairs at AUC, he launched online job-seeking platform Shaghalni.com in 2015. He had a five-minute meeting to pitch the idea to the person who he says inspired him the most, Naguib Sawiris. The pitch resulted in Sawiris investing in the company.

Though Khalifa majored in political science, he still took classes with both his mother and grandmother. He recalls for one of his mother's assignments there was the option to either give a presentation, write a paper, or make a drawing. "I woke up the morning of the class and in minutes I drew a perfect solar eclipse. When I went to class and handed it in, my friend told my mum, 'He just did that ten minutes ago,' so she made me do a presentation instead."

He received no favors from his grandmother either. "During lunch at her house, she wouldn't answer any of my questions about the course," Khalifa says. "Instead, she'd tell me to visit her during office hours."

"Having a family of AUCians—my son, my daughter, my in-laws, and my grandchildren—is really great," says Hassan. "I think we belong to the AUC culture. All of us." It does not end here. Khalifa has a two-year-old daughter, Carla. "The fourth generation of AUCians!" he says hopefully. ✤

"Having a family of AUCians is really great. We belong to the AUC culture. All of us."

Professor emerita
Farkhonda Hassan

37

READ ALL ABOUT IT

Student newspapers have been marking the changes on campus since 1925

After several weeks of posting campus news and photos on a bulletin board, a journalism class issued a four-page newspaper called *The AUC Review* on 9 April 1925. The paper sold for five milliemes, or half a piaster. In the years that followed, the newspaper secured advertising, students purchased subscriptions, and it improved and expanded. Two name changes and ninety-four years later, and it is still going strong. Here, we chart the progress of the paper in six issues.

THE AUC REVIEW
9 APRIL 1925

In this historic first issue of *The AUC Review* the five joint-editors state: "The appearance of this little review is purely and simply an experiment. The students of the class of journalism have wished for some time to start a college publication for AUC. We dare

to hope that this sheet may prove to be the very humble beginning of a future great student publication that will be a source of pride to the college."

The four-page *Review's* contents comprised news on the comings and goings of the American faculty, cartoons, puzzles, poems, and book reviews, and a notice of the intention to sponsor a Miss AUC contest. In English only at first, an English–Arabic issue appeared in the fall of 1930 under the direction of Eva Habib al-Masri (see pp106–07). ≫

▶ Students reading copies of *Campus Caravan* dated 2 November 1939

"Editing *Caravan* helped me get through AUC. It created an identity for me and a pleasure that went far beyond what everybody else was doing."

Eynas Barakat, *Caravan* editor 1989–90

CAMPUS CARAVAN
3 NOVEMBER 1938

In 1936, *The AUC Review* was joined by a rival publication, *The Bore*. The following year the two merged to be relaunched as *Campus Caravan*. The rebranded paper took on a more professional appearance, looking more like a regular newsstand broadsheet. The quality of reporting was also significantly improved. In this particular issue, dated 3 November 1938, there is a noteworthy story on a newly enrolled student who turns out to be the grandson of Haile Selassie, Emperor of Ethiopia.

CAMPUS CARAVAN
31 MARCH 1950

This twenty-fifth anniversary issue of *Campus Caravan*, *above*, pays tribute to the efforts of the original editors of *The AUC Review*, and those who succeeded them. The issue features articles on the history of AUC student publications and comments from the administrators of the university. "Although the *Review-Caravan* has been uneven in its history, the attempt to maintain the publication of a paper through lean years as through better times is laudable," said Dean Worth Howard. Note, the man who is named new

dean in the headline in the 1938 paper, Professor Badeau, in 1950 is now president of AUC.

CARAVAN
27 DECEMBER 1972

The late 1960s and early '70s were a time of political activism, not just in the student body but also among faculty, and this is reflected in issues of *Caravan* around this time. (Note the name change: *Campus Caravan* became just *Caravan* in 1965.) The lead story in the issue dated 27 December 1972, *below*, is about members of faculty protesting against the United States' renewed bombing in Vietnam. Around sixty of them put their names to a petition that was delivered to the Zamalek home of the chief of the American Interests Section of the Spanish Embassy and which also appeared on the front page of local newspapers. The petition said that the signatories were "disgusted by the unabashed manner in which [the US] pursues the diplomacy of murder." The funky lettering used for the masthead is very much a product of its time.

> "*Caravan* was my first journalistic experience and this is where I learned how to write my first article, not just for the professors but for the masses."
>
> Lamees al-Hadidi, *Caravan* editor 1986

CARAVAN
27 SEPTEMBER 1993

Production of *Caravan* has by now become a whole lot easier thanks to the recent introduction of computers and layout programs. The paper benefits from structural and design changes that give it a modernizing facelift, as seen in the issue dated 27 September 1993, *below*, with its screaming headline—"Strike!!" No surprise, the story is about increased tuition fees. The paper has a combative tone, exemplified by an editorial in which *Caravan* aligns itself with the Student Union in fighting university funding cuts for student organizations (including its student newspaper). Elsewhere, the sense of being under siege is

> **"*Caravan* is a living laboratory of how journalism is on the outside. It's a microcosm of the real world."**
>
> Firas al-Atraqchi, *Caravan* editor 1992–93

heightened by stories—including one on the front page headed "A Sense of Security"—following up on the previous month's assassination attempt on the interior minister, which happened "right in front of AUC," a story covered elsewhere in this book.

CARAVAN
4 MAY 2014

Cheap digital printing allowed *Caravan* to go full color in the late 1990s and new user-friendly software provided a platform for posting stories online by the mid 2000s. Then along came social media, an even bigger game changer. These days, when nearly everybody carries a smartphone, *Caravan* engages with far more readers via Facebook, Twitter, and Instagram than it does through hard copies. Articles no longer need to wait for the print cycle but can go out immediately. The print edition has adapted by no longer just

EGYPT'S PLAGUE: SEXUAL HARASSMENT TARGETS ALL WOMEN

reporting but by setting agendas for discussion. This is most obvious in a series of special editions focused on socio-economic issues. The first of these, in 2014, *above*, was on sexual harassment—headline: "Egypt's plague." Articles tackled the subject from multiple angles and called for changes in the country's laws. The issue was quoted in outside media and cited by the organization UN Women. It resulted in the university holding workshops on the subject. Most significantly, it created awareness of the problem among young males, while giving women on campus the encouragement to speak out. Editors have followed up with further special issues on mental health and bullying. ✦

> **"The articles we post on social media get way more attention than those in print. People argue in the comments section."**
>
> Dania Akkawi, *Caravan* editor 2019

38

WELCOME TO LIFE

Before any class graduates, it is subject to the wit and wisdoms of the commencement speech

---

> "We have given you the perfect world. Don't screw it up."
>
> Woody Allen

As an American university, AUC has long embraced the American oratorical tradition that is the commencement speech. As happens at colleges across the United States, a starry roster of statesmen and stateswomen, great figures of learning, and superstar CEOs have taken to the podium to offer words of encouragement, reassurance, and wisdom to departing graduates. In recent history, those delivering addresses at AUC have included then–first lady Suzanne Mubarak, Queen Rania of Jordan, prime ministers Dr. Atef Ebeid and Ahmed Nazif, tourism minister Rania al-Mashat, Nobel Prize winner in chemistry Dr. Ahmed Zewail, two Egyptian presidents of the World Bank in Dr. Ismail Serageldin and Dr. Ibrahim Shehata, the leading Arab intellectual of his time Edward Said, Egyptian–American space scientist Farouk El Baz, and Nobel laureate Mohamed ElBaradei.

It has to be said, delivering a commencement address offers little opportunity for a speaker to shine. For a start, the speech typically follows a well-established formula, honed over centuries. At the beginning the speaker has to indicate very clearly that he or she was young once, but that as they have grown older they have learnt a few things about life and, as a result, offer a few, often contradictory, platitudes that may be of use: be courageous/be yourself; listen carefully to others/don't listen to what people say; follow your dreams/keep your feet on the ground . . . .

Indeed, the conventions of the commencement speech are so well established that in 2018 American humorist Carl Hiaasen ripped apart the genre in *Assume the Worst: The Graduation Speech You Will Never Hear*. In the book, he corrects some of the advice typically proffered by speakers: "Live every day as if it's your last" ("you won't accomplish a damn thing") and "Spend all your waking hours doing only what feels good" ("only if you're a Labrador retriever").

The commencement address also has to be brief. Perhaps not as brief as the one given by the comedian Woody Allen at Cornell University. It was only two sentences long: "We have given you the perfect world,"

he said. "Don't screw it up." But certainly way more succinct than what is often cited as the longest commencement address on record, given at Harvard University in the eighteenth century. It was six hours long; the first three hours were in Latin and the last three in Greek.

Nevertheless, despite the constraints, there is still plenty of room for some good stuff and many worthwhile words have been addressed to AUC graduates. Mohamed ElBaradei, speaking in February 2006, delivered the sort of arresting opening sentence that few others will ever match: "As I was on my way from the palace of the king of Norway to the Oslo City Hall to receive the Nobel Peace Prize, I found myself reminiscing about my life . . . ." Edward Said, who spoke in June 1999, began by pointing out that being at university—and he spoke as someone who had spent his life in universities—was certainly a lot more fun than working. He went on to speak thrillingly on the contribution that historic Arab–Islamic culture made to what is now considered a modern, liberal, and Western education. »

▲ In the earliest days of the university, as no one room could accommodate the crowds who wished to attend, graduation ceremonies took place in a tent on the athletic field. After 1928, they were held in Ewart Hall. Early speakers included Faris Nimr, publisher of *al-Muqattam*, and Talaat Harb, founder of Bank Misr

127

> **"We have not sought to train you to fit your world but to educate you to make that world a better place."**
>
> Professor emerita
> Doris Shoukri

In the year of her retirement, long-serving professor in the Department of English and Comparative Literature Doris Shoukri admitted that for forty-six years she had sat behind commencement speaker after commencement speaker, reading a book, checking her watch, and stifling her yawns. She found herself bemused to now be at the podium, wondering what her colleagues were doing behind her. Her skill at oratory befitted someone who had spent her life in the study of words. "We have not sought to train you to fit your world but to educate you to make that world a better place, so that you will join the ranks of the rational against the rationalizers, the idealists against the ideologues, and the men of faith against the fanatics."

She offered a fine vision of what a university education should be about. "What this university owes to its students is to make accessible to you man's highest achievements, all that is life-enhancing, whether it be great works of art or great thoughts of great minds . . . so that you see life on its highest plane and are eager to accept and embrace it in all its beautiful diversity, knowing that you are privileged to have encountered and lived in the company of giants upon whose shoulders you can stand, and as St Anslem said, 'see further than the giants themselves.'"

Incidentally, almost every speaker peps up their address with choice words spoken by others. Over the years, AUC's commencement speakers have referenced Plato and Rumi, Karl Jung and the Maharishi Mahesh Yogi, economist John Keynes and biologist Louis Pasteur, William Shakespeare and Naguib Mahfouz, the philosophers Isaiah Berlin and Albert Schweitzer, and, most gnomically of all, American baseball legend Yogi Berra ("When you come to a fork in the road, take it").

Like Doris Shoukri, John Waterbury, president of AUB, guesting at AUC in 2003, also commented on the transition from observer to speaker. "Normally I sit where Acting-President Bartlett sits, and I have the luxury of waiting to see if the commencement speaker has anything interesting to say. More often than not, he or she doesn't. So here I am, cast in the same role, obliged by the occasion to try to say something inspirational or profound. I fear I will do neither." He did himself a disservice, because his was a particularly fine address. Along the way, he told a story from when he was a student, of a colleague, Ali, who didn't know what to study and how to direct his life. In despair he went to see an older professor who said to him, "Ali, I am nearing my retirement. My career is behind me. I know what comes next. There are no choices, no surprises. But you are drowning in choices, everything is open before you. You are very,

very lucky." —"My graduating friends," Waterbury told his audience, "please keep that in mind."

The passage of time was also in the thoughts of Nobel laureate Ahmed Zewail during his address in 2002. "As a child I thought I was immortal, but now I recognize how limited a time we all have." Those words carry added poignancy since the scientist's premature death in 2016. More words with particular significance in hindsight were spoken by Suzanne Mubarak in 2000, quoting American cultural anthropologist Margaret Mead: "Never doubt that a small group of thoughtful committed citizens can change the world; indeed it is the only thing that ever has."

The last words go not to a distinguished celebrity but to an AUC student. Every year, one person from the graduating class is chosen to deliver an address. In 2017 it was the turn of Ali Shaltout, a double major in mechanical engineering and accounting. Chuckling his way through his allotted seven or so minutes, he spoke honestly and passionately from recent, raw experience. His basic message was, hey, not all of us will become billionaires or celebrities, and that's okay. "Class of 2017," he said, although speaking perhaps to all generations of graduates, past, present, and future, "just chill." ⬡

▲ In recent times crowds of up to five thousand fellow students, families, and friends have gathered in the ARTOC Sports Court to watch AUCians become alumni. For the year 2018–19, over 1,500 students graduated

39

BACK AT THE OLD STOMPING GROUND

AUC receives a visit from the YouTube queen

▲ "She is very inspiring and she is always helping people out," said Nada Ali, journalism student, interviewed about Queen Rania on the occasion of her 2010 visit to AUC

On 28 February 2010, the woman formerly known as Rania al-Yassin tweeted, "Back at my old stomping ground today, American University in Cairo (AUC). Memories of student life flooding back to me!"

Except this was no ordinary visit. Queen Rania was born in Kuwait City in 1970 to Palestinian parents, who had moved from the West Bank just before the 1967 Arab–Israeli War. She attended the New English School in Kuwait before enrolling, in 1987, at AUC, where she studied business and computer science. She graduated in 1991. By this time her family had moved to Jordan, after Iraq invaded Kuwait in 1990, and she joined them there. In an interview with *Elle* magazine in 2006, Queen Rania discussed the life she had imagined for herself: "Following my studies, I would probably have become a businesswoman." Initially, life conformed to expectations and she landed jobs in marketing at Citibank in Amman and then at Apple. At a dinner party in 1993 she met a man and they hit it off; six months later they were married. In 1999 that man was crowned King Abdullah II of Jordan.

And so in 2010, Queen Rania returned to AUC as both an alumna and visiting royalty. She was here at the invitation of AUC's John D. Gerhart Center (see pp303–05). Never one to choose the easy path, Her Majesty became greatly involved in the public sphere from day one. Passionate about education, she established the Queen Rania Foundation for Education and Development (QRF), to ensure children in Jordan and across the region have access to stimulating classrooms and learning resources that keep up with technology. She has also advocated to draw attention to the global plight of refugees, and continues to speak out against divisive rhetoric that incites fear and hatred.

A thoroughly modern royal, she uses social media to get her message out. Her Instagram account boasts 5.5 million followers, while 10.5 million follow her on Twitter. On both platforms her hashtag is the no-nonsense Queen Rania and she winningly describes herself to followers as "A mum and a wife with a really cool day job."

◀ Her Majesty Queen Rania Al Abdullah, who studied business and computer science at AUC 1987–90

──────

"It's been a long time since I left AUC, but AUC has never left me."

Queen Rania Al Abdullah,
Bassily Auditorium,
28 February 2010

──────

At AUC, Queen Rania spoke about the importance of civic engagement in the Arab region and the role it could play in improving lives and ensuring progress. She called on the next generation of young Arabs who have pursued higher education to accept their obligation to advance their societies. "Because inside each and every one of us," she told a packed Bassily Auditorium, "is the ability to look beyond ourselves and improve our societies for the better [. . .] civic engagement is about looking outside the four walls of your life," she added. She ended her talk by calling for action and change. "What are we waiting for? None of us can hope to fix everything, but each of us can do something," she said.

AUC's president at the time, David Arnold, noted that Queen Rania (the "YouTube Queen," he called her) stood as a role model for young people around the globe, pointing out that she chose "a life of service and volunteer leadership on behalf of others." He added that her example stood "as a testament to all the best qualities that we wish our graduates to strive for"—a sentiment that holds true until today. ⊛

40

EGYPTIAN WOMEN CHANGING THEIR WORLD

AUC women are stand-out achievers in public service

▶ Economics graduate Rania al-Mashat ('95) currently serves as Egypt's first ever female minister of tourism

In 2016, Cambridge Scholars Publishing put out a book called *Daughters of the Nile: Egyptian Women Changing Their World*. It is a celebration of high-achieving Egyptian women, a number of whom were invited by editor Samia Spencer to tell their stories and share their thoughts in print. Some of the stories are truly inspirational and many of the women have achieved firsts not just in Egypt but on a global scale. What is also very interesting, as one reviewer noted, is that of the thirty-seven featured women, a startling sixty percent either attended or have taught at AUC.

One of those contributing to the book is Rania al-Mashat ('95), the first woman to head the Ministry of Tourism in Egypt since its establishment sixty years ago. She graduated from AUC in economics, where, she has said, she was particularly influenced by her professors, Galal Amin, who taught the principles of economic development, and Adel Beshai, who lectured on international trade. While at AUC, al-Mashat was active in numerous extracurricular activities, including the Model United Nations, Model Arab League, and the Arab Cultural Club. After earning her master's and PhD from the University of Maryland, College Park, she returned to AUC to serve as an

> "There are four pillars of success to me, my four Cs. Competence. Connections. Confidence. Charm. These four Cs started for me at AUC."
>
> H.E. Dr. Rania al-Mashat ('95)

▶ Holder of a BA and master's in economics from AUC, Sahar Nasr serves as Egypt's minister of inverstment and international cooperation

adjunct professor, teaching monetary policy and central banking. She has worked with prominent financial institutions in Egypt and worldwide, including the International Monetary Fund, Central Bank of Egypt, and Egyptian Stock Exchange. These days, as minister al-Mashat oversees various boards, including the Egyptian Tourism Promotion Board and the Tourism Development and Investment Board. Throughout her career, she has emphasized being driven by a sense of responsibility to give back to her country. "Serving Egypt by contributing to policies that would make the riches of the Nile flow to all its citizens is not only a mission, it's a passion," she wrote in her piece for *Daughters of the Nile*.

Minister of investment and international cooperation Sahar Nasr also has close ties to AUC. She joined the university first as a student, graduating with a BA in economics in 1985 and a master's in the same in 1990, and then in 2002 became a faculty member and researcher in the department of economics, where she is still an active contributor. She was honored by the Supreme Council of Universities in 2013 for her publications, research, and academic career, during which she published more than sixty research papers, technical reports, and books. Since her appointment to the government in 2017, her most notable achievements include the passing of a long-awaited Investment Law, introducing incentives intended to make Egypt one of the top investment destinations in the region, as well as establishing and strengthening partnerships with the Gulf, Africa, and Asia. She is also a member of the Economic Committee in Egypt's Cabinet of Ministers. "My studies and work at AUC laid the foundations on which I built my professional career," Nasr has said. "With its global focus, the university has fostered my passion for international affairs and my desire to give back to my country and the global community." »

◀ In early 2016, Caroline Maher ('09) became the youngest member to be appointed to the Egyptian parliament. In the event that matters get heated in the chamber, Maher is also a world Taekwondo champion

A third woman at the highest levels of government also has an AUC background. Ghada Waly, who currently serves as minister of social solidarity (the government body responsible for providing social safety networks for Egypt's most vulnerable citizens), may have graduated from Colorado State University in the United States, but her first two years of university study took place at AUC. "It's a place that remains very dear to my heart," she told an audience at the 2015 Annual Research Conference, held at AUC. "It is where I started my college years, it's where my children got their education."

These three women are only the most high-profile among many AUC alumnae in public service. "If you look at our graduates they are salted in the upper reaches of government—and many of them are women," says AUC President Frank Ricciardone. Parliamentarian Heba Hagress ('82, '98) has spent a career championing the rights of women and people with disabilities, most notably as a member of the National Council for Disability Affairs in Egypt and National Council for Women. Mervat Tallaway ('61) paved the way for Egyptian women in 1989 when she became her country's first female ambassador, representing Egypt first to Austria then Japan. She was later Egypt's minister of insurance and social affairs, and also served as secretary-general of the National Council for Women. More recently, Caroline Maher ('09), a graduate of journalism and mass communication, became the youngest member of the Egyptian parliament—this on top of being a former world taekwondo champion, who not long ago ranked third globally and is honored in the Taekwondo Hall of Fame. Since taking up her role in parliament, Maher has drafted a law to amend the penalties for sexual harassment and rape, and fortified the penalty for female circumcision.

It is not just at the top levels that AUC's alumnae are reshaping society, they are also working from the bottom and looking up. When Queen Rania spoke at AUC in 2010 (see pp130–31), her theme was

social progress coming from communities and individuals. She told the story of one particular woman as an example; in her freshman year at AUC, Raghda al-Ebrashi ('04, '07) founded an organization that provides microloans to underprivileged entrepreneurs and vocational training to low-income workers. She was technically too young at the time to run a non-governmental organization and, by her own admission, al-Ebrashi's work distracted her from her studies, but university administrators and many professors encouraged her. Today, Alashanek Ya Balady, the organization that al-Ebrashi heads, has been operating for more than sixteen years and is one of the biggest youth NGOs in the country.

One thing that set al-Ebrashi's organization apart in its early years was that it relied wholly on the work of university students. The group created a model and franchised it to students at other schools— something al-Ebrashi believes was possible only because of the way AUC fosters involvement in student activities as a central component of its liberal arts education.

"It's what makes AUC stand out," says al-Ebrashi. "I think the role of AUC extends beyond the education domain. It's building the personality of students who join to be active citizens." Male and female. ⊕

▲ In 2002, at the age of eighteen, Raghda al-Ebrashi started a student crusade which has grown into Egypt's first employment agency for the underprivileged

135

41

GETTING ON IN BUSINESS

A new wave of
AUC alums are
going it alone

Even during their time at AUC, Tarek al-Nazer ('06), Basel Mashhour ('04), and Sameh al-Sadat ('05), friends and founders of The Bakery Shop, were food-focused. "My favorite memory at AUC is definitely the time we spent in the cafeteria eating the same thing every day for four years," laughs al-Sadat.

Since its founding in 2008, The Bakery Shop, which offers sandwiches and pastries made fresh on the premises, has expanded to several branches across Egypt, including one on AUC's New Cairo Campus. "AUC for us was a great school that helped in sharpening our minds and building the networks we needed to get into the next stage of our lives," explains al-Nazer, who studied accounting. They also credit the opportunities they were given to travel as AUC students: al-Nazer to New York for the Model United Nations, and al-Sadat and Mashhour (both political science students) to the University of Southern California and McGill University, respectively, on summer courses.

"AUC gave me the foundation I needed. It was like a lab where you learn, practice, and share knowledge with different people," says Mashhour. Their advice to budding entrepreneurs at the university? "Learn inside of class as much as you learn outside of class. The more you do on campus and the more you do within the AUC domain—this will have a huge impact on your life later on," says al-Nazer.

Traditionally, large numbers of AUC graduates have gone on to rise to the top in business, heading up national and global companies, such as Saudi Aramco, PepsiCo Egypt, Etisalat, IBM, and numerous banks. The Bakery Shop boys are emblematic of a new breed of business alum— the go-it-alone entrepreneur.

Having a mindset to innovate and inspire is what made Hadeer Shalaby ('11, business administration and marketing) the youngest regional director of Careem Bus, the region's leading app-based car-booking service. Shalaby's first venture was to introduce a car-reservation service on the north coast, called Taxi El Sa7el, in the summer of

2014. "It came out of a personal need to get around the north coast, and I couldn't find anyone to take me," she says. Instead of waiting for someone to make it happen, she decided to start her own business, offering transportation using other people's cars. "At the time, I hadn't heard about Careem," she says. She started surveying people about what they would expect from such a service and investigating the best pricing strategies for the market. "At some point, our drivers decided to quit on us, so I went and drove myself and had my dad, friends, and mothers of friends drive as well. It was so exciting to see your own idea become a reality and actually help people in their daily lives," she says.

After the success of Taxi El Sa7el, the young entrepreneur was approached by the Dubai-based company Careem to launch its operations in Cairo. "They had the technology, and I had the market knowledge in Egypt and experience in the industry," says Shalaby, who in 2017 was recognized by *Amwal al-Ghad* magazine as one of the "Top 50 Most Influential Women in Egypt." »

▲ *Left to right*, Tarek al-Nazer, Basel Mashhour, and Sameh al-Sadat, the three AUC friends and founders of successful chain The Bakery Shop

▲ Mohamed Rafea is the creator of the app Bey2ollak, which allows people to share traffic information in real time

Transportation issues were also the motivation for Mostafa Kandil ('15), who co-founded the ride-sharing business Swvl and—with his partners—sold a stake to Hadeer Shalaby's employers Careem, secured $8 million in venture capital, and began plans to expand from Egypt to a bunch of other countries, as far afield as the Philippines. All of that within three years of graduating from AUC. Kandil says the education he received at AUC helped him focus his ambition: "Everyone is competing globally, and you are part of AUC, which is competing globally. It opens your mind to beyond Egypt."

Kandil and his partners received help in modeling their business from AUC's Venture Lab, a project run by the university specifically to offer support and guidance for start-ups—for more on which, see pp300–302.

Computer science-graduate Mohamed Rafea ('03, '11) is tackling Cairo's traffic with his startup, Bey2ollak, a mobile application that allows people to share traffic updates in real-time. "Through Bey2ollak, we empower people to beat traffic together," says Rafea. Bey2ollak now

> **"Hard work and innovation are key elements for today's entrepreneurs. We do not need more imitation on the market, but unique products."**
>
> Hind Wassef, co-founder of Diwan bookstores

has 1.3 million registered users and is a winner of the NexGen and Start with Google competitions. "We have been creating jobs and helping people lead healthier lives by avoiding problems related to traffic and safety." Rafea is a recipient of the 2015 Distinguished Alumni Award from AUC.

MAKING A BUSINESS OF BOOKS

It would be wrong to suggest that the entrepreneurial spirit in AUC alumni is something entirely new. The Wassef sisters Hind ('92, '95) and Nadia ('94, '96) both earned their bachelor's and master's degrees in English and comparative literature from AUC. (Nadia also went on to get a second master's in social anthropology from the School of Oriental and African Studies at the University of London.) After graduation, both went on to work at NGOs, individually addressing women's issues and education in Egypt. However, the sisters had always talked about opening a bookstore and so, on 8 March 2002—International Women's Day—they launched their flagship Diwan store on 26 July Street in Zamalek, Cairo. It was something quite unique: a warm, welcoming place with books for children and adults in English, Arabic, French, and German; it also sold movies and music, and had a coffeeshop that was a safe and inviting space for women. It was an immediate success and seventeen years on, Diwan remains a cultural landmark in Egypt, hosting talks, workshops, and events at its six stores across Egypt.

▲ Hind *(left)* and Nadia Wassef of Diwan. Nadia recently told an audience at the Abu Dhabi Book Fair that when she and her sister launched the first of their bookstores they were mystified by its success

In 2011, the Wassef sisters received the "Veuve Clicquot Initiative for Economic Development Award;" in 2013 they were presented with the "Best Woman Entrepreneur Award" by the American Chamber of Commerce's Middle East and North Africa Council; and in 2015 they were named among Forbes *Middle East*'s "100 Most Powerful Arab Business Women."

In 2016, the sisters were invited back by AUC to speak at the university's mid-year commencement. "I am overwhelmed by how much this institution has taught me over the years," said Nadia. "First and foremost, I am grateful for the love of reading that AUC instilled in me. This love led to a lifelong relationship with books."

The stores born of that love of reading and books now stand as shining beacons to education, community, social consciousness, and entrepreneurial spirit. ⊛

42

PEAK PERFORMER

If you are willing to persevere, you can make anything happen, says Omar Samra

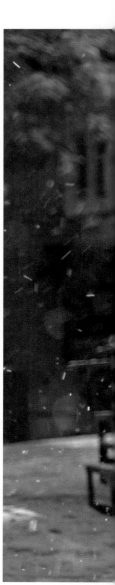

As a child, Omar Samra ('00) was severely asthmatic and breathing was a problem. And yet at the age of twenty-eight he was standing at the top of Mount Everest.

The idea to tackle Everest came when Samra was sixteen and visiting the Swiss Alps. It was the first time he'd ever seen snow and he decided then and there he wanted to climb the world's highest mountain. It seemed like an insurmountable goal so he began breaking it down to smaller, more achievable parts, climbing progressively harder and bigger mountains as the years went by.

Meanwhile, he enrolled at AUC, starting off in engineering before switching to economics. After graduating he took banking jobs in London and Hong Kong, before in December 2002, handing in his notice and embarking on a year-long journey across Asia and Latin America. It was while pursuing an MBA in London he decided it was finally time to tackle Everest. In May 2007 he became the first Egyptian and youngest Arab to summit the 8,850-meter peak.

The following year he set himself the goal of climbing the highest mountain on every continent, which he proceeded to do, ticking them off, one by one: Mount Kilimanjaro (Africa, 2008), Elbrus (Europe, 2008), Carstenz Pyramid (Australasia, 2009), Aconcagua (South America, 2011), Vinson Massif (Antarctica, 2012), and Mount McKinley (North America, 2013). He was the first Egyptian to do this. In December 2014, he became the first Egyptian to ski to the South Pole and in April 2015, the first Egyptian to reach the North Pole. He is now one of only forty people ever to complete the Explorers Grand Slam, defined as summiting the named seven peaks and skiing to the two poles.

When he is not testing himself against earthly extremes, Samra runs Wild Guanabana, an adventure travel company. He also heads a nonprofit (named after his late wife, Marwa Fayed) that provides progressive educational content and tools to underprivileged children and refugee families. And he serves as the United Nations Development Programme's goodwill ambassador to Egypt.

Samra often returns to AUC to talk to students. His message is invariably the same and is always inspiring: "You can break the mold. You determine your destiny." ✤

▲ Omar Samra, whose achievements provide inspiration not just for generations of AUCians, but for anyone around the world with dreams

141

43

SOUND AND VISION

A few of the AUCians who have gone on to make their careers on screen and stage

▲ After graduating AUC with a BA in theatre, Amina Khalil ('09) went on to study acting in New York and Moscow

There is a story in an issue of *AUC Today* from spring 2010 about the Alumni Community Theatre (ACT) group that carries a photograph of four actors in a line on stage. Three of the actors direct their attention on the fourth, a tall woman, head raised, mouth open like maybe she's singing. But looking at the picture today, chances are that your eye is going to catch on the figure at the opposite end of the line up, the shortest of the quartet, a girl all in black with a pink bow in her hair. Is that . . . ? It is, it's Amina Khalil.

Currently topping the A-list with star billing in a succession of Ramadan hit shows including *Grand Hotel* (2016), *Layali Eugenie* (*Eugenie Nights*, 2018), and *Qabil* (2019), and movies such as *Sukkar Murr* (*Bitter Sugar*, 2015), *Sheikh Jackson* (2017), and *122* (2018), Khalil studied theatre at AUC, graduating in 2009. How she got from AUC to hanging out at El Gouna and taking selfies with footballer Mohamed Salah is perhaps partly explained by what she told *AUC Today* back in 2010: "When I began my new job, I told my boss about ACT and that I didn't intend to miss any auditions or meetings, which meant that during peak times at work, I sometimes came home at 6am." Of course, she's also very talented.

While theatre programs are offered at other universities in Egypt, AUC's program is known for its high artistic and academic quality. Numerous other famous Egyptian actors have benefited from the program—even if they didn't necessarily major in theatre.

Asser Yassin ('04) graduated in mechanical engineering but it was at AUC that he got his first taste of performing. "My favorite moment at AUC was my first time being on stage," he says. Since then he has played roles in the TV series *Qalb Habiba* (*Habiba's Heart*, 2006), and in the movies *al-Wa'd* (*The Promise*, 2008) and *Rasayel al-Bahr* (*Messages from the Sea*, 2010), for which he won Best Actor at the Carthage Film Festival and the Malmo Arab Film Festival. He also won Best Actor at the Tetouan International Mediterranean Film Festival for his movie *Aswar al-Qamar*

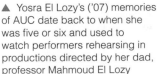

▲ Yosra El Lozy's ('07) memories of AUC date back to when she was five or six and used to watch performers rehearsing in productions directed by her dad, professor Mahmoud El Lozy

(*The Walls of the Moon*, 2015). Most recently, he played the lead role in *Turab al-Mas* (Diamond Dust, 2018).

Yosra El Lozy ('07, political science) has a relationship with AUC that dates back to when she was six years old attending rehearsals held by her father, theatre professor Mahmoud El Lozy. She is now a successful actress with awards under her belt for her roles in *Qubulat Masruqa* (*Stolen Kisses*, 2008), *Heliopolis* (2010), and *Microphone* (2011). Amr Waked ('96) is another political science graduate who began acting at AUC, appearing in several university theatre productions. His acting skills have since taken him to Hollywood, where he has starred in *Syriana* (2005) alongside George Clooney, *Salmon Fishing in the Yemen* (2011) with Ewan McGregor and Emily Blunt, and *Lucy* (2014) with Scarlett Johansson. Most recently he has been appearing in a bald cap playing the father of Ramy in the US TV comedy series of the same name.

ON THE OTHER SIDE OF THE LENS

Yet another political scientist, alumnus Abu Bakr Shawky ('10), wrote in his yearbook that he wanted to direct films. Eight years later and ≫

▲ Abu Bakr Shawky ('10), writer and director of the internationally acclaimed movie *Yomeddine*

the Egyptian–Austrian's movie *Yomeddine* was selected to participate in the 2018 Cannes Film Festival and compete for the Palme d'Or, and was Egypt's entry for the 2019 foreign-language Oscar. Shawky also worked as a consultant and writers' assistant on TV mini-series *The Looming Tower* (2018), which, of course, is based on a book penned by another former AUCian, the journalist Lawrence Wright. Recently, Shawky won *Variety*'s "MENA Talent of the Year Award" at El-Gouna Film Festival.

A native of Saudi Arabia, Haifaa al-Mansour ('97) came to AUC to study English and comparative literature. Fifteen years later she achieved global fame when her movie *Wadjda*, which she wrote and directed, made its premiere at the 2012 Venice Film Festival. It was the first full-length feature shot entirely in Saudi Arabia (a country which at that time had no cinemas). She has since directed the Hollywood movie *Mary Shelley* (2017), starring Elle Fanning. She recently completed shooting her latest film, *The Perfect Candidate* (2020).

VOICES OF AUC

With one notable exception, it is still too early to gauge the impact of AUC's recently introduced music technology and music performance programs (see pp96–97) but, even so, plenty of vocal talent has already been nurtured on campus. Long before he first sang "Habibi da," Hisham Abbas ('88) was a mechanical engineering student but already a star in the making, beating out forty other performers to take first place in AUC's 1987 talent show.

At the time "Habibi da" was soundtracking every Cairo taxi ride, Mohamed Khaled Abou El-Enein was studying business with a minor in economics at AUC. When he graduated in 2002, in his yearbook entry he predicted that ten years on he would be, "a very spiritual religious person." Perhaps he is, but what he failed to predict was that fifteen years on—using the stage name Abu—he would write and perform a song, "Talat Daqqat" ("Three Beats"), that would receive more than 470 million views on YouTube and which would become the unofficial AUC anthem.

By contrast, Gala El Hadidi ('05, '07) was already a star before she arrived at AUC. A week before beginning her freshman year, she joined the Cairo Opera House as its youngest singer, aged eighteen, and went

> **"As an AUC student it doesn't matter what you major in because your experiences go far beyond your major."**
>
> Actor Asser Yassin ('04)

on to perform as a solo artist in Italy, Germany, France, Switzerland, England, Belgium, Denmark, Norway, Finland, Turkey, Morocco, Algeria, and the United States. After graduating in philosophy and English and comparative literature, she received scholarships to attend the International Bach Academy in Stuttgart, Germany and to study for a Master of Music at Yale University. She became the first Egyptian to be nominated for the BBC Cardiff Singer of the World, in 2013, and she is the first Egyptian opera singer to perform the title role of Carmen on the international stage.

Nesma Mahgoub ('13) is a product of AUC's music performance program. She solidified her stardom after winning the eighth season of *Star Academy Arabia* in 2011. She went on to voice Elsa in the Arabic dub of Disney's *Frozen*. In addition to regular public performances (at which she often sings in a variety of languages, including Arabic, English, Italian, German, Latin, French, and Hindi), she has also returned to AUC to teach "singing on stage," teaching students how to perform professionally. She also currently directs the AUC Pop Ensemble, which performs a range of genres including pop, rock, and gospel. ✿

▲ Business major graduate Mohamed Khalid Abu El-Enein ('02), now better known as singer–songwriter Abu, returns to perform at AUC

145

44

AN AUC BOOKSHELF

AUC alumni are well represented in bookshops around the world—here are ten notable titles

The Sixth Day (1960)
Andrée Chedid

Born and educated in Cairo, Chedid ('42) began her first poetry collection while a student at AUC. She moved to Paris in 1946, where she would live for the rest of her life. She published close to twenty volumes of poetry and about the same number of novels, the best known of which is *The Sixth Day*, which tells the story of woman's desperate attempts to take her grandson from a Cairo ravaged by cholera to the safety of the countryside. Youssef Chahine filmed it as *al-Yom al-sadis*.

The Map of Love (1999)
Ahdaf Soueif

In between Cairo University and Lancaster University in England, Soueif completed a masters in English literature at AUC ('73). Her first collection of short stories, *Aisha*, was published in 1983, followed by an ambitious novel, *In the Eye of the Sun*, in 1993. A second volume of short stories, *Sandpiper*, appeared in 1996, followed three years later by the widely praised *The Map of Love*, which was shortlisted for the prestigious Booker Prize and was translated into more than twenty languages, including Arabic. Her most recent book is *Cairo: Memoir of a City Transformed* (2014).

Maq'ad akhir fi Qa'at Iwart (Last Seat in Ewart Hall) (2005)
Mai Khaled

Khaled ('85) began her writing career on AUC's student newspaper, *Caravan*. After graduation, she began to write short stories in her free time. Her first collection, titled *Atyaf December* ('December Phantoms'), appeared in 1998. She followed it with three novels: *Gidar akhir* ('Last Wall') in 2001; *Nuqush wa taranim* ('Carvings and Crenelations') in 2003; and, two years later, *Maq'ad akhir fi Qa'at Iwart*, which is based on Mai's time as a student at AUC. "I discovered myself at AUC," she told *AUC Today* in 2006.

Cairo Stories (2007)
Anne-Marie Drosso

After her graduation ('74), Cairo-born Drosso relocated to Canada, where she did a PhD in economics and later completed a law degree. She began writing while living in London and had a first collection of short stories, titled *Cairo Stories*, all set in modern Egypt, published by Telegram Books. Alaa Al Aswany liked it enough to supply a cover blurb. Her first novel, *In Their Father's Country*, was published in 2009, and a second short story collection, *Hookah Nights: Tales from Cairo*, came out in 2018. She now lives in Vancouver.

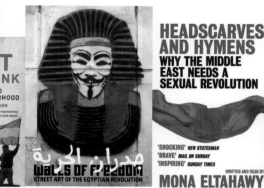
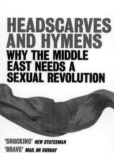

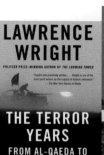
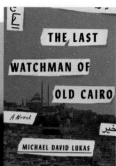

Egypt on the Brink: From Nasser to the Muslim Brotherhood (2013)
Tarek Osman
It was Osman's bad luck that his book on the modern political history of Egypt came out just weeks before the events of 2011, when the dramatic events on Tahrir Square rewrote the country's history. That did not stop *Egypt on the Brink* becoming a best-seller. The AUC graduate ('98) has since updated his text, taking the events up to summer 2013. Since then, he has written and presented several BBC documentary series and he is also a commentator for several leading newspapers and magazines worldwide.

Walls of Freedom: Street Art of the Egyptian Revolution (2014)
Basma Hamdy and Don Karl
Of the many books that have appeared on the graffiti of the revolution, this is one of the most sharply designed. The person responsible for that is Basma Hamdy ('98), who graduated from AUC in psychology with an art minor. She subsequently studied at the Art Institute of Chicago and now teaches graphic design at the Virginia Commonwealth University in Qatar. She is currently working on a book that documents found typography across Egypt.

Headscarves and Hymens: Why the Middle East Needs a Sexual Revolution (2015)
Mona Eltahawy
Eltahawy ('90, '92) is a Muslim, feminist, New York-based journalist and commentator, whose work has appeared in international publications including *The Washington Post*, *Globe and Mail*, *The Guardian*, and *New York Times*. *Newsweek* magazine named her one of its "150 Fearless Women of 2012." *Headscarves and Hymens* is a passionate condemnation of the repression and abuse of women in the Muslim world.

Chronicle of a Last Summer (2016)
Yasmine El Rashidi
El Rashidi ('97) graduated with a bachelor's in journalism and mass communication, which she has since put to use contributing to the *Wall Street Journal*, *Washington Post*, and *New York Review of Books*. In 2011, she published a collection of her dispatches from Tahrir Square as an ebook titled *The Battle for Egypt*. The aftermath of the revolution features in her debut novel, *Chronicle of a Last Summer*, in which an Egyptian girl passes from youth to adulthood as viewed over three particular summers ranged across three decades.

The Terror Years: From Al-Qaeda to the Islamic State (2016)
Lawrence Wright
Wright (MA '71), who as well as studying Arabic also taught English at AUC, is a notable American journalist, author, and screenwriter. He received the Pulitzer Prize for his bestselling *The Looming Tower: Al-Qaeda and the Road to 9/11*. His 2016 book *The Terror Years* analyzes the factors that he believes led to the rise of terrorism in the Middle East. His latest publication is about a politically controversial major oil-producing state with a large Muslim population: Texas.

The Last Watchman of Old Cairo (2018)
Michael David Lukas
A graduate of Brown University and the University of Maryland, American author and creative-writing teacher Lukas took classes in Arabic at AUC in the fall of 2000 as a study-abroad student. He was also a Fulbright Scholar in Turkey, an experience that informed his first novel, *The Oracle of Stamboul* (2011), a finalist for the California Book Award. *The Last Watchman of Old Cairo* revolves around the Ben Ezra Synagogue in Old Cairo and time-hops between the medieval era, 1897, and the twentieth century. ✦

45

THE SENIOR ALUMNUS

Born in 1923,
former student
and lecturer
Wadei Philistin is
AUC's oldest living
alumnus

When Wadei Philistin graduated from AUC in 1942 Farouk was king of Egypt and Sudan. Philistin went on to have a career in journalism and writing, working for *al-Muqattam*, and *al-Muqtataf*, and authoring or translating over forty books. He also taught journalism at the AUC. In 2008, at the age of eighty-five, he was interviewed as part of the ongoing AUC Archives oral history project. Following are extracts from that session, which can be read and listened to in its entirety online as part of the Rare Books and Special Collections digital library.

"I joined AUC in 1938. I was educated in an English school before, so I preferred to come to AUC because it meant I followed a foreign education. But of course I didn't have any idea about what to expect. Although I didn't have any literary or journalistic aptitudes, I joined the journalism section simply because there was a possibility of finding a job when I graduated.

"The full tuition fee at this time was eighteen pounds per year. It was beyond my means, so when I enrolled at AUC they gave me a grant of eight pounds, and I had to make up the other ten. The deal was that when the librarian went to have his meals I took his place, and I also worked as usher at the events hosted by the Division of Extension.

"The university at that time was very small, and everybody knew everybody at least by name from the president, Dr. Watson, down to the hall porter. Dr. Watson taught us the philosophy of religion. He used to tell us, 'Here at AUC we don't educate you. We simply give you keys. And with these keys you can open whatever you want.'

"AUC, this was my first exposure to co-education. My family was Upper Egyptian and I was brought up in a conservative environment, so I found it difficult to mix with the girls.

"AUC was the first institute in the Middle East to teach journalism on an academic standard. When I joined this department in 1939, two classes had already graduated. We studied news writing and editing, editorial writing, and what we call reportage, in addition to advertising,

Exam one week from today.
(+ maybe a pop quiz some time too)

◀ Wadei Philistin graduated from AUC seventy-seven years ago, at the time of writing. He later returned to the classroom to teach journalism

"At AUC we were handed the keys of knowledge."

Wadei Philistin

translation. We had a course in Arabic literature and also a course in English drama. We had the *Campus Caravan*, of which I became editor-in-chief for one year.

"The whole period I spent at AUC, it was during the war and there was censorship of all newspapers. So I had to take the newspaper and go to the Ministry of the Interior to an Azharite sheikh who would read the newspaper and clear it for publication. He used to object whenever we included any jokes.

"At that time we used to read *Time* magazine and in it we would find advertisements for Coca-Cola. What was this Coca-Cola? Maybe some kind of American tomato juice?

"When I graduated I gave myself one month off to rest and then I went to see my professor, Fuad Sarrouf. He asked me had I found a job and I said no and he said, 'Do you want to work at *al-Ahram*?' He gave me a letter for the general manager, who was a cousin of his, and I was employed on the spot.

"I'm grateful to AUC because they have honored me twice. When fifty years had elapsed after I graduated they gave a luncheon and I was presented with a gold medal. And when I reached the age of eighty, they honored me again—and President Arnold gave me a certificate testifying that I was not a failure [laughs]." ✥

46

THE PURSUIT AND EXPRESSION OF TRUTH

AUC alumni working as journalists are inducing positive change around the world

As this book was being pulled together it was announced that Egyptian investigative journalist Maggie Michael and two of her colleagues had been awarded the 2019 Pulitzer Prize for international reporting. The trio, who work for the Associated Press, have been uncovering atrocities and suffering in the ongoing war in Yemen. Michael, who graduated from AUC in journalism and mass communication in 2000, has filed a series of reports, including documenting civilian casualties of a US drone campaign, drawing attention to the presence of child soldiers on the front lines, and showing evidence of torture by both Houthi rebels and US-backed forces. The following month the same team won the Michael Kelly Award, sponsored by the Atlantic Media Company, for "the fearless pursuit and expression of truth."

Michael says she was clear in the career she wanted for herself from around the age of thirteen or fourteen, when she became fascinated by an Egyptian journalist who at the time was uncovering cases of corruption where money and politics intertwined. She came to AUC, she says, because it "provides the best education in Egypt that challenges dogmas and opens up students' minds and hearts to knowledge and new ideas." While at AUC she wrote for *Caravan*—"the best days of my life," she says—and today her Twitter handle is the same name she used for her regular *Caravan* column: "mokhbersahafi" ("detective journalist").

Similarly single-minded, Lina Attalah ('04) is co-founder and chief editor of *Mada Masr*, the independent online Egyptian newspaper, which has frequently locked horns with the authorities in its fight against restrictions being placed on honest journalism. In 2017, *TIME* magazine recognized her as a "New Generation Leader," calling her the "Muckraker of the Arab World," while the previous year *Arabian Business* named her one of the "World's Most Influential Young Arabs of 2016."

Like Maggie Michael, Attalah places a high value on AUC's liberal arts ethos and credits some of the Core Curriculum courses with shaping her thinking, notably the classes on economic history taught

by Abdel Aziz Ezz El Arab. With the support of Ezz El Arab, a core group of students, including Attalah, formed a solidarity movement with Palestinian refugees, visiting camps in Lebanon and Jordan. In 2000, the group protested in solidarity with the Palestinian Intifada and later against the 2003 US-led invasion of Iraq. "It was my entry to politics, really," says Attalah.

Back in the field of TV journalism, Ramy Radwan ('06) is the presenter of *8 al-Subh* on DMC—which previously received audience ratings as the most viewed and popular morning show. Prior to that, he was a presenter on Ten TV, OnTV, and OTV. Yousef Gamal El-Din ('07, '10) is a Bloomberg TV anchor, who has been the host of *Daybreak: Middle East* since 2016. Over the years, he has interviewed heads of state, ministers, CEOs, and billionaires from around the world.

As presenters, they follow in the footsteps of several distinguished alumni, not least Mona Elshazly ('96), an AUC journalism graduate known to millions through her TV interviews with everybody and anybody who matters. She was named as the "Most Influential Presenter in the Arab World" in a CNN poll and "Best Egyptian Media Personality of the Past 25 Years" by Al-Ahram Foundation. She currently presents the program *Ma'kum Mona Elshazly* on CBC.

▲ *Top*, Maggie Michael reporting for the Associated Press in Yemen. *Above*, founder of news site *Mada Masr*, Lina Attalah

»

▲ Former editor of the AUC student newspaper *Caravan*, Lamees Al Hadidi, who has since gone on to be one of the biggest names in Egyptian media

A former editor of *Caravan*, Lamees Al Hadidi ('87, '90) has gone on to do broadcast journalism for Al Arabiya, Al Jazeera, CNBC Arabia, and MBC; hosting *Itkallim* on Egyptian television; and serving as lead anchor and host of CBC's daily news show, *Huna al-'asima*. She co-founded, with Emad al-Din Adeeb, the first daily business newspaper in the Arab world, *al-'Alam al-yawm*. She has been named among the World's Most Influential Arab Women *(Arabian Business)* and 50 Most Powerful Women in Africa *(Jeune Afrique)*.

"Working at *Caravan* made me realize that I wanted to be a journalist," she told *AUC Today*. "What I took from AUC is the value of knowledge, research, accuracy and debate. And, of course, the value of friendship."

Outside of Egypt, Yasmine El Rashidi ('97) is a regular contributing opinion writer for *The New York Times*, a regular essayist for *The New York Review of Books*, and a contributing editor for the Middle East arts and culture journal *Bidoun*. Lawrence Wright, who taught English at AUC and received an MA in applied linguistics here in 1969, is a staff writer with *The New Yorker*, an author (see p147), and a Pulitzer Prize winner. He's probably best known at this point in time for his book *The Looming Tower: al-Qaeda and the Road to 9/11*, which was made into a big-budget television miniseries that screened globally in 2018 on Hulu. He has said of his formative years in Cairo, "A lot of the pleasure I get out of my job as a reporter now derives from that initial experience of being thrust into a world that was so foreign, but at the same time so enthralling and friendly."

Long-established *New York Times* columnists Nicholas Kristof and Thomas Friedman frequently find themselves on opposing sides of an argument, particularly those relating to the Middle East, but both studied Arabic at AUC, Kristof in 1984, Friedman in 1974. Both are winners of multiple Pulitzer Prizes.

Together they are a fitting illustration of what journalism at AUC is all about—finding a voice, and engaging in shared values of freedom and accountability. And maybe winning the odd Pulitzer Prize, too. Congratulations, Maggie. ⚽

LEARNING TO SPELL "PHARAOH"

Small classes, world-renowned professors, and being in Egypt make AUC a magnet for students of Egyptology

There is no better place to study Egyptology than in Egypt itself. Salima Ikram (YAB '86) knew this when she attended AUC as an international student in the 1980s and made up her mind to pursue a career in the field. Now a distinguished professor of Egyptology at AUC, she experiences the magic of Egypt each time she introduces her students to an ancient image of an object and then asks them, "Okay, would you like to go see where it is, in its original context?"

AUC offers a "unique chance to do Egyptology the way you can't really anywhere else," says Ikram, during a break in her work directing a dig at the tomb of Amenmesse in the Valley of the Kings. And it's not just about seeing the important sites. For students from abroad, it's also about experiencing the desert, she says. "I think that ninety percent of a culture is based on the people's interaction with the environments."

Egyptology at AUC is surprisingly young. Related courses were taught from the early 1970s, but Egyptology as a program was launched by President Richard Pedersen only in 1978 with the hiring of Egyptologist Ali Hassan. He was succeeded by Kent Weeks (see pp243–45), who was joined in 1984 by prominent ancient Egyptian language specialist Fayza Haikal and, a little later, by former student Salima Ikram. Since then, aided by more staff, a regular succession of top-rank >>

▲ Former year-abroad student Salima Ikram, now a professor, archaeologist, and leading expert on animal mummies and one of the leading scholars in Egyptian funerary archaeology

"Education and adventure are often the same thing."

Kate Liszka (YAB '00),
Egyptology alumna

visiting scholars, and unrivaled access to all things ancient and Egyptian, the department has welcomed a steady stream of undergraduates and graduates, many of whom have gone on to pursue further studies at the likes of Oxford, Cambridge, Chicago, UCLA, Brown, and Yale, and to enjoy fascinating careers in the field.

American Louise Bertini came to AUC in 2004 as a study-abroad student specifically to work with Ikram, because of their shared passion for old bones. While at AUC, Bertini was able to gain experience assisting on a variety of excavation sites, gathering ancient animal remains, which she studied back in Cairo. She eventually became a teaching assistant to Ikram and later a faculty member in the department. She left in 2017 to become director of the American Research Center in Egypt.

Another American study-abroad student, Kate Liszka, attended AUC in 1999–2000, while studying for her BA at Penn State. In addition to her classes on ancient Egypt, she took Arabic and volunteered for the Theban Mapping Project (see pp243–45). "I wanted to immerse myself in both the cultures of the past and the present," says Liszka. "A year abroad in Egypt was the perfect way to do that." She says her time studying Egyptology at AUC was "one of the most fun and greatest years of my life." There were hiccups. One time Salima Ikram marched up to where she sat with friends and said, "Miss Liszka, if you do not learn how to spell the word 'pharaoh' correctly, I will never write you a letter of recommendation for graduate school."

Liszka now teaches at California State University San Bernardino. In addition, she is director of the Wadi al-Hudi Expedition, mapping and excavating ancient amethyst mines in Egypt's Eastern Desert. And, of course, she now knows how to spell "pharaoh."

Leslie Warden studied at AUC as an exchange student from the University of California, Davis in 2000–2001. "I wanted to study Egyptology, and what better place than Egypt?" she says. She considers the experience seminal for both her personal growth and her career. "While I don't stay in touch with most of my UCD friends, I still talk to many of my AUC friends." The most important thing she learned, she says, was how to live and work in Egypt. "To be an Egyptologist without understanding modern Egypt is to lose something of the Egyptian past." These days she is an associate professor of art history and archaeology at Roanoke College in Virginia. She excavates at Kom al-Hisn, and is head of ceramics on a German Archaeological Institute dig on Elephantine Island in Aswan, and head ceramicist for the North Kharga Oasis Survey, directed by Salima Ikram.

Monica Hanna ('04, '07), who has fond memories of mummifying fish with Salima Ikram, was recognized by the New York–based non-

▲ Leslie Warden's out-of-office email reads, "I am in Egypt with my pottery. I am afraid that between emails and potsherds, the sherds win every time"

profit organization Saving Antiquities for Everyone (SAFE) in 2014 for her outstanding achievements in raising public awareness of Egypt's endangered cultural heritage and the devastating consequences of the illicit antiquities trade. She is currently acting dean of the archaeology and cultural heritage department at the Arab Academy for Science and Technology and Maritime Transport in Aswan.

Majoring in Egyptology at the same time as Hanna, Mennat-Allah El Dorry ('05) is now with the Ministry of Antiquities, where she is working towards establishing an archaeobotanical (the study of plant remains) research unit at the National Museum of Egyptian Civilisation. Another AUC Egyptology graduate attached to the antiquities ministry is Yasmin El Shazly ('98), who has also held the positions of assistant to the minister for museum affairs and head of documentation at the Egyptian Museum in Cairo. During her time studying Egyptology at AUC she was lucky enough to work on the excavation of KV5, the tomb of Rameses II, with Kent Weeks. She is currently on leave from the ministry and teaching Egyptology at AUC.

Salima Ikram, meanwhile, in addition to teaching, reaches out beyond campus to convey her enthusiasm via books and television appearances for the likes of the Discovery Channel, National Geographic, and the BBC. "I just want people to love the ancient Egyptians the way I do," she says. ⊛

▲ Egyptology at AUC is very hands-on. Students get to apply ancient Egyptian methods to manufacture cosmetics, bake bread, shape pottery, and, of course, mummify pets

48

"17 AND IN AUC"

Five years at
the university in
one fifty-six-hour
performance piece

———

Hassan Khan was an undergraduate at AUC from 1990 to 1995, majoring in English and comparative literature because at that time he was focused on being a writer. As things turned out, he is a writer, but he is equally a musician and an artist. He works in a variety of media, from film and video to text, sound, photography, and installation. He has had solo exhibitions around the world, including in Paris (2004), Vienna (2005), London (2006), Berlin (2008), New York (2011), Istanbul (2012), São Paulo (2014), and Frankfurt (2015). He has performed, lectured, and participated in screenings from Abu Dhabi to New York, and, as a musician, he has composed soundtracks for theater and performed his own pieces in numerous venues. In 2017 he was awarded the Silver Lion for the most promising young artist at the Venice Biennale for "Composition for a Public Park," a multilayered sound piece on a series of speakers set in a small garden.

One of Khan's best known pieces is "17 and in AUC." For fourteen nights, from 7 to 20 April 2003, he sat in a soundproofed, one-way mirrored glass room from 7pm to 11pm drinking beer, smoking, and talking. Although people could see and hear him, Khan could not see or hear anything except for himself. ("I don't know if there is anyone [there] except my sister," he says at the beginning, "and who cares who is there, . . . it doesn't matter.") The glass room was constructed in an apartment rented in Downtown Cairo, funded by AUC's Falaki Gallery. Over the span of those two weeks, Khan spoke and spoke and spoke, grasping at foggy memories, meandering through shaggy-dog stories, and analyzing past events in a rambling fifty-six-hour confessional. A video camera recorded the performance and the tapes were broadcast in fourteen daily four-hour segments at the campus gallery.

"AUC was formative in many ways," he says, "and that's partially what '17 and in AUC' is about." Khan was deeply involved in many things during his undergraduate years, some of which included hard-core music experimentation, the theater workshops of fellow student Ahmed

to some conversation and we were going to have our gig me and Sherif in a few
n to come but apparently he missed his stop and everything and so now a story
why but I noticed that I can categorize the stories in different groups there are
at turn them into specific units I noticed that till now the 6th day I told stories
ifference and stories of connection and stories of adventure and stories of
ation yeah till now these seem to be the main themes the question is where will
e's a conflict between the act of remembering and the power of the form itself
value lies in using the form and exploring that side of the form to access
ramed but remembered but the form has its own impetus and as the days go by
ns stronger and stronger so it might be necessary to try to find a way using it
my frame that I think is possible so how to do that exactly? it was funny also
ene at the time I was not part of it I knew friends who were part of it Firas Taji
cene before before the Satanist craze that Satanist craze came three years or 4
ginnings of that but I witnessed the beginnings of that I was definitely not into
t was just a matter of taste not necessarily into the scene either but it was
e of its positive elements is that it did connect people in this city from different
her there was an AUC contingency but there was also a Cairo University touch
people from different language schools who were into it and then there were
of bands coming out of different areas in the city where you would not expect
t was and it came out and the cool thing it was still commercialized of course
difficulties in a city like Cairo because the value of space and because of the
te and it is very difficult to do things outside of that commercialization it is
ere but I think it is extra difficult here because of that but anyway even though
it was still a moment where there were these connections happening of people
ces plugging into something that was definitely against something that was a
was connected to something wider and it could be blunt and stupid for sure but
ing for me seeing it I went to two or three events like that just enjoyed the way
from different places and had something strongly angry and immoral and kind
a positive sense kind of happy to see that and you can draw parallels between
'90s and now with the ecstasy thing but it was very different it was very
k part of adventures and exploring the city like '80s Cairo life these kind of
with new friends not with old friends but I remember I already spoke about the
all the importance and significance of the hall in Sari's house at that time
nber going the first time to a night club a downtown oriental night club with
herif I'm not sure if the first time was just me and Sari or was it all three of us
ure where the city is exotic and it is exotic because you are removed from it so
tic and you are living an adventure OK first time Oriental night club went to
lfy the Alfy street and it was cool the people there thought we were really weird
resting again was searching for these kind of spaces in the city whether in that
her within a something related to a deep direction whichever direction always
es where people mix and are accepted beyond class they can fight each other but
other somehow New Arizona was so different from for example Atlas which was
out for AUC people the point the attitude seemed to be everybody is here to let
matter who you are and if you're weird or fucked up for them or look very strange
tery unclear who you are exactly they'll jut take you as an adventure too and so

I guess I was fascinated by these places because they were places about exotic like each other where everybody is in a way a member and everybody is an exotic element too so so we went there and we were sitting on a table and drinking and watching the belly dancer and she came and she danced on our table and standing on our table and we were of course really young I think it was Sherif 's birthday or something so we were like yeah this was really 17 and we were like blablabla and we danced with her and everything and Sari's like dance with Sherif and we wanted her to dance with Sherif and she in a super bitchy mode said he's too small it won't work and of course we all got the double meaning of that and what's funny in a night club is how we got into this for a few days after laughing about it not funny very expected of people our age in our situation but interesting I had another period later on in my life of going to a lot of places like that but in a completely different mood with a completely different attitude and it had nothing to do with this kind of AUC syndrome at all because by then anyway I was completely outside of it it was just much more personal related to a certain kind of personal darkness and exploring that personal darkness and liking that personal darkness too so we did a bit of that and I think what was that I would call a touching story kind of something that is just so naïve but it was it better intentioned me and Sherif going around from night club to night club from bar to bar in downtown and Ramsis all places completely outside our supposed sphere trying to find jobs as musicians to play there and the music that we were doing was very much like noise improvised feedback not something you'll hear in any night club let alone an Oriental night club but we had this kind of naive romanticism of OK we will somehow take this there and somehow be part of popular culture in a way we tried we actually tried for a few days walking around and offering our services and of course failed completely but what's interesting is that well at least there was the intention of plugging in and you maybe it was also realizing how it doesn't work that way and learning that's the other interesting side that each moment like that there is something being understood as much as there is something that is not understood as much as there is a romanticism a naivete there is a moment where you're getting something acquiring something understanding something else yeah early on I learned the power of being the target in a way I always was conscious of it and I always saw it in games of seduction because a lot of them were based upon this kind of moment of giving away the key offering a certain key to yourself or the illusion of offering a certain key to yourself because in a way you don't really have a key to yourself but because it is easier to communicate with this idea that this exists you can and you offer something and the thing is that this game is not necessarily extremely successful but when it's successful it is extremely powerful because it doesn't necessarily work so well with a lot of people because the moment you offer people something the assumption is that there is a weakness and they want to use it and then they kind of lose interest lose the attraction but for the few who are beyond that and in a way are more interested the fact of offering the key is a seduction itself a challenge to take it somewhere beyond that kind of relationship and I've seen myself do this many times I failed a few times and succeeded a few times but I've seen myself do this many many times and it has something to do with the power of being the target in a way something to do with framing yourself as possibly something very fragile and possibly something that is to be destroyed and there is a magnet here somewhere yeah in a project I did in India there was a question in that project it was a project that had a video in it but it had a lot of other elements in it and the video had six questions in them and one of the questions is who looks at you when you speak and that's an interesting question because it is not about who looks at you when you speak and someone is actually looking at you it is also about who do you imagine seeing you when

El Attar (founder of the Studio Emad Eddin Foundation and Downtown Contemporary Arts Festival), and visual experiments with colleague Amr Hosny (these days an event organizer and graphic designer). All these activities were creative, productive, and social, says Khan, and happened via AUC even if they were not of the university.

For Khan, AUC was a place he could meet like-minded, passionate, critical, and culturally hungry people. In that respect, he notes, the AUC experience was formative, although he suggests that was despite and partially in response to the institution's elitism and conservatism—the boundaries of which Khan frequently tested, on the evidence of his monologue.

The links with AUC continue. In 2014 the university's Sharjah Art Gallery partnered with Khan to produce a specially tailored program titled "Footnotes to Hassan Khan" that included an electronic music concert and a seminar series for students delivered by the artist on his experiences at AUC. ✤

▲ Every audible word of "17 and in AUC" was transcribed and the results were published in a book by Merz and Crousel without any editing or punctuation. The book is organized by day and hour to mirror the structure of the performance

49

DOWNTOWN DAYS

Floating pianos, miniskirts, Pink Floyd's *The Wall*, rats in the walls, earthquakes … life at AUC was, well, different back then

Former faculty and alumni share memories of AUC's Downtown campuses.

THE UNDERWATER CAMPUS

"When I got into Cairo, which was this magnificent city with this little campus set in the middle—because Tahrir Square was not what it is today, it was just a little rotary back then—it was the season of the last flooding of the Nile, so Kasr al-Aini was a little bit underwater. In those days there was no housing office, so I was told to check into the Garden City Pension and they wished me good luck in finding an apartment."

Cynthia Nelson, former professor

"Because we arrived in time to enjoy the last Nile flood—this is the autumn of 1964—there were pools of water in the streets, and an occasional drowned rat or other similar creature. I could see that one of the functions of the flood was to clean out a lot of detritus and a lot of small animals of that kind. The basement of the Khairy Palace was underwater and a Steinway grand piano that belonged to AUC was floating around in it. In charge of operations to get the water pumped out was a rather loony American engineer who we discovered later on was a nudist."

John Rodenbeck, professor emeritus

CAMPUS HANG-OUTS

"At the time when I went to AUC it was not recognized by the state. So it was a place where you sort of hung around, especially if you didn't have very good grades. And it was a hideout for people who didn't want to go to the army. There were a lot of them at the time. You had two main places where people congregated, and you belonged to one or the other. That was the fountain area or the tennis court. The intellectual crowd used to hang around the fountain, while the tennis court was more chic. Those people had designer jeans and the Ray Bans that were very popular at the time."

Paul Geday ('79, '88)

▶ The fountain court was the place for the quieter students and study-abroads. The cats loved it too

"The fountain court was where as a newcomer to the AUC scene I would timidly pull up one of the bamboo chairs at a table, relieved to claim a place to sit alone with a book for company. The fountain area was the quieter side of AUC's social scene, which is why it appealed to me more than the area in front of Hill House, which was where couples would enjoy sitting on the lawn, holding hands. I can even remember the names of the famous couples who were almost permanent fixtures there."
Jehan Attia ('77)

"If you wanted [to find] a study-abroad student, you went to the fountain area, the presidential gate, or the Rare Books Library. If you wanted him/her with their semi-Egyptian friends, you'd find the gang sitting on the platform by the library gate. If you needed an activities dude, you took a trip to the students' lounge or the Greek booths' area. If you were wondering about the latest fashion, pass by the Gucci corner down the platform by the Social Studies building. And, of course, for any technical assistance, you head straight for the Falaki labs. For the

▲ The area around the tennis courts was where the cool kids and couples hung out

'take it easy' chill out, there was always the Social Studies balconies. That was the campus's diverse spirit, and you just had to admire it."
Eman Elba ('07)

INITIMACY

"Classes were very small. A big class was eight people. It was heaven. We felt we were very special and our relationship with our instructors was very different and they could »

◄ "The plat," the raised area leading to the entrance to the Greek Campus library, was a main center of social life and a showcase for student fashion

give us a lot of time because we were so few. And it was magnificent."
Samia Mehrez ('77, '79)

WHAT, NO iPHONE?

"When I first joined AUC's computer center it occupied the entire third floor of Hill House. It was busy with the computing veterans, data entry operators, and the next generation of computing hopefuls (including yours truly). There was a special room with raised floor and freezing air conditioning that hosted our IBM mainframe, nicknamed by all of us 'The Baby.' You had to wear warm clothes in there. This was where the hard drives were, each one the size of small fridge and able to store the amazing amount of (if memory serves me) one megabyte. The entire capacity of the mainframe we had back then can now be placed on a single flash drive."
Sherif al-Kassas, professor

"In some ways, AUC was cutting edge, even in the fall of 1991. We had email, although it was limited to five or six terminals in a Hill House lab; this pretty well met the demand,

as few people in those days knew anyone back home with email to converse with. And there was CNN in the faculty lounge, at a time when very few AUC faculty even owned a TV. This was a big deal indeed, and during breaks between classes it kept many of us feeling in touch with the wider world."
Rob Switzer, Dean of HUSS

THURSDAY NIGHT MOVIES

"We had this guy who was a movie buff. His name was George Makris and he used to make the selection for the Thursday night movies. He used to bring these incredible but sometimes very difficult to understand movies, like you know, Stanley Kubrick's *Barry Lyndon*. God knows how he used to get them because at that time you couldn't simply download stuff, you had to get the actual physical reels of film. So if it was a Russian movie, a Tarkovsky or something, you'd have to get the reels from the Russian Cultural Center or something. It was a big operation, but there was an incredible, incredible selection."
Paul Geday ('79, '88)

DRESSING UP AND DOWN

"I remember attending plays at the Wallace Theatre even before I became a student at AUC. It is also there that I performed for the first time in my life. In those days the students did the actual building of the sets under the direction of a technical director. This took place on Friday and Sunday mornings, the official AUC weekends in those days. While we worked we would play records and tapes on the theatre's sound system. It's in Wallace Theatre that we first listened to Pink Floyd's *The Wall*. In those pre-air conditioning days we would often change into bathing suits during the warm season in order to be able to tolerate the heat as we worked."
Mahmoud El Lozy ('76, '79)

GREEDEES

"I said, 'I want to start a cafeteria in the Greek School,' and I did, in the basement, in the Greek School, called Greedees. I used to wake up at five o'clock in the morning to get everything there and get things started so that people could get their breakfast shakes and their croissants. Because there was no such thing as Hardee's and McDonald's then. No, it was fuul, tamiya, and fatir."
Laila Saad

RATS

"The building of the Falaki Academic Center, or the New Falaki Building as it usually referred to, started in 1994 and was completed in 2001. During this seven-year period, wild life had plenty of time to firmly establish itself in its nooks and

crannies. By the time we moved, the air conditioning ducts were full of rats. I am sure the rats did not like our presence just as much as we did not like theirs, but neither we nor the rats had any alternative but to tolerate each other. The rats could not get out because the building is almost hermetically sealed. It took several months and plenty of rat poison to finally see them off."
Mahmoud Farag, professor

SECURITY

"The campus was more open. Until the late 70s there was no security at AUC, I think on one of the gates, there was a bawwab in a galabiyya, but there was no security."
Mahmoud El Lozy ('76, '79)

EARTHQUAKE

"It's 3:09 pm, six minutes to go [before the end of class]. And then, suddenly, the sound of distant rumbling. Are my ears playing tricks on me? The rumbling grows louder and then the chairs are shaking.

▲ At one time, smoking on campus was almost obligatory

The walls are shaking. The room is shaking. What is going on? My first thought is that the building is collapsing. Is this possible? A terrorist attack? I hear our tutor shout: 'Stand in the doorway! Stand in the doorway!' How? How can fourteen people stand in a doorway? No. We need to get out. It seems everybody is thinking the same. We hear people rushing outside in the corridor, so we all collect our things (!), get up quietly, and leave the room. We go out into the garden and find an incredible number of people already there. The frightening rumbling noise has stopped and the shaking is over. Everybody is talking: 'What is it?' 'What happened?' 'Has there been an explosion on the metro?' 'No,' someone says. 'An earthquake.' I hadn't thought of that. I immediately start to worry about my son at school and family at home (mobile phones hadn't been invented yet). I need to find out where my son is. I rush to the Mohamed Mahmoud gate, find my car, and drive home."
Nagwa Kassabgy, instructor

DRESS CODE

"We dressed in secular modern. Girls were in mini skirts. I think there was one veiled woman on campus and she was the talk of the entire campus. We were far dressier. We came looking very fashionable, in a dress or new boots."
Samia Mehrez ('77, '79) ✾

▲ At AUC in the 1980s there was not a headscarf to be seen

50

ROCK & ROLL HALL OF FAME

A roll call of highlights in the history of student bands

▲ A flyer for a Gama Show concert at Ewart Hall in 1978. The ticket price includes gifts from SIAG cosmetics and Marlboro

What a decade the Fifties were. There were riots on the streets of Cairo; the Free Officers staged a revolution that deposed the king; the joint forces of Britain, France, and Israel attempted to seize the Suez Canal; and AUC was invaded by rock & roll. Well, that's what the headline said—"Rock & Roll invades AUC"—in the *Campus Caravan* dated March 1957. The aggressors were a band called The Skyrockets, who took to the stage at the Howard Theater and got the students so out of control with numbers like "See You Later Alligator" and "Tutti Frutti" that a member of faculty had to tell students to "Relax." Lead singer and guitarist Assad Kelada was an AUC journalism student and actor who appeared in a couple of films. Asked by *Caravan* how he fitted in his studies he replied, "I don't sleep much." After graduating in 1961, he moved to America, where he still works as a director of TV sitcoms.

Meanwhile, in 1965 two teenagers, Mourad Rouchdy and Ali Hazzah, formed a band they called The Mass. Both had British mothers and the boys were inspired by the music coming out of London, specifically the rhythm & blues played by the likes of The Rolling Stones, The Yardbirds, and The Animals. When Rouchdy entered AUC to study physics and mathematics, The Mass effectively became the university's house band, playing parties and providing musical backing for the acts in the annual talent shows held at Ewart Hall. The rock & roll antics spilled off stage when they reportedly tried to beat up a *Caravan* reporter who had given them a bad review. Bassist Rouchdy graduated in February 1973 and later emigrated to Canada before moving to the Gulf. Another Mass member, lead singer Tarek "Ricky" Nour, went on to become a literal icon in the field of advertising, with his silhouetted portrait serving as the logo for his super-successful agency, Americana.

As the seventies progressed, AUCians donned flares and frilled shirts to groove to homegrown bands like Shakti, Highway, and Zie Comes Free, all of which performed covers of tracks by the likes of Queen, Styx,

▲ The Gama Show: Marilyn Coreige (vocals), Mahmoud Nayel (bass), Lamya al-Mugheiry (vocals), Raed Baddar (guitar), Laurette Coreige (vocals), Seif Alla Sadek (drums), Basil Philistin (guitar/keyboards), Hesham Ragab (vocals, guitar, keyboards)

and Deep Purple. A Student Union festival featuring the three in January 1979 drew complaints that it was too loud. A union representative offered to reimburse any members of the audience with ear damage. Around the same time, a bunch of AUC students who had won the 1978 talent show decided to form a band. Led by Raed Baddar (guitars) and Basil Philistin (keyboards) they called themselves Gama Show. Musically promiscuous to say the least, Gama's sets included Greek and Latin American music, sixties classics, and disco. Following a lull in activity, the band reformed in 1981, recruiting another AUC talent show winner, Lamya al-Mugheiry, as lead singer. Lamya later moved to London and New York and sang backing vocals for David Bowie, James Brown, and Duran Duran; she released her own highly regarded album in 2002.

Raed Baddar put aside his guitar on graduating and instead founded the annual Pharaoh's Rally motor race. His partner, Philistin, joined former Mass singer Tarek Nour, writing jingles for Americana, before moving to Canada where he continues to write and record music for television and commercial clients. "Most people go to university to study," says Philistin. "I went to AUC because of Ewart Hall, a place where I could perform and present my music. There was no other place." Baddar and Philistin still speak regularly. "The songs we composed back then still touch me," says Philistin. ⬡

163

51

CAMPUS CATS

For as long as anyone can remember cats have been part of campus life

▲ Design for an AUC mascot and logo by Nourhan Abdel Baki ('16), a graduate of the graphic design program

An article in *Campus Caravan* dated 25 February 1957 visits Hill House, which at the time was the university hostel. "The lounge: 5 p.m. Sami Manna eats his dinner near the radio … Hisham Dabbousy plays tawla with Mohammad Mougazi … Meanwhile, Am Fahim prepares the special food for Little Ambler, Mishmish and their kittens, the cat family of the hostel."

No one knows how long cats have been at AUC but the article proves that felines have called campus home for at least sixty years. Rowaida Saad-Eldin remembers lots of cats roaming wild around campus when she was a student in the 1970s. She never paid much attention, except to throw them a piece of her sandwich. Her attitude changed years later when she was working as an assistant to AUC president Donald McDonald. He noticed an injured cat and decided that something needed to be done. He instructed Rowaida to find a vet, and suggested it might be a good idea to have the cats spayed and neutered. "As a Muslim," she says, "I thought, spay and neuter? Are we playing God?" But she came to see the sense. The treated cats became calmer, friendlier, and generally more "pet-like." They also grew bigger—not least because McDonald gave money out of his own pocket to make sure all the cats were fed twice a day. In fact, the cats looked so healthy that people started assuming they had been imported from America.

Not every president, or presidential spouse, has been a cat fan. Molly Bartlett, wife of Thomas Bartlett, was superstitious about black cats walking in front of her. Often she would encounter two, three, or four cats on the grand stairs leading up to the president's office and if they were black she would walk up the stairs backward to avoid having the cat cross her path. She thought, "Enough already," and pretty soon after that the cats were rounded up and removed.

Similarly, not all students appreciate the cats. "Some are terrified, like they saw Godzilla in the garden," says Ingrid Wassmann, who works in marketing for the AUC Press and is based on the Tahrir Campus. "They've

never had any contact with cats, so this is a perfect chance for them to become acquainted with a fellow creature that inhabits their city. It is another kind of education, beyond the text book."

At the present time, the Tahrir Campus cat population is low, down to perhaps less than ten. One reason is that the cats used to be fed by the campus custodians but since a recent round of redundancies that food source has gone. Wassmann and other cat-loving staff members do their best to fill in, but many cats have gone elsewhere looking for a meal. "There are cats that have been here for decades," says Wassmann. "These are feline alumni. They are part of the heritage of this campus."

Cats are already an integral part of the New Cairo Campus, too. Contrary to popular belief, the animals did not travel with the university when it moved from Downtown. These cats are native New Cairo cats that, like their cousins on Tahrir, adopted the university. Initially, they were neutered and vaccinated, and there was even a budget allowance for cat food allocated to the university's safety department. However, at some point the funds for feeding the cats were stopped. Since then, students have taken up the slack, piling up their kitty offerings beside the bus terminal gate each morning. At last count, there were about forty felines on the New Cairo Campus. In 2017 a student wing of the Animal Rights Association (ARA) launched a "Cats on Campus" project dedicated to maintaining the health and wellbeing of the animals, and finding new homes for any campus-born kittens.

Meanwhile, Rowaida Saad-Eldin no longer works for the president's office but still spends time on both campuses. If you see her she will probably be carrying two bags: one will be a chic bag in which she carries her papers and purse; the other is for her sandwiches, a change of shoes, and, tucked in there as well, a packet of dried food for the cats. ⊛

▲ Students are divided on the issue of cats on campus. While many like having them around and feed them, others consider them unhygenic. Salma Seyam, project director of the Animal Rights Association, points out, "They've been on campus longer than a lot of students and faculty"

52

JOIN THE CLUB

AUC's student
co-curricular
activities are as
important as its
academic offerings

A UC's more than sixty clubs and organizations reflect the university's global character (AIESEC, Black Student Association, Model United Nations), students' professional zeal (associations of accounting, architecture, business, construction engineering, and many more), and a heartening community awareness, with countless groups devoted to charities and causes, including cancer research, disabilities, literacy, refugees, and helping the elderly.

Participating in clubs and activities outside of the classroom has been key to an AUC education since the university's first administration. Early regulations stated that each student had to participate in at least one club or activity, but no more than two at any time. Special activity cards were given to every student, and these had to be filled out by a supervisor, with comments about the student's degree of participation and the value of their contributions. All extra-curricular activities were divided into A and B categories, and students with bad academic grades were not allowed to participate in A-class activities, a list that included athletics, theatre, the orchestra, and working on the student newspaper.

Among the earliest clubs were the Ramses (established 1920–21) and Penatur (1921–22) societies, both dedicated to literature; the Travel and Nature Study Club, which organized trips to places of historic or geographic interest; the Glee Club, dedicated to singing college songs; and the Stamp Club, dedicated to the collecting and trading of postage stamps. Later came the (aptly named?) Bore Club, devoted to publishing pieces of literary criticism, the Maskers, which staged theatre productions, and the Ushers, whose members helped direct audiences to their seats at events in Ewart Hall, and received one complimentary ticket for a friend in payment.

A few other clubs stand out as worthy of description.

THE MOLIÈRE SOCIETY

English and Arabic have always been the main languages on campus, but French has had its supporters too, not least in the Molière Society, which began meeting in 1935 and was active until the late 1940s. Early meets were learned celebrations of classic French poetry, with recitations delivered by members in the surroundings of the Oriental Hall. However, things livened up in later years when music was added and members were a little less precious on the matter of national criteria—performances at meetings included pieces by Mozart, Brahms, and Liszt (Austrian, German, and Hungarian, respectively). A 1940 meeting reported by *Campus Caravan* included a magician turning handkerchiefs into milk and vice versa, with ice-cream and cakes at the interval. However, there was a certain element of selectivity involved because the society seems to have published notices of its upcoming events in French only. »

▲ From the accumulated evidence of stories in *The AUC Review* and *Campus Caravan*, the most popular student activity was a trip to the Pyramids. On occasion, students even spent the night on top of the Great Pyramid

▲ To encourage photography, the Kodak company in Egypt took full-page ads in *AUC Review*, *above*, and offered a discounts to members of the Kodak Club on all developing and printing

THE KODAK CLUB

The hobby of taking pictures took off in a big way in the 1920s, thanks to the arrival of the compact 35mm camera, hence the AUC's own club for "students who are interested in photography and own cameras." The club made regular trips to places of interest where pictures were taken—one year they ventured as far as Khartoum. Later, the "art" was "carefully studied under the direction of a skilled member of Faculty." The pictures taken by the Kodakers were presented annually to the president of AUC and, presumably, some of these images must now make up part of the current University Archives.

AL-QUDS FRIENDS GROUP

There is a long history of Palestinians studying at AUC, and they enrolled in greater numbers following the wars that accompanied the creation of Israel in 1948. They had their own student society, which was cultural, aimed at promoting Palestinian customs and traditions. That changed after 1967. Mahmoud El Lozy, professor in the theatre program, was a student at the time and remembers the club well. "It was probably the most popular club on campus," he told *Caravan*. "At that time we were all politically conscious. We were aware that the Palestinian question was the question of all Arabs." The activism continued into the eighties, re-energized when Israel invaded southern Lebanon in 1982 (it should be noted that by this time there were few Palestinians in the student body and the group's membership was 80 percent Egyptian). Activities included film screenings, notably on the Chatila and Sabra massacres, and hosting guest speakers, including Nabil Shaath, then the special

envoy of Yasser Arafat to the US—his daughter Randa was an AUC student and a leading figure in the Al-Quds club.

As the eighties rolled into the nineties, the club placed donation boxes around campus and sent funds for the "youth of the Palestinian uprising" engaged in the First Intifada. However, by the mid-1990s interest was waning. "There are lots of freshman students who really don't know what is happening in Palestine," said a club spokesperson.

Pro-Palestinian support remains strong on campus—witness the demonstrations on campus in 2017 that greeted President Donald Trump's decision to recognize Jerusalem as the capital of Israel—but the Al-Quds club is no more and the rallying is now led by the Student Union.

Clubs are of their time, they come and go. In 2003, students founded the Anti-Drug Team to warn students off illegal substances, but that has fallen by the wayside. In 2006–2007, there was the briefly popular Bussy Project, inspired by Eve Ensler's *The Vagina Monologues*, raising awareness of women's issues (although it continues as an NGO). There was the Third World Society, a name that now seems as antiquated as the Glee Club. It will be educational to see what comes next. It is unlikely to be a revival of the Stamp Club. ❀

▲ In April 2002, students parked a truck outside AUC and asked for donations of humanitarian aid for the Palestinians. They received enough to fill thirty trucks

169

53

STAGE BY STAGE

Theatre has been an integral part of AUC almost since the university began

While AUC's major and minors in Theatre were only added as recently as the 1980s, students and faculty have been presenting plays since the earliest days of the university. Instrumental in this was an early head of the English Department, C. Worth Howard, who believed that dramatics encouraged self-expression and more: "For students learning a foreign language," he insisted, "there is perhaps no better way of acquiring ease, fluency, and exactness than by appearing in well-written plays in that language." The historic first AUC production took place in 1926 and was *A Night at an Inn*, by Edward Plunkett (also known as Lord Dunsany), a one-act play about jewel

thieves who get their comeuppance in a supernatural fashion. From then on there were usually two productions a year and the boys played female roles when necessary. The students founded the College Players, which later became the Maskers' Club and was active until the Theatre Department was finally established.

The venues were Ewart Hall and the first Howard Theatre, both on the Tahrir Campus. With the purchase of the Greek Campus, the action shifted to the New Theatre in May 1967, which launched with *Othello*. Following a fire in 1977, the New Theatre was rebuilt and reopened as the Wallace Theatre, hosting productions for almost a quarter century until theatre at AUC was moved

▶ Members of the Maskers' Club perform in a production of something called *The Master's Club*, year unknown

to two new spaces on the Falaki Campus in 2001. These days, since the move to New Cairo, the Theatre Department has the use of three performance spaces: the main Malak Gabr Theatre, the Gerhart Theatre, and the Howard Theatre.

Here, current faculty (professor of theatre Jillian Campana; professor of acting and playwriting Mahmoud El Lozy; associate professor of directing and theatre studies Frank Bradley; associate professor of scenic and lighting design John Hoey; and associate professor of costume design Jeanne Arnold) pool to pick out key productions staged at AUC since the creation of the Theatre Department.

1986

Sima awanta by Numan Ashur (Wallace Theatre)

An Egyptian satire from 1958 about the fast-paced world of commercial movie making, this play inaugurated Arabic-language theatre at AUC for the first time in its history. It was also the first AUC play directed by Mahmoud El Lozy, who had to contend with a government curfew and three actors dropping out ten days before opening night. Those who took part included Vanya Exerjian ('84), who later became a theatre actress with al-Warsha independent theatre company until her untimely death in 2004, and Boutros Ghali, who has since acted with al-Warsha and the Temple Theatre Company, and also acts in cinema and on television. Also involved was Pierre Sioufi ('90),

◀ A poster for the 2017 revival of *Sima awanta*, held at the Malak Gabr Theatre

who would go on to act in films, starring alongside Faten Hamama in *Ard al-ahlam*, but would become better known as an unlikely hero of the 2011 revolution for providing a safe house for demonstrators at his tenth-floor apartment high above Tahrir. The play was revived at AUC in 2017.

1999

Al-Sultan al-ha'ir by Tawfiq al-Hakim (Wallace Theatre)

In English, *The Sultan's Dilemma*. The production had a cast of thirty-five students and was notable for being performed entirely in Classical Arabic but with the actors in modern costumes. Also performing in the play, although not an AUC student—she was only about twelve years old at the time—was Yosra El Lozy, who did attend AUC later in life, and has since become a professional actress who has starred in a number of films, including Youssef Chahine's *Alexandria–New York*, and has also acted in TV series.

2001

A Traveler without Luggage by Jean Anouilh (Falaki Studio Theatre)

Written in 1936 by one of France's most respected playwrights, *A Traveler* is an intense and bittersweet drama in which a soldier who lost his memory in the Great War discovers the sordidness of his past life. As staged by AUC, it **≫**

▲ *A Traveler Without Luggage* by Jean Anouilh (Falaki Studio Theatre), 2001

▲ *School for Wives* by Moliere (Malak Gabr Theatre), 2009

featured a particularly fine country house set and evocative lighting by Stancil Campbell, and fabulous period costumes by Jeanne Arnold.

2002
Antigone by Sophocles (Falaki Mainstage)

A city lies in ruins after a revolution. A young woman refuses to obey the law of the state as she seeks to give her dead brother a proper burial. One of history's greatest plays was given a post 9/11 interpretation in this production. It was later performed at the Cairo International Festival for Experimental Theatre. The production was included in *Antigone on the Contemporary World Stage* (Oxford University Press, 2011).

2004
Sulayman al-Halabi by Alfred Farag (Falaki Mainstage)

The play was originally about the French invasion of Egypt in 1798 (al-Halabi was the Syrian Al-Azhar student who assassinated General Kleber, commander of the French army in Egypt), but this production was reframed to echo the recent US invasion of Iraq. It opened memorably with a group of soldiers rampaging through the auditorium, waving guns and screaming orders and insults at the audience in distinctly American accents. With parts for fifty-five students and alumni, it boasted probably the largest cast ever in an AUC production; among them were Asser Yassin ('04), who has appeared in many films and TV series since, Yosra El Lozy ('07), and Layla Soliman ('04), now a

playwright/director with a number of works to her credit.

2008
The Fever Chart by Naomi Wallace (Falaki Mainstage)

An almost world premiere by internationally acclaimed playwright and MacArthur Genius Grant award winner Naomi Wallace, who came to AUC for ten days to work with the cast and director Frank Bradley. Taking the form of three mini-plays, each set in a different location in the Middle East, it was a highly political piece of work. This production preceded and influenced the May 2008 New York opening.

2009
School for Wives by Molière (Malak Gabr Theatre)

Significant for being the first

production on the New Cairo Campus, this was a suitably ambitious production that featured contributions from all of the AUC theatre faculty, who acted, directed, and designed. This included notably Leila Saad, who attended AUC in the 1960s, then spent twenty-five years in the United States before coming back to Cairo and returning to AUC to teach acting. Some of the student cast have gone on to acting careers overseas, including Waleed Hammad ('09), who recently appeared in *Anthony and Cleopatra* with Ralph Fiennes at the UK's National Theatre, Nezar Alderazi ('11), who is also acting onstage in London, and Dahlia Azama ('10), who is working in New York.

▲ *Menein agib nas* by Naguib Sorour (Gerhart Studio Theatre), 2011

2011

Menein agib nas by Naguib Sorour (Gerhart Studio Theatre)

This production (in English, *Is Anybody Out There?*) was entirely designed by students. The rehearsal process was often interrupted by the events of January 2011 and by the street violence that followed. It was held as a rehearsal of a supposed production and in between scenes the various actors fell back into their real personas. It starred Nezar Alderazi (see *School for Wives*), Samia Assaad, who now acts in cinema, and Sara Shaarawi ('11), now a playwright in Scotland.

2017

Dream Hope Wish Desire: Stories of the People of Cairo (Malak Gabr Theatre and Falaki Theatre)

Reflecting a recent global trend for documentary theatre, this new play was collaboratively written by Theatre students and Professor Jillian Campana. Together they interviewed over sixty Cairenes on the subject of their personal, professional, and national hopes. The responses were transcribed and then used to write the text of the play, which used direct quotes and "real-life" people. With a cast of ten students plus Campana, it was performed in English on the New Cairo Campus in the spring and in Arabic at the Falaki Theatre, Downtown in the fall of 2017. The play featured in an article in the journal *Arab Stages*. ❧

▲ *Dream Hope Wish Desire* (Malak Gabr Theatre and Falaki Theatre), 2017

54

THE AUC PYRAMID

When healthy bodies were as important as healthy minds

In the early days of AUC, each boy was required to spend regular time dressed in short pants and an undershirt engaged in physical training. AUC's founders considered physical health almost as important as the exercising of the mind that went on in classes. Students were not always keen—many associated physical activity with the lower classes and were embarrassed to be seen partially dressed in public. Crowds often gathered outside the fence to watch the exercising. Despite this, the boys

took two hours of calisthenics and gymnastics each week, usually on Friday and Saturday afternoons. Each spring, the university sponsored a Sports Day with inter-class competitive drills, acrobatic stunts, parallel bar and mat-work, and the forming of the AUC pyramid, made by boys standing on each others' shoulders. This became a sort of trademark of university athletics events. Health and safety would not allow it these days. ❧

▲ AUC students form themselves into a pyramid in 1924

55

MAKING A SPLASH

Funds invested in state-of-the-art sports facilities are paying off, particularly in the swimming pool

When the Paul B. Hannon Swimming Pool opened in 2010 it marked the completion of the New Cairo Campus sports center, as well as an extraordinary turn-around in AUC sports facilities. Rewind to 2007, when AUC was still Downtown and pretty much the sum total of the offerings was a couple of outdoor courts, used for tennis, volleyball, and basketball, and two gyms. Athletes at AUC were forced to make use of facilities elsewhere, typically the city's sporting clubs. Three years later and the university had gained more than 40,000 square meters of indoor and outdoor facilities. Indoor includes three weight and exercise-machine rooms, an aerobics studio, six squash courts, a table tennis area, martial arts room, and billiards hall, and a gym for basketball, volleyball, and handball; outdoor are the pool, a 400-meter track, six tennis courts, two all-weather basketball/football courts, two volleyball courts, a handball court, and two grass fields.

AUC went from next to nothing to having, according to Chuck Gordon, director of athletics from 2008–11 and again in 2018, "the best facilities in Egypt as far as size of gymnasiums and courts, and their finishes and equipment."

No surprise then that in the last decade AUC has really started to make a name for itself in the inter-collegiate sporting world. Nowhere have the results been more dramatic than in the field of swimming. AUC has had excellent swimmers among the student body in the past, who have grown up swimming for their clubs—Karim El-Shazly, for example, who was a medal winner for the Alexandria Sporting Club before enrolling at AUC, where he became captain of the AUC swim team for the 2009–10 academic year. Such students traditionally competed for AUC but as individuals. The opening of the pool marked the first time the AUC swim team had a home pool and could grow together as a team.

While the men have posted some great recent results, the real success story has been the women's swimming team. A significant part in that success was played by American Louise Bertini, who was the

aquatics director and swimming coach from 2008 through 2016. She came to AUC in 2004 as a study-abroad student in Egyptology. However, Bertini had also swum backstroke for the University of New Mexico in college and had gone to the US Nationals a number of times. In 2007 she met Chuck Gordon, who invited her to get involved with the new pool being built on the New Cairo Campus. "I got to do the two things that I've always been really passionate about in my life, which is Egyptology and swimming," says Bertini. "An odd combination," she admits.

The first season that Bertini coached, she took men's and women's swimming teams from AUC to the Egyptian Nationals, where they failed to even place in the top ten. The second year both teams did achieve top ten placings, but only just. But then the following year, 2011, the women came in first. In fact, AUC's women swimmers ended up being national champions five times in a row. Not only that, but AUC had three female swimmers qualify for world championships and one, Reem Kassem, for the 2016 Olympics (see pp180–81). On the men's side, AUC went from never placing in the top ten to winning the Nationals two years running, in 2015 and 2016.

▲ Basketball has a long history at AUC, dating back to at least 1925, when the university was one of just five teams in Cairo that formed the first Egyptian Basketball Union

>>

177

The mixed relay team who won gold in the 4x50m Freestyle Mixed Relay at the ACG 2019 International Sports Festival held in Athens, Greece. *From left to right*: Reem Kassem, Yasmine Helmy, Aly Kassem, and Omar Elewa

Key to the successes, says Bertini, was the building of a team culture. Her successor as swimming team head coach, Adham Aly, agrees. "Although swimming is an individual sport," he says, "the best quality I've observed is the teamwork, and the discipline and dedication." All the swimmers train on campus five times a week, Sunday through Thursday, this in addition to their academic workload, and further practice with their local club teams.

As if that were not enough, in 2013 the swimmers started an academy offering swimming lessons to kids in the local community. "We weren't trying to create competitive swimmers," says Bertini, "we just wanted kids to enjoy the pools and learn to swim." The youngsters in turn have become part of the extended swim team family, turning up at competitions to cheer on their instructors. "It's a small sport," says Bertini, "and you give back to the sport that gave to you."

And the successes continue. In the most recent Nationals tournament, held in fall 2018, of the thirty-eight competing Egyptian universities, AUC's women again ranked first place overall, with the men placing fifth. Meanwhile, since graduating (architectural engineering) in 2019, long-distance specialist Reem Kassem has been preparing for the African Championships, which will determine qualification for the 2020 Tokyo Olympic Games, where she hopes once again to represent her country. "I believe that the support I received at AUC is one of the major reasons I am where I am," says Kassem. "The facilities that the university offers helped me pursue both my athletic and academic dreams, and I don't think I would've had the same opportunities anywhere else." She says that while she doesn't know what the future holds, she hopes she can raise more awareness of sports in Egypt, and help more athletes to achieve their dreams, especially female athletes. ◉

▶ Graduating senior in computer engineering Aliaa Ashraf in the AUC pool. She joined the swimming team in 2015, and has since represented the university both nationally and internationally

56

THE OLYMPIANS

AUC has a proud modern tradition of its students competing in the world's greatest athletics event

The Olympic Games are always an exciting watch but if you were an AUC student in 2016, they were even more compelling than usual. In that summer's games, held in Rio de Janeiro, the AUC community was represented by no less than six members of the competing Egyptian team, all women. Leila Mohammed Abdel Moez and Samia Hagrass Ahmed were both part of the synchronized swimming team; Reem Kassem competed in the 10k open swim; Reem Mansour shot in archery; and cousins Yossra Helmy and Dina Meshref were both part of the table tennis team.

They were following in the footsteps of other AUCian Olympians, notably Dalia al-Gebaly, Mai Mohamed, Nour al-Afandi, Shaza Abdelrahman, and Yomna Khallaf, who were all part of the synchronized swimming team at London in 2012; Mohamed Elwany (swimming), Heba and Sara Abdel Gawad (both synchronized swimming), and Mohannad Seif Eldin Sabry (fencing), who all competed in Sydney in 2000; Sharif al-Erian (pentathlon) who competed at Barcelona in 1992; Nihal Meshref (table tennis) who was at Barcelona in 1992 and Seoul in 1988, on the latter occasion along with fellow AUCian Sherif al-Saket (table tennis); and Ahmed Said who, as well as being president of the Student Union, swam butterfly for Egypt at the 1984 Los Angeles games.

Rio was particularly special in that the two women from AUC helped Egypt to a best-ever seventh out of twenty-four competing nations in synchronized swimming. Abdel Moez, an architectural engineering junior, told an interviewer, "The best moment was after I finished the second routine and was standing on the podium waiting for our score and seeing in the eye of my coach how happy and proud she was."

For economics alumn, Reem Mansour ('15), who competed in archery, the 2016 Olympics were, among many things, an invaluable learning experience. "The main lesson I learned from Rio is that it is absolutely necessary to take yourself out of your comfort zone and constantly challenge yourself," she told an AUC News reporter.

▲ Yossra Helmy ('20, far left) and Dina Meshref ('17, in red) with other members of the Egyptian table tennis team in Rio in 2016

Reflecting on the most memorable moments of competing for the Egyptian women's table tennis team, Yossra Helmy says, "I think the best moment was being able to be with athletes from all the other sports and taking pictures with them. I met [swimmer] Michael Phelps, and [tennis players] Rafael Nadal and Novak Djokovic. I also watched [sprinter] Usain Bolt win one of his gold medals. It was a surreal experience."

Both Yossra (whose mum is Olympian Nihal Meshref), who is still at AUC majoring in accounting and will graduate in spring 2020, and teammate and cousin Dina Meshref ('17), now a full-time athlete, hope to compete again in Tokyo in 2020. "The hardest challenge is balancing my studies and grades on the one hand and going to table tennis practice daily," says Yossra. "AUC has been supportive in terms of their flexible absence policy that allows me to reschedule my workload and exams to fit in with my practice and tournament schedule." Dina used the leave-of-absence policy to spend a whole semester training in China and in Germany before the 2016 Olympics.

"AUC also organized a ceremony to honor us athletes on our achievements," Adds Yossra, "and I received a reward that I keep on my desk at home." ⚽

57

A CULTURAL CENTER FOR CAIRO

For over ninety
years Ewart Hall
has provided
a forum for
engagement with
the leading minds
of Cairo, Egypt, and
the world

*"Let us show you
to your seat..."*

EWART
MEMORIAL
HALL

▲ A renovation in the 1990s
gave donors the opportunity to
attach their names to a seat

During the 1930s when the great Egyptian
writer and intellectual Taha Hussein
had nowhere else to go, AUC offered him its
largest auditorium—Ewart Hall—as a platform.
Dismissed from his position as dean of the
Faculty of Arts at Cairo University because of
his controversial writings, for four years Hussein
lectured regularly at AUC, confirmation that in a
very short time since its founding the university,
and in particular its main hall, had already
become one of the most vital intellectual and
cultural spaces in Egypt.

The cornerstone for a new auditorium was
laid in February 1927 and the building was
inaugurated the following year. Executed in a neo-
Islamic style sympathetic to the existing university
structures, the hall was both beautiful and spacious—
with seating for 1,150 it was at the time the largest public
space of its kind in Cairo. The idea was that it would be used
by the university's Extension Division for events that would exert "a
wholesome influence" on the local community. In the early days this
meant lectures on public health, including famously a series of talks by
Dr. Fakhry M. Farag on venereal disease, as part of which he advocated
locking up infected prostitutes. Even more controversial was a lecture
he delivered in February 1930 on the topic "Shall Women Have Rights
and Obligations Equal to Men?" When it became clear to the audience
that Farag considered that, yes, they should, there was a near riot, with
a crowd of al-Azhar students attempting to rush the stage and the police
having to be called to restore order.

In part to overcome the adverse publicity following the Farag event,
AUC arranged for the Egyptian State Broadcasting company to put

Ewart Hall lectures on the radio. To further expand its reach—and raise money—the university also embraced cinema. Starting in 1931, it began screenings of the biblical epic *King of Kings*, a 1927 silent movie directed by Cecil B. DeMille that depicts the last weeks of Jesus Christ before his crucifixion. The film was so popular that in one season AUC ran it over twenty times and it was seen by around 25,000 people. The screenings were repeated every Easter through until the 1950s (after 1939 with a sound version of the film) and they continued to draw massive audiences. In the early fifties, DeMille happened to be in Egypt, filming *The Ten Commandments*, and he came to see for himself the crowds that turned up at Ewart Hall to watch his old movie. From 1938, AUC extended its film program, although limiting it to "educational cinema" only. So, while the Metro up the street was showing things like *The Adventures* »

▲ What a capacity audience looked like, as viewed from the stage of Ewart Hall some time back in the 1930s

of Robin Hood, starring Errol Flynn, AUC offered *The Birth of a Baby*, an American instructive film about childbearing. Even so, the screenings were always well attended, possibly because Ewart Hall was the only place that conservative families allowed wives and daughters to go to see films.

The hall was the venue for landmark musical occasions, including a series of concerts given by Umm Kulthoum—for more on which, see pp212–13—and in January 1937 two performances by the Palestine Philharmonic Orchestra, which was almost entirely made up of Jewish musicians who had fled the rise of the Nazis in Europe, conducted by maestro Arturo Toscanini. A key contributor to Cairo's cosmopolitan music scene, Ewart Hall competed with the opera house to host the top international talents, including French chanteuse Edith Piaf, German pianist Wilhelm Kempff, and Franco-Swiss pianist Alfred Cortot.

In its desire to serve the needs of the wider community, the university allowed outside organizations to use the hall, when it didn't conflict with its own activities. This arrangement was subject to stringent rules including no events on Sundays except religious services, and strictly no stage dancing or "erotic" music.

All the while, the hall fulfilled its other role, which was to provide a venue for the milestones in academic life. Until the move to the New Cairo Campus, Ewart Hall was also the venue for the Freshman Seminar, Model United Nations, and Model Arab League conferences, and, until 1989, for annual graduation ceremonies, not to mention all varieties of student performances.

Above all remains Ewart Hall's significance as an open forum for sharing ideas and knowledge, with a commitment to free speech. Taha Hussien and Dr. Fakhry M. Farag were only the first to benefit from this. The main stage of the American University has been used frequently to question American foreign policy, notably by Egypt's foreign minister in 1948 when the United States backed Israel, and in more recent times by Edward Said, whose ringing critique of US policies always challenged his adopted country. An address by Moroccan nationalist leader Abdel Karim once resulted in all staff of the AUC being taken off the French Embassy's

WHO WAS EWART?

In 1925, a friend of the university was on a tourist steamer when she overheard a fellow passenger say she had received three million dollars from her grandfather and wanted to do something in his memory. She was taken to AUC where she was given a tour, at the end of which she agreed to make a donation eventually totalling $100,000. The money funded the building of a new auditorium, which the woman, who wished to remain anonymous, stipulated be named for her grandfather, William Dana Ewart, who had experienced great kindness once when taken ill in Cairo.

invitation list for many years. Not that speakers need necessarily be controversial to inspire with their speeches. Audiences at Ewart Hall have been privileged to receive addresses by the likes of Hassan Fathy, whose architectural genius won him international acclaim, Ahmed Zewail, whose sober thoughts aimed to inspire his original homeland, and Hillary Clinton, who at the time of her visit was making her case as an up-and-coming American politician.

It was said a long time ago now (in 1943, in fact), but the words spoken by a former Egyptian minister of social welfare still hold true: "This university has not limited its learning to its students; it has not kept its riches within its walls. It has been sending its light all over Egypt, indeed all over the Near East through its lectures and forums in which mind and tongue compete." ❁

▲ Ewart Hall as it appears today, renovated, thanks to a grant from USAID, to suit modern demands with, among other improvements, a new sound and light system

58

THE EWART HALL HOARD

In 2011, a series of thefts threw the spotlight on a forgotten antiquities collection

▶ About the only antiquity on display at AUC is this pharaonic head, which sits on a cabinet in the Rare Books and Special Collections Library. However, it is a fake, a prop that once belonged to the photographer Van Leo

One of the more intriguing stories to emerge in the wake of the 2011 revolution concerned the theft of antiquities from a storeroom under Ewart Hall. The intrigue was not so much the theft but the revelation that AUC had antiquities. Who, of the hundreds of thousands of students and members of the public that have attended events at the Ewart Hall over the decades, knew that beneath their feet lay a stash of ancient treasures? And what were they doing there?

The roots of the collection lie with former AUC president Richard Pedersen, who presided over the university from 1977 to 1990. He had a great interest in heritage and was keen to establish a museum on campus like many universities back in the United States. The Board of Trustees okayed him to buy antiquities for a university collection and allocated a modest budget. Buying antiquities was legal back in the 1970s, and there were a number of dealers in Khan al-Khalili and Downtown Cairo.

Pedersen made the purchases on his own, spending time at weekends visiting the dealers' shops. He bought small pharaonic, Coptic, and Islamic objects. He was not the only collector at the university. George Scanlon, who taught Islamic studies at AUC, amassed a selection of old pottery and textiles as a result of the university's excavations at

Fustat—antiquities Law 215/1951 used to allow foreign expeditions excavating in Egypt the right to 50 percent of whatever was dug up. And then there was also Robert Gene Pippin, who taught comparative literature in the 1970s and was a published poet, and who had a liking for Greco-Roman objects such as lamps and terracottas. All three collections ended up with AUC, either bequeathed or on indefinite loan, altogether numbering 1,664 objects.

We can be so precise because in 1983 the Egyptian government passed Law 117 outlawing trading in Egyptian antiquities and requiring those who owned such things to register every item with the Supreme Council of Antiquities—which AUC did. When, under Pedersen's leadership, AUC decided that the university's Ali Fahmy villa would become the home of the Rare Books and Special Collections Library, part of the plan was that the building should serve as an archaeological museum displaying items from the AUC collection. But while the library duly opened, for reasons now unknown the museum was never realized. The antiquities remained in the basement below Ewart Hall and, as faculty and staff left and retired, the number of people who knew about them dwindled.

It was not until the theft of a reported 145 pieces, undertaken during the chaos of the revolution, was revealed in March 2011 that AUC was reminded of its collection. The police were called in, the culprits were identified (members of AUC security), and sentences handed out. Meanwhile, elements of the national press had their fun with the story. One newspaper invented a scenario in which there was an underground tunnel connecting the Egyptian Museum with AUC, through which the university smuggled artifacts.

In the aftermath, AUC moved the antiquities to secure storage on the New Cairo Campus. President at the time Lisa Anderson stated that AUC had "no interest in being an antiquities warehouse" and appointed a committee, headed by Egyptologist Salima Ikram, tasked with evaluating the collection and deciding what to do with it. Ikram reported that the collection was not particularly valuable and contained no great masterpieces. She recommended that after restoration some of the objects could be put on display, others could form a useful teaching resource.

In the event, once again it proved not possible to display any of the collection—despite provision being made for a small museum building as part of the new campus plans. So in June 2017 AUC donated its entire collection of antiquities to the SCA. The plan is that the objects will now be displayed at the National Museum of Egyptian Civilization in Fustat—which is entirely fitting, given that Fustat is where many of the objects came from in the first place, and a neat end to the story. ✿

PRESIDENT #7
RICHARD PEDERSEN (1977–90)
Richard Pedersen is surely the only AUC president to have a wiretap placed on his phone by the United States White House. It happened in 1970 when Pedersen was serving as counselor to the US State Department under a Nixon administration, investigating leaks about its invasion of Cambodia. Following a spell as American ambassador to Hungary, he left Cold War politics to join AUC. He led curricular expansion and efforts to attain full accreditation in the United States, and pursued his interests in history by pushing for the creation of AUC's Rare Books and Special Collections Library. He died, aged eighty-six, in Greenport, Long Island in 2011.

59

THE NUBIA PROJECT

Established in 1953, AUC's Social Research Center earned its spurs in Nubia in the 1960s

In the late 1950s a sense of urgency swept across a dispersed but deeply concerned community of historians, archaeologists, anthropologists, and documentary filmmakers with the realization that the land of Nubia was under sentence of imminent death by drowning. This was the drastic price to be paid for the new Aswan High Dam, constructed to supply the country with electricity for industry and domestic use, and a year-round water supply for existing and new farming areas. The countless small villages scattered along the twisting Nile Valley south of Aswan and well into northern Sudan would disappear beneath the backed up waters of the world's largest artificial body of water, Lake Nasser.

International rescue efforts focused on the great pharaonic monuments that would be swallowed by the rising waters, notably Abu Simbel and Philae. A mission spearheaded by UNESCO was planned to dismantle, move, and reassemble these on higher ground. But there were also over fifty thousand Nubians living within Egyptian territorial borders whose homes, land, and physical heritage were going to be lost, too. The

plan was to resettle them around Kom Ombo, north of Aswan.

As part of an effort to record as much as possible about the Nubian people before their living culture was irreversibly changed forever, staff at AUC's Social Research Center (SRC) mounted a salvage anthropology project led by the ethnographer Robert Fernea. Fernea had joined AUC in 1959 upon completing his PhD in anthropology at the University of Chicago. His doctoral research had been on issues of irrigation and development in southern Iraq. He approached the SRC's director Laila al-Hamamsy with a proposal that the center undertake a study of the Nubians and their relocation, and she enthusiastically agreed.

The SRC was established in 1953 to conduct and encourage multi-disciplinary research and training in the social sciences and social policy in Egypt and in the Middle East. For over sixty-five years, the center has been reaching out to local communities to tackle everything from female illiteracy to the ecological development of Cairo and evaluation of family planning programs. Recent research activities have examined ≫

▲ Abdul Fattah Eid, an Egyptian professional photographer seconded to the project from the Ministry of Culture, compiled a unique pictorial record of the last days of Old Nubia

▲ Egyptian architect Hassan Fathy was employed by the High Council of Housing Research to draw house façades and plans, and take photographs. Fathy participated in activities with the SRC team and contributed to the 1964 Aswan symposium

population and fertility, poverty, political participation of women, the effects of economic liberalization, urbanization, social epidemiology, maternal and child health, and the environment.

Speaking at the SRC's fiftieth anniversary in 2003, AUC's president at the time, David Arnold, explained, "Service to Egypt continues to be an essential part of who we are and what we do, and the work that the SRC does is key to our ability to fulfil that very critical part of AUC's mission."

But of all its activities, the survey of Nubia stands out for its scale, scope, and cultural significance. Financed by two Ford Foundation grants, it took the form of a demographic study of the whole area, from Aswan south to the Sudanese border. Nubian families who had migrated to work in Cairo and Alexandria were also studied, while another strand of the project focused on a Nubian community, known by the pseudonym Kanuba, which had been established near Kom Ombo after their lands in Nubia had been flooded in 1933–34. A second phase examined the process of settlement and the adjustment of the Nubians after their resettlement in Kom Ombo.

The team consisted of Americans, Europeans, and Egyptians. Some of them had been students in social science courses at AUC; others came from Cairo University and other national universities. Some had already worked on previous projects. For most of them, as for many other Egyptians at the time, Nubia was unknown territory. Families of the assistants were sometimes reluctant to let them join the project. Before Nawal al-Messiri could join the project her brother made an exploratory trip to confirm that it was safe for his sister. Al-Messiri, who combined the survey with fieldwork for her Masters, spent much of 1961 and '62 in the village of Dahmit, close to Aswan; she remembers the field conditions: "We didn't have running water, or latrines. To wash your hands someone has to pour the water for you. You walked a kilometer to the Nile to get the water because the water in the wells had worms in it. You had to check before putting on your shoes because there were so many scorpions."

The Nubians who were in touch with the researchers were generally active participants in the process, even if they were not always sure what the purpose was. "We really never entirely understood what you were doing and why," a village leader once said to SRC team member Hussein Fahim. "But we liked you very much." On another occasion the chief said, "You were under the village scrutiny for a long time. As you proved to be good people, I instructed the people to cooperate with you and have you go to their homes."

Over the years that the project ran (1961–64), the team generated enormous amounts of quite diverse data about the nature of Nubian society, and the resettlement process and its implications for the Nubian population. Then it had to reach conclusions. Some of these were presented in a symposium on contemporary Egyptian Nubia that was held in Aswan, in January 1964, to present the major early findings of the ethnographic survey.

Since then, more than a hundred publications have emerged from the Nubian survey. Many of the papers from the 1964 Aswan conference came out in an informal publication edited by Robert Fernea in 1966. His wife, Elizabeth, published an account of life in Egypt, *A View of the Nile,* with a lengthy section on Nubia, in 1970. Robert Fernea put out a book of his own, *Nubians in Egypt: Peaceful People* (1973), a collaboration with project photographer Georg Gerster. Most recently, Nicholas Hopkins and Sohair Mehanna edited *Nubian Encounters: The Story of the Nubian Ethnological Survey 1961–1964* (AUC Press, 2010).

Many of the students who took part in the survey were subsequently sponsored by the Ford Foundation to do PhDs in the United States. Some, including Nawal al-Messiri, afterwards returned to the SRC to teach. The project was the nursery for a generation of Egyptian anthropologists.

"The story of the Nubian survey," write Hopkins and Mehanna in the introduction to their book, "is a chapter in Egyptian history, in the history of the social sciences in Egypt, and also in the history of anthropology in general. . . . Moreover, it is an excellent example of cooperation among people of many different backgrounds, from the researchers who took the lead to the assistants they recruited and trained, and to the Nubians, experts on their own life, who guided them in the research." The hugely valuable material gathered by the survey is now available through AUC's University Archives. ❀

▲ Egypt-based Swiss artist Margo Veillon traveled through Sudanese Nubia in late 1962, producing drawings and notes that were later published in book form

60

A FAME OF SORTS

How AUC has been portrayed in film and literature has changed over time

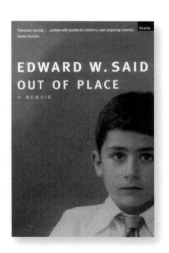

▲ Although Edward Said was never an AUC student, the university is recalled fondly in his fine memoir

▶ Very appropriately the part of the rebellious girl who goes to AUC in the classic movie *Ana Hurra* was played by Lubna Abdel Aziz, an alumna and one-time Miss AUC

A select few universities become far more than just places of learning. Over time they lodge themselves in the popular imagination, becoming associated with specific qualities, whether that's rarified academia, privileged wealth, political radicalism, or sporting prowess. AUC can count itself a member of that select "iconic" group—at least within Egypt and the Middle East. The university frequently appears in film and literature, often used as a shorthand sketch for a certain archetypal character: "AUC girl," "AUC boy." What is interesting is that those terms have not always meant the same thing. Over time, AUC has moved from being something apart from Egypt to becoming an integral part of the nation's identity.

In *Out of Place*, the late Edward Said's captivating memoir, we encounter an AUC that was part of a Cairo where the cultural life was dominated (as Said saw it) by European colonial élites. Said writes of attending his first concert at Ewart Hall, some time in the late 1940s. For him, it represents one of the markers of his Palestinian family's insertion into the cosmopolitan Cairo scene. "I was once taken to the Ewart Hall . . . to attend a concert by the Musica Viva orchestra conducted by one Hans Hickman, a careful time beater who buried his head in the score as if in his pillow. The soloist in, I think, either the First or Second Beethoven Piano Concerto was Muriel Howard, wife of AUC's dean, mother of Kathy, a schoolmate of mine at Cairo School for American Children. My father was close to Dean Worth (a name whose solid ring for me had the power of the American continent) Howard, and insisted on taking me and my mother up to him and his, I thought, strangely retiring wife, who had just completed a breathlessly rapid rendering of the concerto."

In time, Said's insular AUC gradually opens up to the growing Egyptian middle class. This is captured in Ihsan Abdel Quddus's classic novel *Ana hurra (I Am Free)*, which was adapted for the cinema in 1959 and starred actress Lubna Abdel Aziz, herself an AUC alumna—a former Miss AUC, no less. She plays Amina, a rebellious young

»

انتاج
رمسيس نجيب
يقدم
لبنى عبد العزيز
شكري سرحان
أجرأ قصة كتبها
احسان عبد القدوس
وأخرجها
صلاح ابو سيف
تصوير محمود نصر
انا حره
مطبعة انور ٤٨١٦٦
توزيع شركة الشرق لتوزيع الأفلام

▲ In October 2018, Mohamed Henedi revisited AUC as part of a symposium in his honor. During the event he unveiled plans for a sequel to his movie *Sa'idi fi-l-gama'a il-amrikiya*

woman who practically tricks her father into enrolling her at AUC, which at the time offered degrees unrecognized by the Egyptian government and was definitely not a place through which this middle-class girl could secure a job. Amina is depicted as an intruder into a community of foreign and aristocratic students, for unlike them she did not come to the university from one of Cairo's many private foreign schools, but rather from a public girls' school. But, for Amina, AUC represents a social shift that will distinguish her from her neighbors in Abbasiya, who all go to Cairo University. It gives her a sense of personal freedom.

The trend for diversification of the student body continued. In the blockbuster comic film *Sa'idi fi-l-gam'a il-amrikiya (A Sa'idi at the American University)*, released in 1998, Khalaf is an underprivileged Upper Egyptian who wins a scholarship to study at AUC. Unlike Amina in *Ana hurra*, who had to assimilate to succeed, Khalaf remains defiantly a Sa'idi, sending up the other more privileged students. When AUC got wind of the film, as it was being shot, the university's head of public relations forbade the movie-makers from filming around the university. This was terrible PR. Thankfully, President John Gerhart was more savvy and stepped in to invite Mohamed Henedi, the actor playing Khalaf, to visit the campus in order to show that the institution could take a little ribbing.

◀ Ahmed Alaidy's funny and angry journey through the insanity of present-day Cairo, *An takun 'Abbas al-'Abd*, includes a character who is an AUC student. AUC Press published the novel in English as *Being Abbas al-Abd*

> **"Enter a buxom daughter of the gentry from AUC (a.k.a. the American University in Cairo, or, according to some smartasses, 'Are U a Charlatan?')."**
>
> *Being Abbas al-Abd*

In Ahmed Alaidy's novel *An takun 'Abbas al-'Abd (Being Abbas al-Abd)*, the narrator is set up by Abbas, his streetwise friend, on a double blind date with two girls. One of them is an AUC student. However, rather than being something "other," she is simply one of Egypt's young generation, engaging in social media and pharmaceutical abuse just like everybody else.

By the time we get to Mai Khaled's *Maq'ad akhir fi Qa'at Iwart (Last Seat in Ewart Hall)*, written in 2005, the narrator is an AUC alumna herself. As she sits in dense traffic in Tahrir Square, she contemplates the American University in Cairo sign, written in both English and Arabic. She regards it as emblematic of her own split identity. "Here you are, with your head wrapped in a veil and wearing long sleeves so that the upper part of your body gives an incontestable Islamic impression. But if the onlooker were to direct his gaze towards the lower part of your body he would notice your tight jeans or your denim skirt with lace and patches and would discover the split within you."

Crisis of identity is also at the heart of hit US TV comedy *Ramy* (Hulu, 2018). When the Egyptian-American title character leaves North Jersey in search of his roots, he's bewildered to be met at Cairo Airport by a cousin fluent in New York street speak. "My English is premium," he says. "I went to AUC. American University in Cairo, baby!"

Weclome to the new Egypt. ⊛

61

HERE COMES THE SUN

With help from AUC, a Delta village pioneered sustainable energy in Egypt

"There is a vital need to connect teaching in the classroom to work, community, and the environment."

Professor of physics
Salah Arafa

In spring 2018 international media reported extensively on what was being called the "world's largest solar farm," under construction in the Western Desert near Aswan. It will, claimed the *LA Times*, single-handedly put Egypt on the clean energy map. It has been a long time coming, in the opinion of AUC professor of physics Salah Arafa. He can point to another article in the US press, this one published by *The New York Times*, dateline 'Basaisa, Egypt, June 1978;' the opening paragraph describes the inhabitants of this small village of 250 gathered in a communal hall watching television. The small, orange, portable set is a wonder because it is powered by the sun—or, to be more precise, by a solar cell on one of the village's mud-wall buildings.

Solar power was introduced to Basaisa by Arafa as part of a project to improve living conditions in this small village in the Sharqiya district, where he grew up. It began in 1974, six years after Arafa joined the faculty of AUC. His idea was to introduce basic sustainable technologies in order to induce real development in rural areas, not by enforcing change from the outside, but by involving the members of the community every step of the way. In addition to the sun-powered TV, Basaisa was also provided with solar-powered water heaters for the local mosque, some households began using biogases produced from organic matter, and there were early experiments in wind-generated power.

By utilizing local resources and engaging village residents, Arafa created an "integrated approach to development." His program included training sessions in agriculture, efficient use of natural resources, literacy, group collaboration, creative thinking, and community building. Initially, Arafa worked on his own, visiting Basaisa every Friday, but later AUC students, faculty, and staff began to volunteer. "When people started to learn about what I was doing in Basaisa, they became enthusiastic and wanted to participate," Arafa explains. The sociology and anthropology departments took a particular interest, and Basaisa quickly became a truly interdisciplinary project. "In the end, everyone found something to

contribute and a way to share in the responsibility," says Arafa.

In 1992, building on what he had learned, Arafa launched another project, New Basaisa, in a small desert community in Ras Sudr, in Sinai. There he introduced many of the same sustainable technologies he pioneered in the original Basaisa. Meanwhile, back on campus, every April since 2004 AUC has hosted an annual Basaisa Day. It brings together NGOs from all over Egypt to display and promote their developmental programs, and display and sell regional handicrafts. At the same time, AUC students get to experience the diversity of traditions and cultures within Egypt. Some even sign up to volunteer on projects. "It's an excellent example of the university's outreach," says Arafa.

After working at Basaisa for some forty-five years, Arafa measures the village's transformation by the positive impact on the people. He says his proudest moment was attending a conference on desertification and meeting the new Basaisa-born deputy of AUC's Desert Development Center, who was only twelve years old when Arafa first visited the village in 1974. "My real reward is knowing that we were able to positively transform conventionally accepted beliefs and ways of thinking in the village over the years," said Arafa. "That's a real step forward." ⬡

▲ A photo from the early days of the Basaisa project, showing a villager and volunteers examining a solar panel. This charged a twelve-volt car battery during the day to provide television viewing for the village in the evening

197

62

CONSERVING EGYPT

The work of the Rare Books and Special Collections Library

▲ ▶ The Van Leo collection includes not just images, such as the surreal triple self portrait, *opposite*, but also the photographer's equipment, such as this light unit, *above*

Van Leo (the working name of Levon Boyadjian) was a high-society portrait photographer who captured in lustrous prints the glamour of cosmopolitan, mid-twentieth-century Egypt. At his studio on Cairo's Sharia Fouad (present-day 26th July Street) he posed and shot the likes of Roushdy Abaza, Samia Gamal, Faten Hamama, and a fledgling Omar Sharif. In between glitzy assignments, Van Leo also staged a series of avant-garde self-portraits in which he took on a multitude of roles and guises, prefiguring by decades the similar work of celebrated modern American photographer Cindy Sherman. After fifty years behind the lens, Van Leo called it quits in 1998. When it came to the safekeeping and preservation of his archive of over twenty thousand negatives and prints, he decided to bequeath the lot to AUC.

Associate dean for the Rare Books and Special Collections Library (RBSCL) Philip Croom was present at AUC's first meeting with Van Leo. He remembers the photographer was so weak with illness that he feared he would not last until the end of the interview. He did, and as well as taking care of Van Leo's archive, Croom and his colleagues called in a doctor and managed to have the photographer admitted to a hospital for vital surgery.

In addition to the negatives and prints, AUC took possession of Van Leo's huge box-like cameras, as well as his lights, props, and furniture. "We can totally recreate his studio," says Croom. What Van Leo wanted from AUC, in Croom's view, was for the university to enhance his reputation. AUC immediately started exhibiting the photographer's work, both in Egypt and abroad. In 2000 it nominated him for a prestigious Dutch Prince Claus Award for his life's body of work, which he won. By the time the photographer died in 2002 he was well on his way to achieving the international acclaim he desired, in no small part thanks to the efforts of Croom and his team.

The conservation and promotion of the cultural heritage of Egypt and the Middle East region is at the heart of what the Rare Books and ≫

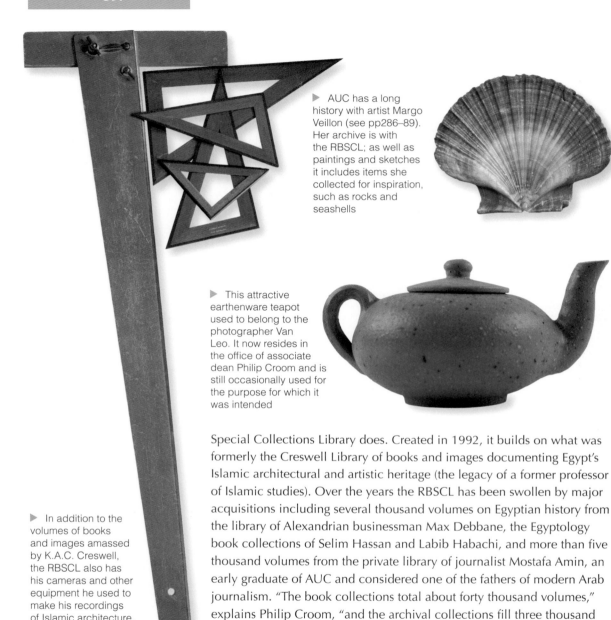

AUC has a long history with artist Margo Veillon (see pp286–89). Her archive is with the RBSCL; as well as paintings and sketches it includes items she collected for inspiration, such as rocks and seashells

This attractive earthenware teapot used to belong to the photographer Van Leo. It now resides in the office of associate dean Philip Croom and is still occasionally used for the purpose for which it was intended

In addition to the volumes of books and images amassed by K.A.C. Creswell, the RBSCL also has his cameras and other equipment he used to make his recordings of Islamic architecture, including this T-square and array of set squares

Special Collections Library does. Created in 1992, it builds on what was formerly the Creswell Library of books and images documenting Egypt's Islamic architectural and artistic heritage (the legacy of a former professor of Islamic studies). Over the years the RBSCL has been swollen by major acquisitions including several thousand volumes on Egyptian history from the library of Alexandrian businessman Max Debbane, the Egyptology book collections of Selim Hassan and Labib Habachi, and more than five thousand volumes from the private library of journalist Mostafa Amin, an early graduate of AUC and considered one of the fathers of modern Arab journalism. "The book collections total about forty thousand volumes," explains Philip Croom, "and the archival collections fill three thousand linear meters of cabinets."

Significant in the RBSCL's holdings are numerous illustrated pre–twentieth-century travel accounts of the Middle East and a 1591 Arabic–Latin volume of the New Testament printed in Rome. Several hundred of the library's books were printed between 1537 and 1800. But it's not just old books; the library is also a cabinet of curiosities with maps, personal documents, medals, memorabilia, drawings, and a great many other miscellaneous artifacts. There are political cartoons from the pen of Ahmed Toughan; seashells and rocks collected by artist Margo Veillon;

▲ The RBSCL has a collection of musical instruments donated by artist and newspaper columnist Hussein Bicar and by AUC Arabic-language alumnus and exhaustive world traveler Ted Cookson

▲ These glasses once belonged to architect Hassan Fathy. They feature a small reading light set into the frame. Among other items, the library also has Fathy's pipe and his collection of classical records

▲ Among the tens of thousands of images held in the RBSCL are stereographic cards designed to be viewed in a special 3D viewer. The collection also includes the taxiphote viewer, *above*, which uses similar technology to view glass slides in 3D

musical instruments from the collection of Hussein Bicar; photo albums recording the diplomatic travels of former secretary-general of the United Nations Boutros Boutros-Ghali; watercolor sketches by Egyptologist Susan Weeks; handwritten placards that were wielded by protestors on Tahrir Square in 2011, as well as spent tear-gas canisters from the guns the police shot at them. (The RBSCL, incidentally, also maintains AUC's University Archives, without which the book you are holding in your hands could never have been written.) In order to make all these valuable intellectual assets available to the widest audience, the RBSCL is busy preserving them digitally and making them available for study online.

One of the most frequently consulted collections in the library is the archive of the world-famous Egyptian architect Hassan Fathy. This comprises drawings, paintings, architectural models, and documentation—not to mention Fathy's cases of classical music LPs and his pipe. In 2018, architectural conservators consulted some of these drawings to help them in their work restoring Fathy's New Gourna village in Luxor, built between 1946 and 1949. Donors have been willing to give to the RBSCL because they know their donations will be preserved and made available for scholarly resources. "It is a great comfort to know we have saved so much that otherwise would have disappeared," says Philip Croom. ❁

63

A BETTER ORANGE

How citrus strains developed at AUC have brought billions of dollars to Egypt's farmers

From the perspective of AUC, Adli Bishay might be considered the 'father of science.' An ex–Cairo University student he gained his PhD at Sheffield University in the UK in 1955 and six months later parlayed it into a faculty position at AUC. Here, he initiated a materials engineering department and solid-state science program. He was then instrumental in lobbying for, planning, and kitting out a new six-story science building on the Tahrir Campus, dedicated in September 1966. And so the teaching and study of science came of age at AUC. (Although not all at once, because the purchase of the science equipment specified by Bishay was more than the university could afford. A compromise was reached: only three floors of the new science building were completed and equipped, the other three had to wait some years until more funding could be found.)

All of which would have been more than enough to earn Bishay the gratitude of decades of graduating biologists, chemists, and physicists. But then, in the 1970s, then-president Anwar Sadat threw down a challenge to Egyptians.

It is commonly stated that about ninety-seven percent of the Egyptian population lives on three percent of the land, in the Nile Valley and Delta, and that even there agricultural land is shrinking every year through new construction and other uses. "It was 1973," Bishay told an interviewer. "Sadat kept repeating, 'Let us go to the desert.' The engineers said they would build buildings, the social scientists that they would study the desert, the agricultural engineers that they would plant the desert. But something," he asserted, "was

not quite right. I thought all these elements had to come together and work as one." It was with this vision that Bishay founded AUC's Desert Development Center (DDC) on 575 feddans of unreclaimed desert land in South Tahrir, in Beheira governorate, donated by the government.

Established in 1979, the DDC was originally a research station and training center for the promotion of sustainable development in desert areas. This involved not only agriculture but also technological aspects like renewable energy, and special architecture for the desert. Over the next thirty-five years, the DDC worked on improving soil, water, and sanitation management in different parts of Egypt, developing small-holder livestock enterprises, and increasing crop yields.

The DDC was the first venture to tackle these issues in such an integrated way and it helped foster a national approach to development. (AUC professor of physics Salah Arafa had been undertaking work of a similar nature at Basaisa since 1974 (see pp196–97) but that was an effort by a group of independent faculty. The difference is one of »

▲ When the South Tahrir research station was first established it was a remote facility in the middle of the desert, but later Sadat City grew up around it

▲ The built structures on the South Tahrir research center, like the one shown above, were inspired by the work of architect Hassan Fathy, who revived traditional forms of construction

scale: Bishay managed to get AUC to adopt his DDC as a university research center.)

"I like to start new things and nurture them, and watch them grow. Many years later, when they've developed and spread, then been copied, people will look back and say, 'Yes, Bishay was the one that planted this.' That," he told *Al-Ahram Weekly*'s Yasmine El Rashidi, "makes me happy."

Among its notable achievements, the DDC was instrumental in introducing and applying tissue culture techniques to the propagation of banana varieties in Egypt. It was also a leader in integrating crop and animal production in desert areas. However, the Center's biggest research contribution has been the improvement of citrus production. In the 1980s and 1990s, the DDC carried out field tests to determine what combinations of rootstocks (the part of the plant underground) and fruit varieties were best adapted to desert conditions. A broad selection was tested, including oranges, grapefruits, mandarins, lemons, and limes. Within a few years it was observed that the Sour Orange rootstock that predominates in the Nile Valley and Delta is not suitable for desert conditions. By contrast, something called *Citrus volkameriana* turned out to be tolerant to drought. Combined with a variety of Valencia orange this produced a high-quality fruit with excellent juice. The DDC began growing these trees in its nurseries and selling them—at below cost—to farmers. As a direct consequence, says Richard Tutwiler, who became director of the DDC in 2001, "Citrus is now Egypt's number one agricultural export commodity, more than rice, more than cotton, and is worth well over $1 billion per year." Egypt is now ranked second in citrus exports worldwide. It was not, Tutwiler notes, a significant part of the export economy thirty years ago.

"Another major impact of the DDC was on the educational front," says Tutwiler. "An evaluation by the Ministry of International Cooperation cited the DDC training as the best program of its kind in Egypt. We are particularly proud of that."

Closer to home, the staff of the DDC were also heavily employed in applying their expertise to the planning of the New Cairo Campus, which, although it is easy now to forget, was originally a desert site. The Center collaborated on the design and execution of the landscaping,

grew new plant material on the South Tahrir station, and then transplanted it to the new campus. It also oversaw the installation of the irrigation system—for more on all of this see pp274–77.

In 2012 the the lease on the land in South Tahrir lapsed and the role of the DDC was reconfigured. It morphed into the cutely named Research Institute for a Sustainable Environment, or RISE. Housed on the New Cairo Campus, RISE was given a much broader mandate than the DDC, which had been focused very much on desert environments, whereas RISE was to consider any environment, in Egypt or beyond. From its launch in 2013, RISE projects involved solar energy, the treatment of wastewater, and garbage recycling. "We are much more in the field than we were before," says Tutwiler. "Because we don't have the research stations, almost all our work is in villages in the field. There's not a week goes by when we don't have a team somewhere in Egypt. This is a good thing."

In 2018 RISE was merged with another center to form the even more cutely named Center for Applied Research in Environment and Sustainability, or CARES. ❀

▲ The oranges grown in the gardens of the New Cairo Campus are strains that were developed by the DDC to improve the yield of desert farmers

64

GOING PUBLIC

The School
of Continuing
Education extends
the resources of
AUC to Egypt and
beyond

For Iman al-Zayat, studying at AUC's School of Continuing Education (SCE) in the 1980s was not just a memorable experience, but one that left an imprint on her career and helped her become who she is today—chief of Arabic translation at the International Monetary Fund for the past fifteen years.

"The basic and most valuable difference between the School of Continuing Education and formal education was that it was more career-oriented rather than theoretical," explained Zayat. "It provided students with a practical tool kit for immediate application in real life, and this particular emphasis has enriched my versatility and breadth of knowledge in a positive and focussed manner, which was reflected in my fast career progression, whether as an instructor at the school, a translator and interpreter, or chief of Arabic translation later on at the IMF."

Established in 1924 as the Division of Extension, the SCE is almost as old as AUC itself. It was part of Charles Watson's original vision to have a public service component to the university. He realized that a program of lectures and evening courses, similar to extension programs in the United States, would benefit many additional people beyond the day students and enlarge the impact of the new institution.

The Division of Extension began as a forum for lectures by well-known speakers on topics of "immediate concern to Egypt," including population growth, education, and social and economic reform (see "A Cultural Center for Cairo," pp182–85). In addition to lectures and film screenings, it worked on improving people's well being, for example through development projects in villages, such as a contest to make eye hygiene posters to help prevent blindness. In the 1940s the Division of Extension became the "evening college," targeting those who had completed college work and would like to earn another degree. Some twenty years later, it was renamed the Division of Public Service (DPS), offering non-credit evening programs in business, consumer education, playwriting, language studies, accounting, fine arts, and family

education. At the same time, it continued with sponsored lectures and seminars, as well as public film showings and art exhibitions.

In the 1980s the center grew tremendously under the guidance of Ralph Nelson, dean of adult and continuing education, expanding its offerings in Arabic and business; creating its own English-language curriculum, tailored to the needs of Arabic speakers; introducing one-year and two-year professional certificates, not just individual courses; and initiating evaluative techniques for faculty members, as well as English proficiency entrance exams for participants. An off-campus extension in Heliopolis was also established to accommodate the increasing number of students.

There was another name change, this time to the Center for Adult and Continuing Education, as the program expanded to include outreach and full-time career programs in different parts of Egypt, such as Alexandria and Tanta, as well as further afield, including Saudi Arabia and Abu Dhabi. In 2006–07, the center was renamed again; now it was the School of Continuing Education, enrolling approximately twenty thousand students per year.

When AUC moved most of its operations to New Cairo, the SCE remained mainly in Tahrir, although, since then, the numbers of SCE students attending the New Cairo Campus have rocketed and the split between the two is approaching fifty–fifty. "We are certainly

▲ The School of Continuing Education has traditionally served as a sort of night school, providing for those who have completed college and are looking to add new skills

"SCE transforms the perception that AUC is only for high-end students with money."

Alia Shoeib,
interim dean 2018–19

▶ The School of Continuing Education helps around twenty thousand students achieve their dreams every year, whether that is improving their English or learning to play guitar

"We give the masses the skills and languages that will enable them to enhance their employability."

Alia Shoeib,
interim dean 2018–19

part of AUC," said Deena Boraie, who until 2018 was dean of the SCE. "That's why the SCE was re-established as a school, to integrate it more with the rest of the academic schools."

With its diversity of programs, the SCE remains a real-life manifestation of Watson's dream of AUC's outreach and service to a wide spectrum of the Egyptian public. "Through the SCE, the university opens it doors every year to thousands of Egyptians from all areas," said Boraie, adding that the school's main drive is being responsive to market needs.

"We are a needs-driven business," she explained. "We are conducting needs assessments all the time, working to identify and understand clients' desires and requests, and use this information to develop new products and services. So, in the 1980s, our focus was on secretarial certificates and IT, and we were one of the first institutions to offer courses in computer studies. Today, we still offer those courses, but our portfolio has expanded to include sales, marketing, human resource management, international accounting and auditing certificates, legal, UN, media and literary translation, TOEFL preparation, teacher training, youth programs, and much more."

And, of course, there are the English courses, which remain the hallmarks of an SCE education. "Right now, there is a tremendous need for English-language training," says Boraie. "Within the SCE, there are thousands of students who want to learn how to speak and write English

properly. It's an unfortunate reflection of Egypt's school system, and, in that sense, we are providing a form of remedial education."

Besides English, one of the strengths of the SCE is its professional career certificates, which complement, rather than duplicate, a four-year university degree. "We are giving our students the practical skills they need to understand the theory behind what they're studying, or have studied, at their universities," says Boraie. "This is an added value."

And students testify to that. "My studies at the School of Continuing Education have added value to my competencies and increased recruiter interest, so my AUC experience has always been a positive asset for me in receiving good job offers," said Raafat Donia, head of compliance at Sandoz Pharmaceutical, a division of Novartis. "The diversity of students in terms of culture, work experience, and demographics has also enriched my learning experience and outcome, both when I was a student and when I worked as a part-time instructor at the school."

For Ahmed Kamel, regional sales director for Travco, the "sharing of experiences and exposure to different industries through the student mix" were some of the main benefits of studying at the SCE. More importantly, the communication and presentation skills he acquired, in addition to time management, have helped him become "adaptable and flexible as a professional," which paved the way for him to be in the leadership position he holds until today. ◈

65

READING WRITING ON BUILDINGS

The department of Islamic art and architecture preserves the narratives of Cairo's past

Cairo has the richest legacy of historical architecture of any city in the Islamic world. Over four hundred mosques, madrasas, mausoleums, and other monuments, ranging from the eighth to the nineteenth century, are listed as worthy of protection by the Ministry of State for Antiquities. They range from simple mosques to complexes that are among the world's architectural masterpieces. These structures collectively constitute a great open-air living museum of architecture, crafts, and traditions. In addition to the domes, minarets, and decorative stonework, another distinctive feature of many of these monuments is their inscriptions.

"These inscriptions provide a wealth of historical information about the patrons of buildings and the date they were erected," says Bernard O'Kane, professor of Islamic art and architecture at AUC. "They provide historical and social context to scholars and students, and show how the manifestations of artistic traits change over time." Most of the inscriptions are Qur'anic and serve to sanctify the building on which they are placed, but there are also *waqf* inscriptions that detail endowed properties.

"Inscriptions really mattered in medieval Cairo," says O'Kane, who has been teaching at AUC since 1980. "They could convey information in many ways, either directly by their content, or indirectly as indicators of prestige, or even as assurances that God's word was being proclaimed from on high."

One major problem facing today's scholars is that due to degradation caused by natural abrasion, wind erosion and dust, and the rising water table, the inscriptions are becoming ever less legible. To help combat this problem, starting in 1997, and with funding from the American Research Center in Egypt and AUC, O'Kane began working on a project to photograph, transcribe, and translate all the inscriptions on pre-1800 monuments in Cairo. (Why only pre-1800? Because the budget did not stretch to buildings of the nineteenth century.)

The gathering of the data took seven years and along the way O'Kane drew on the help of two assistant directors (initially Tarek Swelim, then

for much of the project Lobna Sherif), and a host of AUC students of Islamic art and architecture. Buildings that had been locked for years occasionally even had the padlocks prised off before being sealed again after the researchers' visit. The team was able to visit almost all of the monuments, although a few, whose entrances were completely bricked up, resisted even the antiquities authority's best efforts to gain access. Sherif, who was a visiting assistant professor at AUC at the time, teaching a course on the art and architecture of Cairo, has fond memories of visiting obscure and off-the-beaten track monuments. "These were trips in time, to neighborhoods that seemed to belong to a different era, rich in monuments and poor in urbanization."

In the years since the project, some monuments have been subject to extensive restoration. The treatment of the inscriptions on the monuments has ranged from careful cleaning to making them look like new. The latter approach makes O'Kane thankful that his team were able to record what was there before the interventions. Since 2017, the complete searchable database, consisting of some 3,250 inscriptions and 11,000 photographs, has been available for scholars online.

Meanwhile, O'Kane's continued researches into historic Islamic architecture, along with more than five hundred of his own photographs, also fed into the sumptuous *The Mosques of Egypt,* which was published by AUC Press in 2017. ✤

▲ Professor of Islamic art and architecture Bernard O'Kane photographing inscriptions in the interior of one of Cairo's magnificent Mamluk-era monuments

66

AL-SITT SINGS AT EWART

In the late 1930s, AUC was honored to provide a platform for the greatest Egyptian singer of all time

▲ Too salacious for the Christian backers of AUC?

In 1937, Umm Kulthoum was around twenty-seven years into a career that began when she was all of twelve years old and started singing with her father at weddings in the villages and towns of the eastern Delta. By now she was already possibly Egypt's highest paid artist, her fee per performance on a par with, if not greater than, that of the legendary Mohamed Abd al-Wahab. That year she began the venture that would see her eclipse every other performer and cement her reputation as the greatest Arab cultural figure of the twentieth century. She signed a contract to give a concert on the first Thursday of every month, which would be broadcast live. The first of these historic performances took place on 7 January 1937 at the old Cairo Opera House. It marked the beginning of a golden age in the singer's career.

AUC had a policy of making Ewart Hall available to organizations that wanted to sponsor cultural events. At some point in 1937, the university was approached by Egyptian State Broadcasting, the body responsible for producing and transmitting the "First Thursday" concerts. It wanted to use Ewart Hall as one of its recording venues because of its fine acoustics. AUC consented and for three successive winter seasons Umm Kulthoum's performances at Ewart Hall were beamed out to millions of radio sets in households and coffeeshops in Egypt and across the Arab world.

Not everyone was happy, however. Members of the Egyptian Evangelical Church—a Protestant church that was founded in Egypt by the American Mission—flooded the office of the AUC president with complaints and urged him to halt the concerts. The church's attitude was that women singing in public was immoral, doubly so when they were singing the sort of passionate love songs that made up much of Umm Kulthoum's repertoire. "Such songs," raged one clergyman, "serve as an open revolt against Christian principles and an open call to licentiousness." The university reassured the church that it had carefully scrutinized the reputation of Umm Kulthoum, as well as the

▲ A relatively youthful-looking Umm Kulthoum on stage at Ewart Hall in May 1939

subject matter of her songs, and it felt that they were no more salacious or suggestive than songs accepted in Christian social life in America. Further, the university argued, the association with the broadcasting company represented a serious effort on the part of AUC to guide and uplift the recreational programs that penetrated so widely and deeply into the life of the Egyptian nation.

Even so, AUC was reluctant to antagonize the Christian community in Cairo and so certain conditions were agreed. It requested that the performances include fewer love songs and perhaps more of the "patriotic or idyllic." It also asked that broadcaster ensure that audiences were well behaved and that the concerts were finished by midnight. In practice, it was impossible to enforce any of this. The great lady felt no need to abide by anyone's restrictions and the audiences, regrettably as far as the university was concerned, continued to be unrestrained in their enthusiasm, cheering wildly. Despite being asked not to do so, audience members also smoked profusely and drank openly from bottles of alcohol they had smuggled into the hall. Performances consistently overran thanks to the singer's unrepentant habit of turning up late. In January 1940, a frustrated university council could placate the Christian zealots no longer and finally gave in, pulling the plug on the concert series. Relations with the radio station were unaffected and it continued to broadcast other programs from the university's halls. Umm Kulthoum simply went elsewhere, continuing her regular Thursday performances through until 1973, just a couple of years before she died. ✤

AND THE KING OF THE OUD CAME TOO
He didn't play Ewart Hall but on Friday 17 May 1940 Farid al-Attrache entertained 150 guests at a dinner held in the garden outside the Oriental Hall—presumably what is now the fountain courtyard. The *Caravan* reported that he "sent his audience into fits of ecstasy and loud 'Allah's at the end of every verse."

67

A VISIT FROM THE KINGS

The day Martin Luther King and his wife visited AUC and no one was home

▲ In 1959 King was already well known for leading a boycott of segregated buses in Montgomery, Alabama

In February 1959, leader of the civil rights movement in America Martin Luther King traveled to India to learn at first hand more about the principles of Mahatma Gandhi, who he considered a guiding light for the kind of nonviolent social change he was striving to bring about back home. Afterwards, rather than fly straight home from New Delhi, he took a detour via Karachi, Beirut, Jerusalem, and Cairo. While in Egypt he met his friend Jimmy A. Beshai.

Beshai was born in Luxor, where his father was a teacher at the American Mission. Later, the family moved to Cairo and James was enrolled at AUC, graduating in 1947. At the age of twenty-three he left for the United States, where he enrolled at Crozer Seminary, a theological college in Pennsylvania. Crozer students lived in a dormitory on campus and in the room next to Beshai was an equally young, black American by the name of Martin Luther King Jr. Recalling his dorm mate in 2012, Beshai remembered that even then he already possessed great skills as an orator and had a fine intellect. He was already then a student leader, representing a largely white student body.

Following a year at Crozer, Beshai returned to Cairo, where he became an instructor in psychology at AUC. He corresponded with his former dorm colleague a few times, as King became famous around the world for leading the Montgomery bus boycott in Alabama, a seminal event in the civil rights movement. In 1958, Beshai received a letter from King saying that he would be in Cairo the following spring and that during the visit he would be going incognito and enjoying a little downtime with his wife, Coretta. This duly happened. The King party spent two days at the Continental-Savoy hotel, Downtown, doing a little sightseeing. Beshai met the couple and took them to the AUC campus on Tahrir Square. It was a weekend and there were few people around but Dr. King was introduced to Alan Horton, dean of the graduate school, whose father was a professor of divinity at Harvard. Horton invited King to address the students at an assembly the following week, but the

Dexter Avenue Baptist Church

DEXTER AVENUE AT DECATUR STREET
MONTGOMERY, ALABAMA
PHONE 3-3970

Martin L. King, Jr., *Minister*
309 South Jackson Street

January 7, 1957

Mr. Jimmy A. Beshai
American University
Midan Tahrir
Cairo, E G Y P T

Dear Jimmy:

Thanks for your very kind letter of December 4. I can assure you that this was a real pleasant surprise to begin the new year with. I had been wondering how you were getting along.

As you know, I have been deeply involved in a struggle for justice and freedom here in the state of Alabama. It has kept me working under a great deal of pressure for more than twelve months. We have been able to continue in the struggle because we have had the moral support of men and women from all over the world.

I have been keeping up with the situation in Egypt, and as you know this is one of the most important issues in the world today. It will determine whether we will live in peace or whether we will die in war. Naturally my sympathies are with Egypt, rather than with the Western Colonial and imperial powers.

I plan to be in Asia and Africa during the months of March and April and it might be possible for me to come to Cairo. I hope this will be the case. If this can be worked out, I will be sure to write you in advance so that we can definitely see each other.

Again, it was a real pleasure hearing from you. I will extend your best wishes to our mutual friends.

Very sincerely yours,

M. L. King, Jr.,
Minister

MLK:mlb

American activist had to decline because he was leaving the next day.

Apart from Jimmy Beshai, who received an inscribed copy of King's book *Stride Toward Freedom*, sent as a thank you, hardly anyone is aware of this great man's visit to Egypt, let alone to AUC. Nevertheless, his legacy does live on on campus, as each year as part of the Core Curriculum's Celebrating Ideas program students get to dissect the "I Have a Dream" speech delivered by King in Washington on 28 August 1963, in which he called for civil and economic rights and an end to racism in the United States. ✸

▲ A letter sent by Martin Luther King to his old Crozer dorm mate, Jimmy A. Beshai. Although King says he will be in Africa and Asia in spring of that year, 1957, it would be another twenty-four months before he made the trip

215

68

A VISIT FROM THE POLICE

In March 1980, as part of a massive global tour, one of the hottest bands in the world dropped by to play a gig at Ewart Hall

In October 1979, British rock band The Police released its second album *Reggatta de Blanc*, which topped the UK albums chart and spawned a handful of singles—"Message in a Bottle," "Walking on the Moon," and "So Lonely"—that became international hits. To promote the album, the band embarked on its first world tour: 127 concerts in nine months, taking in around twenty countries, including several rarely ever visited by working Western musicians. Egypt was slotted in between India (Mumbai) and Greece (Athens). The venue for the Egyptian gig was AUC's Ewart Hall; the date, Friday 28 March 1980.

This was a homecoming of sorts for The Police's drummer Stewart Copeland, who, for a few years from the age of two months, was brought up in Cairo, the family then resettling in Lebanon until his dad's CIA cover was blown and they all had to be evacuated. Copeland's older brother Miles was educated at the American University of Beirut and as The Police's manager it was probably he who decided that the Middle East's other American university would be the right sort of place for the band to play. (Beirut, of course, was not a consideration, Lebanon being in the middle of its civil war at the time.)

In Mumbai a journalist had asked why they had chosen to play to non-Western audiences. "We figured that sooner or later some decadent, greedy, capitalistic Western rock'n'roll band was gonna move in and exploit the s**t out of them," answered Stewart Copeland, "and we agreed it might as well be us." In Cairo, at least, it did not quite work out like that.

The band came on late—the tour's sound system had been locked up in customs at the airport until just a couple of hours before the performance was due to start, and there were also problems with the lighting. Even so, as the first number started the hall was less than full. Lead singer Sting was also visibly put out to see that most of those who were there were expat Americans and British. "Open the doors and let Cairo in!" he shouted at the empty spaces in the stalls. The doors at the

THE POLICE

Message In A Bottle
Regatta De Blanc
It's Alright For You
Bring On The Night
Deathwish
Walking On The Moon
On Any Other Day
The Bed's Too Big Without You
Contact
Does Everyone Stare
No Time This Time

Regatta de Blanc

JUNE 13th LYCEUM THEATRE, LONDON

◀ A number of AUCians were roped in to help out at the gig, notably operating the lighting because The Police had not brought any lights of their own. As a thank you those who assisted were given official tour T-shirts and pins

back of the hall were duly opened and four street kids cautiously stepped in. At least that is the way one British journalist who accompanied the band remembers it.

Part way through the set the band played three of their biggest hits in a row prompting the enthusiasts down at the front to get up on their seats and dance, only for security to come running down the aisles to order them to sit back down. As the concert went on more people filtered out than in. Speaking to a journalist afterward, Stewart Copeland admitted that it had been the quietest reception so far of the tour.

The local press were also unimpressed: a write up in the *Egyptian Mail* expressed disappointment that lead singer Sting had been billed as the new Mick Jagger when, in fact, wrote the journalist, he "has all the sex appeal of a hover fly." ❦

ALSO APPEARING . . .
International artists rarely include AUC on their tour schedules but there have been a few exceptions. The Billy Taylor Trio played Ewart Hall in 1982, as did David Byrne, ex-Talking Heads frontman, in December 1994, and jazz keyboardist, composer and bandleader Herbie Hancock in April 2001. Most illustrious of all though, French superstar Edith Piaf performed at Ewart Hall on the evenings of 22, 23, 24 and 28 February 1949.

69

HILLARY CLINTON

In March 1999, the then–US First Lady visited Egypt as part of a short North African tour. She delivered her only public address in Egypt to a crowded Ewart Hall

On 21 March 1999, Hillary Clinton, wife of US president Bill Clinton, disembarked from her thirteen-hour flight from Washington at Cairo Airport. This was not an official presidential visit, it was just Hillary and nineteen-year-old daughter Chelsea doing their own thing. "I am here on behalf of my husband and of the American people to strengthen the bonds of friendship and partnership between our two countries, deepen our dialogue and see first hand how Egyptians are moving toward the future while preserving their extraordinary culture and heritage," she explained. After two days being whirled around the city and meeting the Mubaraks, Clinton gave her only public addresss, which was to a packed house at AUC. Her speech was a crowd pleaser, referencing shared touch points—America has a pyramid on its dollar bill—quoting Umm Kulthoum, and using a metaphor of the things we carry into the Afterlife as a framework for her message of tolerance and understanding. Many in the audience, however, were more interested in her new look: short, slicked-back hair, and a sharply tailored black suit with leopard-print lapels. Afterwards, Hillary met with students. In Cairo again in 2012, this time as secretary of state meeting with Mohamed Mursi, her motorcade was pelted with tomatoes. How she must have longed for the more welcoming days of her visit to AUC. ◉

70

EDWARD SAID

The academic, critic, author of the groundbreaking *Orientalism*, and leading voice in the field of post-colonial studies, delivered a commencement address in 1999

Although he lived most of his life in America, the Palestinian Edward Said was born in Jerusalem and grew up in Cairo. He attended the American College in Maadi and Cairo's Victoria College, before continuing his education in the United States. However, in the commencement address Said delivered at AUC on 17 June 1999, the distinguished visiting Columbia University professor told a Ewart Hall audience how AUC was the first university he had anything to do with. Two of his cousins were students here and his father was a close friend of President John Badeau. More recently, in 1994, Said's son studied Arabic in the CASA program. "I am honored to be here today, first as a Palestinian and a child of Egypt's immense and unparalleled cultural history and, second as an American," he began, noting that the combination of these two different strains in AUC, and in its students, has the potential to be both enriching and highly challenging. Since Said's death in 2003, AUC has hosted an annual Edward Said memorial lecture. ✆

> "It is salutary indeed to realize that our Arab–Islamic culture contributed substantially to what later was to become the system of education which we call modern, liberal, and Western."
>
> Edward Said, 17 June 1999

71

NOAM CHOMSKY

The eminent scholar visited AUC in 2012 to discuss America's fear of democracy in Middle East

When eighty-four-year-old American linguist and author Noam Chomsky stepped on stage at Ewart Hall in October 2012, the capacity audience rose to offer a standing ovation. This was not his first time at AUC but it was his first appearance here in nineteen years. Chomsky has long been a cult figure in Egypt for his stinging critiques of American imperialism and Israeli treatment of Palestinians. In 1993, his target was the Clinton administration, in 2012 it was American belligerence toward Iran. Chomsky cast this as part of America's efforts to reverse a decline in its geostrategic position in the world. The waning of American power, he explained, can be mirrored in the rise of China, independence in Latin American states, and in the Arab Spring. Said Chomsky: "Movements to independence and democracy are the biggest threat to [American power] . . . control interests rely on dictators that ensure that public opinion does not democratically manifest in policy." It would be fascinating to hear what he would have to say were he to revisit AUC today. ⊛

> **"I can't help thinking more and more of the world that we are bequeathing to our children and grandchildren, and it's not a pretty picture."**
>
> Noam Chomsky at AUC, 23 October 2012

72

SIR MAGDI YACOUB

One of the world's most prominent and renowned heart surgeons maintains close and fruitful ties to AUC

In April 2018, the distinguished professor of cardiothoracic surgery at the National Heart and Lung Institute at Imperial College, London, founder and director of research at the Harefield Heart Science Centre, and founder of the Magdi Yacoub Heart Foundation appeared at AUC to speak at the university's annual Research and Creativity Convention. The event marked the continuation of a close relationship between the eminent doctor and the university that stretches back at least three decades. Yacoub received a honorary doctorate from AUC as long ago as 1989, and a Global Impact Award from AUC in 2015, recognizing work that "advances Egypt and the world." In addition, in 2010, Yacoub delivered a lecture at AUC titled "In Search of Excellence." Even more significant is the collaboration between AUC and the Magdi Yacoub Foundation, which was inaugurated in 2015. Researchers from the university's School of Sciences and Engineering work with the Foundation on advancing technologies that support cardiac procedures and heart surgeries in Egypt, notably at the Aswan Heart Center, which was established by the Foundation to provide free medical services to those in need. Speaking at the Research and Creativity Convention, Yacoub emphasized the importance of such collaboration: "You cannot clap with one hand. You really need two hands. You need everybody." 🌐

73

KOFI ANNAN

The then–UN secretary-general delivered the inaugural Nadia Younes Memorial Lecture at AUC on 8 November 2005

Kofi Annan, the first black African and the most charismatic individual to occupy the post of secretary-general of the United Nations, was no stranger to Egypt. Soon after joining the UN he was made head of personnel for the mission in Cairo. Throughout his career he made frequent return visits to the country, including in 2005, when he delivered the first AUC lecture in memory of Nadia Younes, the Egyptian UN official who died of wounds sustained in a 2003 bomb attack in Baghdad. "I am deeply honored to be invited to deliver this lecture in memory of my dear friend and colleague, Nadia Younes," he began. "How I wish she were still alive, and did not need to be commemorated." He called Nadia a "true daughter of Egypt," and expressed his gratitude to Egypt, not only for giving birth to her but also for seconding her to the cause of humanity. There has been a speech in honor of Nadia every year since, delivered variously by a former president, a former prime minister, and two former foreign ministers. As stimulating and engaging as their words have been, it is unlikely any have been as warmly received as the words spoken by the gentle, dignified, and much missed global statesman, who passed away in 2018. ☺

"If we allow conflict to persist between nations we all lose."

Kofi Annan at AUC, 8 November 2005

WE ARE HONORED THIS EVENING...

The list of famous guests to grace AUC is lengthy and diverse

Do you remember Agnes Moorehead? Does anyone remember Agnes Moorehead? She was an American actress whose career began in 1941 with *Citizen Kane* and wound up with 218 appearances on the American sitcom *Bewitched*. For reasons now forgotten she visited AUC in March 1961 and was presented to students in a Ewart Hall assembly, at which she talked about her life and career. Afterwards, President McLain and his wife held a reception in her honor and students peppered the actress with questions for an hour-and-a-half.

What about Gene Tunney, the American boxer who held the world heavyweight title from 1926 to 1928? He was another visitor, addressing the student assembly in 1931 on the topic of athletics and their role in developing the character of nations. He offered to spar with the dean, who declined. Or the American Helen Keller, who was the first deaf–blind person to complete a bachelor of arts degree, and who became famous when her life story was turned into a bestselling book and a hit stage play and film. She visited AUC in 1952, when over eight hundred people crushed into Oriental Hall to see her. Questions were invited from the audience, which an assistant tapped out on Ms Keller's hand.

The names of other historic visitors have more resonance. Egyptian presidents Mohamed Naguib, Gamal Abdel Nasser, »

Anwar Sadat, and Hosni Mubarak have all been visitors to AUC. On the occasion of his first official visit, shortly after the Revolution, in March 1953 Colonel Nasser, as he was, was guest of honor at the annual Arabic Language Day. He arrived at Ewart Hall to a cheering crowd and was welcomed by a performance of the Liberation Song sung by future Miss AUC and media personality Laila Rostom. He sat through a program of sketches and speeches, after which he addressed the audience, then went straight outside to light a cigarette, smoking being banned in the hall.

Nasser's status as possibly the most charismatic figure to grace AUC was challenged in December 2006 by the arrival on campus of actor and director George Clooney. Clooney was in town with actor Don Cheadle, the Kenyan long-distance runner Tegla Loroupe, and the 2006 US Olympic speed skater William Joseph Cheek to raise awareness of the humanitarian crisis in Darfur. It was a closed session, attended by selected AUC students—who were informed that questions about films or other entertainment topics were not permitted—but as Clooney and colleagues left Oriental Hall there was a mob of screaming fans outside, some of whom managed to grab some prized selfies.

Clooney is not the only Hollywood A-lister to have appeared on campus. In 1998, John Malkovich was in Egypt heading the judging committee at the Cairo International Film Festival when he accepted an invitation to take part in the AUC student union's *On Air* program. Two years previously, *Pulp Fiction* star Samuel L. Jackson dropped in to pay a call on Egyptology professor Kent Weeks, to receive a first-hand update on the latest developments surrounding the exploration of the KV 5 tomb. He came with his wife and daughter, and in the serene surroundings of the Rare Books Library Jackson chatted with Weeks about Egyptology, the Valley of the Kings, and Jackson's daughter's favorite subject in school, archaeology. Who would have thought it, Hollywood's coolest badass a trowel and brush fan?

Less surprising, although no less welcome, have been the visits by Egyptian cinematic legends, including directors Youssef Chahine and Salah Abu Seif, and actors Yousra, Adel Imam, Mohamed Sobhi, Nour el-Sherif, Mahmoud Yassin, Mohamed Henedi, and, of course, Omar Sharif. The redoubtable Sharif attended the gala dinner for the 50th anniversary of the AUC Press in 2010, held in Oriental Hall. AUC has a strict no-alcohol policy, but there was a fear Sharif would not stick around when he discovered this was the case, so, rumor has it, he was discreetly served red wine instead of the karkadeh everyone else was drinking.

From the world of politics, the 1999 visit of then–first lady Hillary Clinton is described elsewhere, but the link between AUC and American politicians extends much further back. In 1953, Adlai Stevenson was

▲ Actor John Malkovich took time out from judging at the Cairo International Film Festival to drop by AUC in 1998

guest of honor at the annual commencement; he had run for US president the previous year and been beaten by Dwight Eisenhower. US senator Edward Kennedy, younger brother to the assassinated president John Kennedy, visited AUC in November 1966. In 1994 it was the turn of 45th vice-president of the United States, Al Gore, who took to the stage on crutches to speak on population and development. In 2005 it was Condoleezza Rice, former US secretary of state and the first African American woman to serve in that position; her visit fell shortly before Egyptian presidential elections and she called on the Egyptian government to have faith in its people and stated that it "must fulfil the promise it made to its people to be free to choose." In 2008 Jimmy Carter, 39th president of the United States and recipient of the 2002 Nobel Peace Prize, came to share his dream of peace in the Middle East.

The tradition continues. The year of AUC's centenary began with a visit from US secretary of state Mike Pompeo, who delivered a controversial speech that was picked up by media around the world. People might not always agree with what AUC guests have to say, but the university remains committed and proud to provide a platform for dialogue from a diverse array of global voices. ⬡

▲ George Clooney at AUC in December 2006. With him is AUC alumnus Amr Waked ('96), who had recently acted alongside Clooney in the international hit movie *Syriana*

75

GENUINE LITERARY CELEBS

The starry guests (and non-guests) of the English literature department

If you were a fan of English literature and were in Cairo in the 1960s, '70s, and '80s, then AUC was the place to be. Under the leadership of professor Doris Shoukri, the Department of English and Comparative Literature ran a distinguished visiting professor program that pulled in not just professors but genuine literary celebrities. Their assembled works could constitute a bookshelf of required reading for English-language writing in the second half of the twentieth century.

The program was born, Shoukri has said, out of a fit of pique. She had met the great American poet T.S. Eliot and felt that he could be persuaded to visit AUC, except the university administration said they didn't have any money to bring people over. Shoukri petitioned President Bartlett and eventually succeeded in securing a modest budget. What the department could offer was to cover flights and two weeks in Egypt, one in Cairo at a good hotel—typically the Nile Hilton (as it was)—and one in Luxor and Aswan on a cruise. In exchange, the writer would give one public lecture and one seminar class. It came too late for Eliot (who died in 1965), but the deal proved attractive enough to reel in an astonishingly good list of novelists, poets, and dramatists including Pulitzer Prize–winners John Updike, John Cheever, Robert Lowell, Robert Warren Penn, and Arthur Miller, as well as William Styron, Marguerite Duras, and John Fowles. "They liked coming to Egypt," said Shoukri. "They enjoyed it, they were pleasant, and they made themselves available to the students." English author Angus Wilson (now largely forgotten but a big name at the time) enjoyed himself so much he stayed on for six weeks. Short-story writer John Cheever enjoyed himself too, but in a different fashion (he was struggling through a period of alcoholism), and afterwards wrote Shoukri an embarrassed letter of apology saying he wanted to come back and redeem himself. John Fowles (best known for *The French Lieutenant's Woman*), visiting in 1972, expressed his thanks by providing an introduction to the AUC's first English-language Naguib Mahfouz translation, *Miramar*.

> 9th August 1987.
>
> Dear Doris Shoukri:
>
> Thank you for your renewed invitation to visit Cairo. My present difficulty is that, I'm simultaneously making a 90-minute documentary in India and trying to finish an immense novel that won't be done until next Feb. or March. So I simply can't come to Cairo or anywhere else at present, much as I should like to. Perhaps if we could talk again during next year
>
> —you'll understand my reluctance to commit myself too far in advance — I might be able, should you wish it, to visit sometime between Oct. 88 and May 89?
>
> Sorry to disappoint, and many thanks again for the invitation.
>
> Yours sincerely,
>
> Salman Rushdie.
>
> P.S. I do not know Kundera; have never met him. Perhaps you have confused him with Calvino? Or Grass? Both of whom are / were friends. SR.

Salman Rushdie's letter expressing regret that he would be unable to visit AUC in 1987 but holding out hope for a future date

Naturally, not everybody approached said yes and among those who passed are film-maker Jean Luc Godard (invited on the occasion of the introduction of a film minor in the Department of Comparative Literature) and Anglo-Japanese novelist Kazuo Ishiguro ("I'm afraid I'm going through a very busy time at the moment"). Similarly busy in August 1987, "trying to finish an immense novel that won't be done until next Feb. or March," was Salman Rushdie. He might, he offered, be able to visit next year. As the author of one of the most highly praised books of recent times, *Midnight's Children* (1981), Rushdie was a big deal and a further exchange of letters saw a visit scheduled for spring 1989. Before then his "immense novel" was published, which was *The Satanic Verses*. Not long after its release in the States, Ayatollah Ruhollah Khomeini denounced the book as an attack on Islam and another Iranian cleric offered a bounty of $2.6 million to any Iranian who killed Rushdie and $1 million to any other Muslim who succeeded. AUC's student newspaper *Caravan* reporting on the story carried a comment by an unnamed AUC source: "I guess he won't be coming, not now, or ever." ✥

76

A WORLDLY FRATERNITY

The international
make-up
of the 1950
student body

For the first thirty years, Christians predominated within the AUC student body. Copts, Greeks, and Armenians all constituted a higher percentage at AUC than in the population of Egypt. Which meant the university could, with some justification, present itself as "an interdenominational Christian institution serving the Near and Middle East," as it did in this piece of marketing collateral, opposite. The message is designed to appeal to Christian "friends in America," without whose money AUC could not exist. The proposition is enhanced because any donations go to educate not only the students of Egypt, but those of the world, from the Adenese to the now equally obsolete Yugoslav. Of the twenty-five nationalities illustrated, Egyptians at this time represented approximately sixty percent of students. Up until recently, Greeks and Armenians had been the second most populous on campus, followed by Italians, but Italian numbers had diminished during World War II when that country found itself fighting against the Americans and British. But by 1950, even the Greeks and Armenians were outnumbered by Palestinians, whose families had fled the fighting that accompanied the declaration of the state of Israel. It is illuminating to see how multicultural AUC was even seventy years ago, with students from as far distant as Brazil, China, Cuba, and Indonesia.

In one way, this advertisement marks the beginning of the end of a particular phase in the history of AUC. A series of changes adopted by President Thomas Bartlett encouraged more Muslims to enroll. These included dropping requirements for studies in Christian religion and ethics, and bolstering the English Language Institute so that young students from Arabic-speaking families could improve their English enough to benefit from AUC. By the early 1960s, Christians and Muslims were roughly equal in numbers at AUC and by the end of the sixties, Muslims were in the definite majority. As for the different nationalities enrolling, that number has doubled since 1950. ⊕

▶ This appeal for donors was published in *The Chronicle*, an AUC newsletter circulated to friends of the university in America, in 1950

228

THE AMERICAN UNIVERSITY AT CAIRO

INCORPORATED AT WASHINGTON D.C. IN 1919

AN INTERDENOMINATIONAL CHRISTIAN INSTITUTION SERVING THE NEAR AND MIDDLE EAST

THE 1950 STUDENT BODY AT A.U.C. INCLUDES MANY NATIONALITIES

ADENESE

AFGHAN
President of Student Council

AMERICAN
Exchange Student

ARABIAN

ARMENIAN

BRAZILIAN

CHINESE

CUBAN

EGYPTIAN

ETHIOPIAN

GERMAN

GREEK

HUNGARIAN

INDIAN

INDONESIAN

IRANIAN

IRAQI

ITALIAN

LEBANESE

MALTESE

PALESTINIAN

SUDANESE

TRANSJORDANIAN

TURKISH

YUGOSLAV

THE AMERICAN UNIVERSITY AT CAIRO IS SUPPORTED BY TUITION FEES IN
EGYPT, A SMALL ENDOWMENT AND CONTRIBUTIONS FROM FRIENDS IN AMERICA.

WON'T YOU BECOME A PARTNER BY SENDING YOUR CHECK TO
THE AMERICAN UNIVERSITY AT CAIRO
800 LAND TITLE BUILDING
PHILADELPHIA 10, Pa.

Gifts are Deductible from Federal Income Tax

"A MYSTIC BOND
OF BROTHERHOOD
MAKES ALL MEN ONE" - Goethe

77

FROM ALL CORNERS OF THE WORLD

International students reflect on their experiences in Cairo

▲ Shan Yang, who, at the time of writing, continues her MIddle East studies at AUC

Each international student—from the United States suburbs to the edges of the African continent—comes to AUC with a purpose: to learn Arabic, to choose a field of study not offered in universities at home, or to explore the beginnings of civilization up close. Many of them get more than they expected.

Below, four such international students describe in their own words why they're here and what knowledge they're bringing back home. Yang came to Cairo to broaden her understanding of the region. Amir Ben Ameur has discovered a knack for policy and economics. Nour Elhouda Bouzahzah, who studied abroad in Washington, DC at a pivotal moment in American history, found her ideas shifted by international exposure. Erick Dokalahy, the only student from Madagascar at AUC, wants to learn how best to preserve fresh food grown in his country.

SHAN YANG
Middle East Studies Graduate Student, China

"I am from a small village in China, so they didn't understand my decision to come here. Even though my family supports me studying abroad, they still said, 'Why not Europe? Why not the United States? Why are you going to Egypt?' They have major misunderstandings. To be honest, even when I was in China, I had almost no Muslim friends. Minorities in Shanghai are relatively few. Shanghai has about seven small mosques, but only when they go there to pray do they wear scarves. They are under huge social pressure not to.

"People who live here must think it is ridiculous to have to prove themselves as 'normal.' But the first thought in my mind was to 'normalize' Islam and the Middle East. It's normal to wear a scarf, to pray five times a day, and to go to a mosque—and it's normal to choose not to do any of those things. People here care about family, safety, inflation, graduation, and jobs, just like people elsewhere. The deeper I

go into society, the more strongly I feel that we belong to one common community. Nationality, ethnicity, language, faith—these should never be obstacles for us to be united. Now, although I have lived in Shanghai for eight years, I call Cairo home. I feel more relaxed in Cairo and have developed a good sense of humor here. I like drinking tea with sugar or lemon or mint.

"I want to bring this knowledge, this sense of shared community—and maybe even a new way of drinking tea—back with me to China, where we have many US or European study experts, but lack people who know about this area. We should have more professors who have lived here for some time. Inshaallah, I will return to China to do this."

AMIR BEN AMEUR
Economics Senior, Tunisia (Tomorrow's Leaders Scholarship Recipient)
"I got a scholarship from the US Department of State to attend AUC, and I came because the School of Business here is one of the best. Honestly, after these years, I have learned so much from AUC.

I've taken courses that have changed the way I see the world. Before my education here, I used to just criticize and complain. Now, I'm giving recommendations. I'm trying to solve problems. I want to offer constructive criticism. I was telling my professor recently that now I can read parliamentary budget line proposals and can do analysis. I understand what they mean. I have different ideas now about politics and the economy as systems that regulate individual lives. It's healthy to be skeptical about these systems, but I believe that we must suggest good alternatives and young people should be engaged and work to ►►

► Erick Dokalahy from Madagascar, who currently works in the department of chemistry, AUC, doing research in food science and chemical thermodynamics

become responsible citizens capable of making change.

"I believe in the importance of international work. I am currently a post-conflict adviser in the United Nations–Habitat Youth Advisory Board and have been previously involved with the United Nations Development Programme. We Youth, my nonprofit in Tunisia under the National Youth umbrella, is one of the biggest youth NGOs in the Middle East and North Africa region. We work a lot on engagement, involving youth in socioeconomic political uplifting. We work on decentralization, elections, political accountability with Parliament, and engaging youth in democracy. Having a liberal arts education here has helped me make a healthy transition from a radical to a practical mindset. I want to tell other young people: You're wise enough. Start engaging and acting instead of agonizing and rejecting. Idleness won't lead to any improvement."

ERICK DOKALAHY
Food Chemistry Graduate Student, Madagascar

"At an early age, my love for manufacturing science was nurtured by a TV documentary series, which triggered my interest in food processing. We produce a lot in Madagascar, but we do not produce raw material for food, we export it. So this is a burden for the country. That triggered my interest in agricultural science and galvanized me to become what I call an 'ambitious food technologist.' That's why I am here, studying food chemistry at AUC.

"I hope to establish my own start-up on fortified food one day. I want to participate in the fight against food insecurity by making high-quality, locally produced, and affordable food for the Malagasy people. No matter where I end up, I'll use the skills and experiences I've gained at AUC to pass the torch to the next generation.

"Here at AUC, everything is different from what I've experienced before. There is an emphasis on the student's well-being and personal development, not just academic achievement. I always keep myself busy volunteering in extracurricular activities, such as being the Graduate Student Association representative in the University Senate, a member of the Chemistry Club and Black Student Association, as well as a teaching assistant in the School of Sciences and Engineering.

"Being out of one's comfort zone is always difficult. When I came to Egypt, I had to manage my finances, learn Arabic to be able to deal with the basic things in my everyday life, and make new friends—all while focusing on my studies. They say 'life is the best teacher,' and I think that's completely true. Since I started my international student life journey here at AUC, I've had a mind shift and new vision of how things should be in my country."

NOUR ELHOUDA BOUZAHZAH
Business Administration Senior, Algeria (Tomorrow's Leaders Scholarship Recipient)

"As a study-abroad student at the American University in Washington, DC, I met people who have different arguments and thoughts, and heard them explain their points of view. It was really enriching. In my dorm, I got to interact with a lot of Americans, and we talked about politics. They had never traveled to Africa, so they had a different view of the continent. We discussed women's issues and other topics.

"What really impacted me was the Women's March in Washington, DC. It was incredible. Everyone had these pink hats, and they were marching literally throughout all of DC. The metro was so crowded you could not get on.

"The Women's March also reminded me of the startup that I worked for a year ago, ScaleUp Ventures, which was founded by a female CEO. We weren't a lot of people at ScaleUp, only five, but the CEO promoted hiring women. I liked the idea.

"My goal is to establish my own startup that would employ more women while also doing something beneficial for my country. I will make sure to transfer all the priceless knowledge that I learned at AUC and in Washington, DC to young people in Algeria. My startup will be built for youth, by youth." ❀

▲ Nour Elhouda Bouzahzah, who came to AUC from Algeria and is now an event officer in the AUC alumni office

233

78

TALK LIKE AN EGYPTIAN

AUC boasts the
world's premier
full-immersion
Arabic-language
program

It is a paradox that one of the teaching departments that does most to promote the name of AUC around the world—and particularly in the United States—is one of the least heralded in Cairo. The clue to that is in its name, the Center for Arabic Study *Abroad* (CASA). The nature of CASA is that it trains non–native Arabic speakers from other countries, who come to Cairo for a year of intensive language study then typically leave again, having only limited involvement in the wider AUC community. However, meet any US career diplomat posted in the Arab world or any leading US academic researching the Middle East and North Africa and there is a reasonable chance that they went through CASA—not least because the program has been running for over fifty years now.

Its origins go back to 1966 when the US-based Joint Committee of Near and Middle East Studies decided to establish an Arabic-teaching program abroad and chose AUC as its location. "The reality was that the United States needed a capacity that it did not have—people who knew about the Arab world who could speak Arabic," recounted Thomas Bartlett, who was AUC president the year CASA was founded. A consortium of eight prominent American universities, including AUC, came together to set policy. A curriculum was drafted, applications solicited, and instructors recruited. The first intake was scheduled to start classes in October 1967 but safety fears following that summer's war with Israel pushed back the start to January 1968.

CASA introduced a groundbreaking change in the way Arabic was taught. In years past, Arabic at AUC meant the old School of Oriental Studies with its Arabists and Azhar sheikhs, or night school classes run by the Division of Public Service (now the School of Continuing Education) for foreigners living in Egypt who wanted to speak a little of the local language. CASA was a serious Cold War language-training program that took students who could already speak some Arabic and raised it up to near fluency. "The CASA method focused on Arabic as a 'living spoken language,'" says John Swanson, associate provost for assessment,

▲ An exercise from an early Arabic-language instruction book used in the Center for Arabic Study Abroad program

evaluation, and special projects at AUC, who co-directed CASA in the 1980s. "I think the most unique thing about CASA is that it gave highly motivated students of the language an opportunity to spend a whole year focusing on developing their Arabic skills at the highest level, without any outside academic interference."

"I started studying Arabic with a visiting professor in college at a school without a formal Arabic program, and I was determined to find a way to continue," explains Eleanor Ellis, a Harvard University graduate student and a 2017–18 CASA fellow. "It was my dream to do CASA because it's not only textually immersive but you are also really pushed to learn and use *ammiya* [colloquial Arabic] and be immersed in Cairo."

"You can never learn enough to become fluent if you take only four years of Arabic in college," says Alice Duesdieker, also a 2017–18 CASA fellow. "CASA is the only program that I'm familiar with that takes you above and beyond to the point of being truly fluent." Since finishing her studies at CASA, Duesdieker is back in her hometown of San Francisco, working as a community manager at TechWadi, a ≫

nonprofit that builds bridges between Silicon Valley and the Middle East.

CASA has provided a base for many careers built around a proficiency in Arabic and knowledge of Egypt and the Middle East. Paul Wulfsberg was in the program in 2004–2005. He became an Arabic instructor at Harvard before joining the US State Department. Most recently he was based at the American embassy in Amman. Just as significantly, while on the course he met and later married a fellow student, Iraqi-American Rana Abdul-Aziz, and they now have two children, to whom they only speak Arabic at home—"True to the spirit of CASA," says Wulfsberg.

One of the most striking novels of post-revolutionary Egypt has been Basma Abdel Aziz's *al-Tabur* (2013), published in English in 2016 as *The Queue*, in a translation by Elisabeth Jaquette, who attended CASA in 2012–13. "I wouldn't have the career I do today without CASA," says Jaquette, who is the executive director of the American Literary Translators Association. "It's no exaggeration to say that I wouldn't have been able to achieve the Arabic proficiency needed to work as a translator without the CASA program."

Denis Sullivan (CASA '84, '09), professor of political science and international affairs, co-director of the Middle East Center and director of the Boston Consortium for Arab Region Studies at Northeastern University, is another proud CASA*wi* who believes his studies helped him secure a tenure position. He notes that his favorite night in Cairo was his first. He recalls "breathing in the feel of Tahrir" and making a lifelong friend through a random encounter. "He taught me more Arabic than any language partner I ever had," Sullivan says. "He taught me about 'real life' in Egypt, especially about the majority of *al-sha'b* [the people] and the Egyptian underclass."

Such is the importance of exposure to the street life of Cairo in the program that when AUC moved to the New Cairo Campus in 2008, CASA students rejected the spacious new classrooms, state-of-the-art library, Olympic-size swimming pool, and lush gardens, and said they didn't want to be there. The course directors agreed and within two years the CASA program moved back to the old Tahrir Campus and the clamor and din of Downtown.

AUC's provost at the time would surely have understood the reverse move: before her time as provost (2008–10) and then president 2011–15, Lisa Anderson attended CASA ('76) at AUC. "CASA crystallized my lifelong love of Egypt, of Arabic and of learning," she told *AUC Today*. "I have had the immense good fortune of having a career that I have found to be—like the city and the language CASA taught me about—endlessly fascinating. *Alhamdulilah*!" ☙

> **"In academic circles related to the Middle East CASA is regarded as almost an essential step along a career."**
>
> Former CASA co-director
> John Swanson

79

INTERNAL AFFAIRS

For almost forty years, an AUC program has been giving American graduates a foothold in the wider world

O n 15 September 1981, recent Princeton graduate Frank Packard stepped off the boat in Alexandria harbor, took a three-hour taxi ride to Tahrir Square, Cairo, and presented himself at AUC. Neither student nor faculty, Frank was something new—AUC's first-ever presidential intern. It was an eventful time to have arrived: three weeks into Frank's stay, President Sadat was assassinated. Despite this, Frank remembers feeling safe as an American in Egypt, particularly with the goodwill generated by the attendance of United States president Jimmy Carter and two former presidents, Nixon and Ford, at Sadat's funeral.

The idea for the internship came from AUC president Richard Pedersen. The university would offer free accommodation, Arabic-language tuition, and organized trips, plus a modest stipend, in exchange for a commitment to work in the president's office for a full academic year. Frank's tenure was considered sufficiently successful that the next year there were three interns, one for the president's office and two assigned to the office of planning and development. The following year there were four. Presidential administrator Rowaida Saad-Eldin was tasked with overseeing the program: "We wanted them to bring in their expertise and knowledge from their prestigious universities. But we also wanted them to have a wonderful experience so that when »

▲ The Presidential Associates of 2018–19, drawn from across the United States, most with academic backgrounds involving some form of Middle Eastern or Arabic studies

they went back they'd say AUC is wonderful and Egypt is wonderful, and they'd become our ambassadors."

In 2019, almost forty years since launching, the program is still going strong. These days it offers positions for up to twelve overseas graduates a year—although now that the word "intern" is viewed as a synonym for slave they have been rebranded "associates." They are distributed across the university, working variously in the offices of the president, dean of students, and provost, and in advancement and communications and the rare books and special collections library, among others.

Competition for places is keen. Not only do candidates have to be graduates of top-end US universities, they have to show a credible interest in Egypt, the Middle East, or the Arabic language, and/or have skills that relate to the specific position for which they are applying. To date, 290 associates have passed through the program, in the process enhancing their CVs, honing their Arabic, getting to know Cairo, Egypt, and the region. "[The program] has everything I wanted out of a post-college experience," says 2018–19 associate Claire Davenport, "except being paid a lot. Although, for Egypt, it's probably pretty good."

Some have stayed on for a second year, or longer—in which case, they are no longer associates and instead become local-hire staff. Some married Egyptians, which, says Rowaida Saad-Eldin, who retired from running the program in 2010, was definitely contrary to her advice. "I always told them, don't fall in love with an Egyptian, you'll suffer."

Most, however, left and got on with their careers. After Cairo, the original intern, Frank Packard, resolved to develop a career outside of America; he moved to Tokyo, then Hong Kong, then back to Tokyo, where he founded a boutique investment company. He says of his time at AUC, "I think it set me on a journey that continues to this day."

Other former interns have made similarly fascinating journeys. Elizabeth "Libby" Thompson, who was in the second-ever intake (1982–83) went on to become an associate professor of history, specializing in the Middle East, at the University of Virginia. Her book, *Justice Interrupted: The Struggle for Constitutional Government in the Middle East* was published in 2013. Eve Troutt (1983–84), now Dr. Eve Troutt Powell, is a distinguished professor of history at the University of Pennsylvania, where she is an expert on Egypt, Sudan, and slavery in the Nile Valley. Sarah Albee (1985–86,) worked on *Sesame Street* before becoming a bestselling author of more than one hundred books for kids. Alicia Sams (1987–88) went into film production and her credits include *Chocolat*, *The Shipping News*, and *Amreeka*. Nathan Martin (1988–89) became a rabbi.

Katherine "Amira" Bennison (1989–90) is now a lecturer in Middle

> **"I think the program set me on a journey that continues until today."**
>
> Frank Packard, AUC's first ever Presidential Associate

Eastern studies at Cambridge, England, and regularly appears on British TV and radio speaking on Islamic history, while her colleague Suzanne Malveaux (1989–90) became an Emmy award-winning anchor for CNN's *Around the World*. She covered the White House for ten years, interviewing presidents George Bush, Bill Clinton, George W. Bush, and Barack Obama. Also from that year's intake, Peter Vrooman (1989–90) joined the US State Department, serving in Djibouti, Ethiopia, Somalia, Algeria, Beirut, Israel, and Iraq; he is currently ambassador to Rwanda. Twelve years after interning in the president's office, Bradley Cook (1990–91) made the shortlist for the AUC presidency itself, narrowly losing out to David Arnold. He is now the provost and executive vice president at Southern Utah University.

In 1991–92, Hanif Vanjaria of Duke University, interning in development, met Patricia Lally of Fordham University, interning in rare books, and the two went on to marry. Charles Duhigg (1997–98) became an award-winning journalist for the *New York Times* and an author. Ryan Greene-Roesel (2001–02) is a transport planning consultant in San Francisco and plays *nay* (Egyptian reed flute) in a local orchestra. Graeme Wood (2002–03) is a correspondent for *The Atlantic* magazine, a lecturer in political science at Yale University, and author of *The Way of Strangers: Encounters with the Islamic State*. Anders Blewett (2003–04) became a representative in the Montana State Senate from 2011 to 2015 and is now an attorney. He married former intern Celia Smalls (2007–08).

As 2018–19 associate Aaron Blinderman says, "Never underestimate the value of spending a year in a place like Cairo." ⬡

▲ In exchange for working five days a week at AUC, presidential associates receive accommodation, a stipend, Arabic-language tuition, organized trips, and plenty of opportunities to travel in Egypt and the region

80

GOING GLOBAL WITH MAHFOUZ

The championing of Naguib Mahfouz by the AUC Press ultimately paved the way for successive generations of Arabic writers to get their work read around the world

▶ There are now some 600 editions in more than forty languages of the works of Naguib Mahfouz published or licensed by the AUC Press

When one afternoon in October 1988 Naguib Mahfouz was woken by his wife telling him there was someone on the phone saying he had won the Nobel prize, he told her, "Enough of dreams." But it had been predicted. In October 1982, the then-director of AUC Press, John Rodenbeck, asserted in a letter to the editor of *World Authors 1975–1980* at the H.W. Wilson Company of New York that Mahfouz "will certainly win the Prize itself someday before he dies." Rodenbeck was even more strident in correspondence with the publishers Heinemann the following month: "The fact is that it is about time that Mahfouz had his Nobel. If he had defected say to Israel he would have had one long ago."

In 1972, the Press had made an extraordinary commitment by signing agreements with Naguib Mahfouz to publish nine of his novels in English. It was the sort of risk only a university press could take because for all his stature in the Arab world the Egyptian writer was unknown elsewhere. To help spread the costs, licensing deals were made with Heinemann and Three Continents Press to produce editions in Britain and United States, respectively. One of the Press's translations, *Awlad haratina* (in English, *Children of Gebelawi*), was published only in foreign editions as the book was banned in Egypt. Sales were modest, particularly outside Egypt. The Press consistently sold more copies of its *Miramar* in Cairo alone than Three Continents did of its licensed version throughout the States

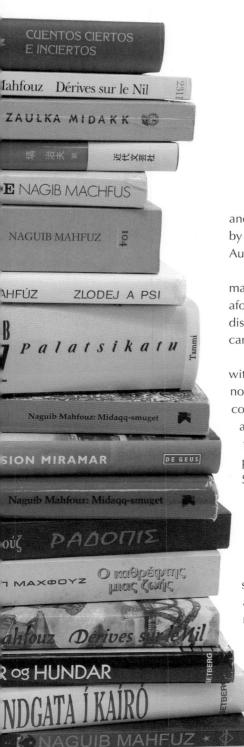

and Canada. However, to put that in perspective, the royalty fees paid by AUC Press to Mahfouz for *Miramar* for the twelve-month's sales to August 1982 amounted to a less-than-life changing LE74.

To sell more books the Press embarked on a publicity campaign, making sure Mahfouz was included for the first time in the aforementioned *World Authors* reference book, and printing and distributing an English-language pamphlet about him. Then in 1988 came the news from Stockholm.

As soon as the award was announced, the Press was besieged with orders for Mahfouz's books. The problem was that there was not much existing inventory, so instant reprints with newly designed covers were ordered. Meanwhile there was a deluge of faxes, letters, and telephone calls from publishers around the world seeking translation rights. The major issue was finding an appropriate partner for the future publication of Mahfouz's works in English. Several big publishing houses in London and New York expressed interest, but the Press went with Doubleday, with whom it had been in sporadic dialogue for several years. Doubleday boasted an enthusiastic champion for Mahfouz's work in the form of former first lady turned editor, Jacqueline Onassis, who had read the first volume of Mahfouz's *Cairo Trilogy* in French. She loved it, she said, because it chimed with her love of Mediterranean culture, acquired while married to her second husband, Greek shipping magnate Aristotle Onassis.

A deal was reached—for a six-figure but very reasonable sum, remembers Doubleday editor Martha Levin—for the US publisher to acquire seventeen titles by Mahfouz over the next two or three years. Jacqueline Onassis's first job was to edit the Press's translations of the trilogy, which were brought out in hardback starting with the first book, *Palace Walk*, in 1991. According to Levin, who was Doubleday's »

▲ Various works by Mahfouz translated into (from top left) German, Japanese, Norwegian, Dutch, Polish, French, Icelandic, Greek, Finnish, Portuguese, Spanish, and Slovakian

managing editor on the Mahfouz project, the publishing program was a big success, both critically and financially. The onset of the first Gulf War provoked a great need in American readers to understand more about the region and with his "brand name" recognition as the winner of a major literary prize, Mahfouz was an obvious first read for a lot of people. For Doubleday (and its paperback imprint Anchor), its success with Mahfouz paved the way for an extensive and successful publication program of both fiction and non-fiction written about Egypt and the Middle East, by many writers whose work had not previously been published in the United States.

Meanwhile, the AUC Press continues to translate and publish Mahfouz's works. The list currently stands at some thirty-six novels, collections of short stories, and memoirs—Doubleday/Anchor publishes thirty-three of these—and it is not finished yet. One imagines that the family of Mahfouz—he died in 2006, aged ninety-four—receives considerably more these days than the LE74 annually of old.

The awarding of the Nobel prize ensured that the name of Mahfouz is now enshrined in the canon of world literature, alongside the likes of Ernest Hemingway, Albert Camus, Günter Grass, and Gabriel García Márquez. Mahfouz acknowledged the role that the AUC Press played in this when he wrote in 1992: "It was through the translation of these novels into English . . . that other publishers became aware of them and requested their translation into other foreign languages, and I believe that these translations were among the foremost reasons for my being awarded the Nobel prize." ◉

EBOLA'S RISING TOLL

TIME

SECRETS OF THE LOST TOMB

The discovery of a crypt fit for 50 princes sheds new light on the epic life of Ramesses the Great

81

HANDS-ON EGYPTOLOGY

Kent Weeks's discoveries at KV5 opened a world of opportunities for AUC students

I n May 1995 AUC achieved a first. A member of faculty was the subject of a cover story in *TIME* magazine. In fact, during that year AUC Egyptology professor Kent Weeks would make many more newspaper and magazine covers around the world. The reason was the "rediscovery" and subsequent exploration of tomb KV5 in the Valley of the Kings. The tomb was known to earlier excavators, who dismissed it as not worth bothering with. Howard Carter used its entrance as a place to dump his debris when he was clearing the access to Tutankhamun's tomb. But Weeks's modern explorations revealed the forgotten tomb to be among the largest ever found in Egypt and the likely burial place of the sons of Rameses II. It was hailed as the most dramatic find in Egyptology since Tutankhamun, back in 1922.

Weeks actually rediscovered the entrance to KV5 in 1987, but it was not until eight years later, when it became apparent just how large the tomb actually was, that the international media took notice. Weeks, who holds an MA in anthropology from the University of Washington in Seattle and a PhD in Egyptology from Yale, first taught at AUC in the anthropology department in 1972, while conducting field work at Giza. In 1974, he moved to Luxor as field director of the Chicago Oriental Institute's epigraphic and architectural survey. It was while there that he became aware of the need for an accurate and comprehensive mapping of the numerous ancient monuments on Luxor's West Bank, ≫

▲ The exploits of AUC Egyptology professor Kent Weeks made the front cover of *TIME* magazine in May 1995 when he uncovered a mammoth tomb in Luxor

243

▶ Pages from the sketchbooks of Susan Weeks, wife of Kent and a member of the KV5 team. A collection of her work is held in the AUC University Archives

Dira' Abu an Naja, Qurnah.   1993 80   Qurnah, Mar '94   1993 80.

PRESIDENT #8
DONALD McDONALD
(1990–97)

McDonald came to AUC from Texas A&M, where he had been provost and then vice-president for academic affairs. He had only been AUC president for one day when Iraq invaded Kuwait. "That event changed any expectations I may have had," he said. He moved quickly to establish a scholarship fund for affected students. As part of AUC's 75th anniversary celebrations, he commissioned a task force to determine the optimal areas of expansion for AUC; the resulting report led directly to the decision to create a new campus on the outskirts of the city.

burial place of generations of pharaohs and nobles, and so, in 1978, he established the Theban Mapping Project.

After he returned to teaching at AUC in 1988, Weeks continued working on the Theban Mapping Project, and selected two or three students each summer season to join his team in Luxor. "We were laying the foundations for topographic maps of the Valley of the Kings and making detailed plans of each tomb," says Weeks, "and the AUC students learned the basics of proper land surveying and something of the history of Egypt's New Kingdom and of the Valley of the Kings. Several of them proved to be very good." The team used hot-air balloons to scientifically survey and photograph the ground. Infra-red cameras also recorded what was going on beneath the ground. All this information was then computerized and used to generate 3D maps so users could walk through the Valley of the Kings without ever leaving their desks.

The main goal of the project was, as its name suggests, mapping. But when the local government in Luxor decided to widen a road, Weeks wanted to be sure that the work would not destroy anything important, like the old dumping ground that was KV5. He wanted to give the forgotten tomb one final exploration. Its three rooms, which had previously been explored in 1820, were filled with rubble to the ceiling. In the process of clearing them, a handful of small items were found that persuaded the authorities to give the team more time. Eventually Weeks was able to pry open a door blocked for thousands of years and announce the discovery of a lifetime. "We found ourselves in a corridor," Weeks told *TIME*. "On each side were ten doors, and at the end there was a statue of Osiris, the god of the afterlife." KV5 was huge.

Coincidentally, the announcement of KV5 occurred as the American University marked its seventy-fifth anniversary. The two were celebrated

in an event entitled "The Future of Egypt's Past" at the Explorer's Club in New York. "Happy birthday AUC," Weeks said in his opening remarks. "You have a new tomb."

After 1995, the focus of the work on KV5 grew to include its clearing. AUC president Donald McDonald and the provost George Gibson encouraged the excavation and steered small grants to Weeks. In return, Weeks made sure to credit AUC in all KV5-related press interviews. Over the next few years, several AUC students took part in the ongoing dig, recording pottery and small artifact finds, and helping record wall decoration.

Today, the Theban Mapping Project has its main office on the New Cairo Campus. There is also a second office in Luxor, with an Egyptological and community/children's library, both open to the public. The AUC office employs one full-time and two part-time staff plus about six work-study students, some of them Egyptology graduates. Both offices are presently preparing a new version of the Theban Mapping Project website, developing an Egyptian Archaeological Database, and readying a new edition of the *Atlas of the Valley of the Kings*. As Weeks says, this presents an unrivaled opportunity for AUC students, "Doing Egyptology, not just reading about it." ❦

▲ Kent Weeks aboard the dahabiyya that for many years was his home in Upper Egypt while working on the Theban Mapping Project and excavation of KV5

82

MODELING SUCCESS

How changing
the world starts
on campus

In 2018, for the ninth year in a row, a team from AUC was recognized with the "Outstanding Delegation" award, the highest award at the National Model United Nations Conference in New York. Sounds impressive, but what is a Model United Nations?

It is an educational simulation of a United Nations (UN) council in which delegates are placed in committees and assigned countries to represent, along with topics for discussion. Teams then debate with their fellow delegates. At the end of a conference, the best-performing delegations are recognized with awards.

In 1989, AUC was invited by the United Nations Association (an organization that exists to raise public awareness of the UN and its work) to send a Model United Nations (MUN) delegation to its conference in Moscow. Tim Sullivan, provost emeritus and former political science professor, who had experience with MUN back home in the United States, recruited a number of AUC students and took them off to what was then the Soviet Union.

Sullivan remembers the conference as being "somewhat chaotic at times" with the Soviet students having trouble role playing, particularly when asked to represent the views of countries that were not part of the Soviet Bloc (which in 1989 was in the process of coming apart, so AUC students got to be eyewitnesses to history at first hand).

As the conference ended, the Egyptian team told Sullivan that they thought AUC could do a better job. Sullivan agreed and in the coming months he taught students how to organize a debate, chair a meeting, and deal with the protocols of discussion and resolutions. The culmination was the first Cairo International Model United Nations (CIMUN) conference, hosted by AUC later that same year with the participation of students from other universities in Egypt. It was a resounding success, so much so that it has been repeated annually ever since, supplemented from 1990 onwards by a Cairo International Model Arab League (CIMAL).

Although CIMUN is considered as an extracurricular activity, it has flourished at AUC to become the largest and most prestigious MUN conference in Africa and the Middle East, as well as the largest student-run activity on campus, with more than five hundred members. Each year, participants engage in lively discussions about a variety of challenging and controversial topics on the agenda of the UN and international community.

In 2019, twenty-two-year-old Marwan El Sayed, majoring in actuarial science, is current secretary general of CIMUN. He joined the organization as a freshman, impressed by its scale—CIMUN's board alone is bigger than the entire membership of many university clubs—and reputation. "Minister of foreign affairs Sameh Shoukry attended two of [CIMUN's] last four opening ceremonies and UN secretary general Kofi Annan attended the opening in 2004," says El Sayed. "This is an organization that can give you a head-start in your career."

Indeed, the leader of that first CIMUN team in Moscow, Mohamed El Farnawany ('89), went on to become deputy chief of mission at the Egyptian Embassy in Paris and work at the UN in New York; >>

▲ In the Model United Nations teams of students take the roles of countries and are assigned topics that they then debate with their fellow delegates, who are playing the roles of other nations

▲ Shaden Khallaf ('98, '04) took part in CIMUN while at AUC and on graduating joined the United Nations High Commission for Refugees. "I immediately knew that this was what I had always wanted to do," she said

he is now a director at the International Renewable Energy Agency (IRENA). "CIMUN prepared me for the real UN," he told *AUC Today* in 2010. "It helps develop skills such as research, negotiation, public speaking, and organization of events. It prepares you for the real world where you can help make a difference in the lives of people in need."

Many other CIMUN participants have also gone on to work for the actual UN, including Reem Al Salem ('97, '00), who served as president of CIMUN's International Court of Justice and judge at the National Model United Nations in New York. "MUN was a game changer for me in terms of my ability to develop my personality, self-confidence, and self-expression," says Al Salem. "It also gave me a glimpse of the real world as I had to learn how to design and implement projects from A to Z, and navigate the complexity of dealing with different stakeholders with different interests." On graduating she joined the United Nations High Commission for Refugees (UNHCR) and spent seventeen years with them operating in countries around the globe. In 2018, she founded her own consulting company, Global Humanitude, through which she continues to provide support on humanitarian response to NGOs, UN organisations, and academic institutions.

AUC graduate Shaden Khallaf ('98, '04) also went on to work at the UNHCR. "CIMUN provided me with excellent exposure to the international legal framework within which the United Nations operates and how that impacts people's lives on a daily basis," she told *AUC Today*. She is now a senior policy advisor specializing in the Middle East and North Africa and lectures at AUC in the Center for Migration and Refugee Studies and the Department of Law.

But according to Marwan El Sayed, participation in CIMUN has other benefits. He is heavily involved in organizing events, including a junior conference, held each fall semester, that brings in two thousand high-school students from all over Egypt, introducing them not just to CIMUN but also to AUC. "It's the best feeling in the world when a high-school student comes to me on the last day and says, 'Thank you. I've actually learned something from you.' I'd work for years just to hear that sentence."

El Sayed's parents, incidentally, now want him to pursue a career in international affairs, despite, he notes, paying "all that money" for him to study mathematics. ⬡

83

HELPING PEOPLE HELP OTHERS

AUC's double role in a refugee success story

———

Clad in a white shirt decorated with scarlet red and fiery orange patterns, Dawood Mayom scanned the aisles of books in the library before hand-picking his next read: *Public Policy Analysis and Program Evaluation*.

Born in what is now known as South Sudan, Dawood was the youngest of seven siblings when the second Sudanese civil war broke out and his father was killed. The widowed mother fled with her children to Jabarona Camp for internally displaced people near the Sudanese capital of Khartoum, where they stayed for nearly eight years.

At Jabarona, Dawood struggled to convince his mother to let him attend the camp school. In the daily battle to survive, education was a low priority. His unwavering habit of watching other children walk to class every day eventually tugged at her heart. At the age of nine, Dawood's family was able to move to Khartoum, where he was finally able to attend school regularly. Although the setbacks he faced as a child meant that he would have to make up for missed years of school, he was up to the challenge and managed to graduate from high school and enrol in university.

However, in his freshman year Dawood was to experience forced displacement for the second time when he had to flee Sudan and ≫

▲ Dawood Mayom, a refugee from South Sudan who is now studying for a master's in public policy at AUC's School of Global Affairs and Public Policy

seek safety in Egypt. "Being displaced is the worst ever experience, one that separates a person from his loved ones," says Dawood, who came to Cairo on his own. "I was responsible for myself, and I had to find ways to build my future," he added. He started involving himself in volunteer activities in the Sudanese community, teaching children maths and Arabic. In 2010, he enrolled in a distance-learning law degree at Cairo University. In 2012, through the United Nations High Commission for Refugees (UNHCR) he secured a scholarship with the Albert Einstein German Academic Refugee Initiative (DAFI), which gives access to higher education for refugee students in their country of asylum. With DAFI's help, Dawood pursued a full-time bachelor's degree in economics, graduating from 6 October University in 2016. All of which then led him to AUC, where he expects to graduate with a master's in public policy in 2019, courtesy of an African Graduate Fellowship.

The masters in public policy is intended to prepare students for leadership positions in public service and for careers as policy analysts. Its mission is to support better public governance in Egypt and the Middle East. The program is part of the offerings of the School of Global and Public Policy, or GAPP. Led since its founding in 2009 by former Egyptian ambassador to the United States and Japan Nabil Fahmy, the school includes the Law, Journalism and Mass Communication, Public Policy and Administration departments, the Kamal Adham Center for Television and Digital Journalism, the Prince Alwaleed Bin Talal Bin Abdulaziz Alsaud Center for American Studies and Research, the Cynthia Nelson Institute for Gender and Women's Studies, and the Middle East Studies Center. It also incorporates the Center for Migration and Refugee Studies, where Dawood has worked as a volunteer translator, supporting Sudanese refugee communities in Cairo. "The Center has a great value not only as a research institute but also as an advocate for refugees," says Dawood. "Many recommendations for improving the life of migrants come out of it."

It was a former GAPP student who brought Dawood's inspirational story to light. Yasmine El-Demerdash double-majored in political science and communication and media arts at AUC. She originally thought she might join the Ministry of Foreign Affairs but she graduated in 2014 at a time when the number of people being displaced by war in Syria was at a peak and so she volunteered to work on a blueprint for an income-generating project for female Syrian refugees in Egypt. "I just wanted to help out, I never had any plan in mind." When that came to an end she simultaneously interned with two other agencies dealing with refugees, until one of them,

the UNHCR, offered her a full-time position handling media. "I like to meet people and listen to their stories. I want to know how they lived and what happened to them." One of her jobs is to find success stories to highlight the work of the agency, which is how she learned of Dawood and went back to AUC to interview him. "It is very rare you find a refugee doing a masters at somewhere like AUC. He is one of the very few who made it."

Dawood is not sure what comes next. Since 2018 he has been working with the Psycho-Social Services and Training Institute in Cairo, which, in collaboration with AUC's Center for Migration and Refugee Studies, offers mental health and psychosocial support for refugees, but his long-term goals lie in South Sudan. "I hope my studies in public policy will allow me to help shape the future of those young men and women in my home country. I want to contribute to poverty reduction by helping the youth in my country to achieve their dreams through education."

And, of course, there is also the small matter of reuniting with his mother, brother, and sisters in South Sudan, none of whom he has seen since 2010. "Hopefully I will see them as soon as possible," he says. ☸

▲ Yasmine El-Demerdash ('14), *left*, who graduated from AUC's School of Global Affairs and Public Policy and now works with the United Nations High Commission for Refugees in Cairo

84

TIME TO GO

Taking the biggest decision in one hundred years of AUC history

In 1996 AUC took one of the most important steps since its founding back in 1919. The previous academic year saw approximately 4,500 students enrolled with the university, compared to approximately 600 three decades earlier. This was a number that placed a barely manageable strain on the physical infrastructure. Over the previous three-quarters of a century the university had made regular piecemeal expansions into a scattering of neighboring Downtown properties, most notably the sites that became the Falaki and Greek campuses. It had even shipped out some administrative offices into rented apartment buildings. Even so, the landlocked university had run out of space. Serious attempts were made to purchase the large French Lycée that lay immediately behind the main Tahrir Campus but they failed. There was nowhere else to go.

An advisory committee presented the Board of Trustees with two options. One, to cap the number of students or, two, set up a satellite facility. The board decided to do neither and instead opted for a third way forward, which was to go for a completely new campus.

The decision was not taken lightly. AUC's chief financial officer at the time Andrew Snaith used the analogy of an airliner. If a company is flying a 747 and it's half full, it is losing money; if the plane is something approaching full, then it is more than likely making money. If the company then decides to accommodate more passengers by buying a second 747 it has a huge extra cost for a marginal change in the number of customers, and it is suddenly plunged into a huge loss. Who knows if it will ever achieve enough passengers to fill the second aircraft? The investment represents a substantial risk.

Some on the Board of Trustees argued that AUC was never going to be a big player (in terms of number of students, it is dwarfed by other Egyptian universities) and the best strategy was to stay small and niche. The institution was very comfortable and cozy the way it was. The counter-argument was that as Cairo expanded and rival educational institutions opened, a static AUC ran the risk of becoming irrelevant.

The expansionists carried the day. A "new campus development" team spent a year looking into sixteen different potential sites around Cairo, aided by the reports of no less than five outside urban planning offices who had been asked to submit their analyses on each of the options. The combined results indicated that east of Cairo was better than west. East was where the majority of AUC's students lived, with a center of gravity around the Heliopolis–Nasr City area. West also suffered from major transport access problems.

The consensus settled on what was then just a great empty expanse of desert east of Nasr City, marked on city planners' schematics with a promissory label of "New Cairo." The trustees were taken out to what one described as "Siberia with sand." One flatly stated, "This won't do." While it seemed impossibly remote—more than thirty kilometers from AUC's campus on Tahrir Square—and barren, the government's future projections had New Cairo rapidly growing to accommodate »

▲ The graphic shows the outline of the New Cairo Campus superimposed on Downtown Cairo. In total, the Tahrir Campus amounted to 2.7 hectares; the New Cairo Campus is over 100 hectares

253

▲ The 105 hectares of land purchased by the Board of Trustees constituted a virgin desert site or, as one trustee described it, "Siberia with sand"

two to three million people, a population comparable to Paris or Chicago. Added to which, the price was good: AUC was able to purchase the plot at a fraction of what developers would be fighting to pay just a few years later.

On 25 August 1997 the final decision was made to purchase the 105-hectare site. It would not only relieve the space limitations of the existing campus but would also provide the facilities and infrastructure to expand educational, sports, and extracurricular activities at AUC. Although faculty and students were not involved in the decision, sample groups from both were polled by a campus research group. In both cases the percentage of those in favor of the move was almost exactly the same as those against.

On 25 September, President Donald McDonald signed the contracts. The handover of the land took place five days later. Those tasked with envisioning the new campus estimated that a master plan for its design would be ready within two years and that construction would take another eight. Those predictions proved remarkably accurate. ⊛

> "There were alumni who totally opposed the move because they met their partner on the Tahrir Campus and so it was special to them."
>
> Hussein El Sharkawy, VP for new campus development

85

THE VERTICAL CAMPUS

Before the move to New Cairo, there was another ambitious plan on the drawing board

———

The decision to purchase land for a new campus was taken in 1996, but had things worked out differently it might never have happened. Just a few years previously, in the early 1990s, the university was pursuing a scheme to build a new campus not far from Downtown, on the island neighborhood of Zamalek. It was a complex intended to house the Center for Adult and Continuing Education (now the School of Continuing Education, see pp206–09), which for the previous thirty years had called the Greek Campus home. Moving it out would free up considerable space for expansion of other parts of the university.

The site was on the corner of Ismail Mohamed Street and Mansour Mohamed Street, one block away from the university's Zamalek student dormitory. An architect was commissioned, who developed a scheme. The design was for a single large building of nine stories, organized in two sections, each with its own internal courtyard. All rooms and corridors were oriented toward the courtyards rather than the streets outside. The two sections were offset from each other by half a story, but there was complete access from section to section anywhere in the building via a series of ramps and terraces. These terraces were to be planted with greenery and be big enough to serve as outdoor assembly places. The idea was that this should work as a "vertical campus," with the terraces as alleyways in the sky. Beside ample classroom and office space, the scheme also included a 150-seat theatre, a cafeteria, and underground parking, and the entire complex was to be centrally climate controlled.

Construction was scheduled to begin in late 1995, with the completion date set for 1998. Unfortunately, changes in building regulations reduced the maximum allowable height, which would have meant the building could deliver only around half the required space. This rendered the project unfeasible and it was dropped. The architect for the scheme, selected via a competition between three local practices, was Community Design Collaborative (CDC), led by Abdelhalim Ibrahim Abdelhalim, who would go on to be the major contributing architect for the New Cairo Campus. ⬡

▼ The architect's impression of the unbuilt Zamalek campus for the CACE. Elements of the design would find their way into the New Cairo Campus

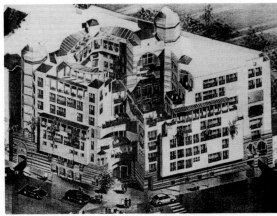

86

A CITY FOR LEARNING

The design and building of AUC's new campus in the desert

———

Few universities in the world have the chance to do what AUC did. With the purchase of a vast plot of desert land way outside the city limits, the university was presented with the opportunity to dream up an entire new campus from scratch.

1999: A COMPETITION

Shortly after AUC bought the land in New Cairo from the Egyptian government, it began a process of space programming. Nothing to do with NASA, this was the translation of the university's educational requirements into physical space. From this "wants list" came a brief and a budget of US$200m.

In 1998 an announcement regarding the proposed new campus was placed on professional architectural websites and in the international trade press with a request for interest. Fifty-three American, Egyptian, and European architectural practices responded. Credentials were reviewed and eighteen firms were long-listed. Those firms were put through a technical prequalification cycle, resulting in a press conference on 1 June 1999 at which AUC president John Gerhart announced a shortlist of six practices that had been invited to develop plans for the campus.

Representatives from the practices were flown to Cairo for three days of discussion, and to tour AUC's existing campus and visit the virgin site. During this time they were provided with the university's competition guidelines, which began with a statement that was neither technical nor even architectural in nature. It consisted of four words: "Learning is human nature." Competitors were put on notice that a successful proposal, in addition to being aesthetically satisfying, culturally responsive, and environmentally sensitive, had to celebrate learning above all else.

The practices were given approximately six weeks to develop their ideas, with a submission date of mid-August. The judging took place at the headquarters of the American Institute of Architects in Washington,

where a seven-member jury examined the six schemes. On 16 September 1999, at a dinner at the Cairo Capital Club, AUC announced the winner as two Boston firms working in partnership: the Boston Design Collaborative (BDC) and Carol R. Johnson Associates. According to the judging panel, their winning concept envisioned a campus at once intimate, interactive, and conducive to diverse intellectual and extracurricular pursuits. The inspiration was the medina, where it is not the architecture that is the defining characteristic but the public spaces. "We designed the voids first," Mozhan Khadem, BDC's director of design told *AUC Today* in early 2000. "The architectural approach in this part of the world, unlike in the West, has to be in designing the open spaces first, not the solids."

2000: THE MASTERPLAN

Actually, the competition had had two components, the masterplan and the architecture, and while BDC's masterplan was adopted, its architecture was not. In fact, the jury had a problem with the architectural component in all six schemes. They found them all too homogenous, with architecture that repeated itself. The comparison

▲ Assistant director for special events Ranya Boraie presents the New Cairo Campus to, *from left*, AUC president David Arnold, Egypt's minister of planning Faiza Abou al-Naga, and chair of the Board of Trustees Boyd Hight, observed by architect Ashraf Salloum, November 2007

▲ The library building rises from the desert sands. This photograph was taken in March 2007. The building would be ready by the end of that year

was made with the Tahrir Campus, where no two buildings were the same and the campus was all the more interesting for it. Tahrir, obviously, was shaped by eighty years of organic growth, while the new campus was all going up at once. The jury's recommendation was to move forward with the masterplan but to hire several different architects in an attempt to encourage the variety in the built environment deemed appropriate for a liberal arts institution.

For the next stage, AUC appointed a joint American–Egyptian partnership of Sasaki Associates, Inc. of Boston and Abdelhalim CDC of Cairo. The two practices were invited to work together with AUC's in-house New Campus Development Office (NCDO) to flesh out the masterplan, resolving practicalities such as traffic access and the interface between the campus and the community. Sasaki/CDC were also tasked with pinning down the exact location of campus buildings and their limits, and formulating the design principles for all the architects who would work on the project. "These were not design guidelines," stresses NCDO architect Ashraf Salloum, "but design principles. The difference is huge. A design guideline is a strict set of instructions you have to follow to the letter. A design principle sets an understanding or an approach, leaving room for the architects to do their own thing."

The refined masterplan was presented to the university's Board of Trustees during its November 2000 meeting. It was approved and the new campus moved from planning to the building design stage.

2001–03: BUILDING DESIGN

Sasaki and Abdelhalim CDC were made the lead architects for the campus. Between them they were assigned approximately sixty percent of the university buildings. For the rest, the university engaged the services of an experienced array of international specialty architects. Hardy Holzman Pfeiffer Associates of Los Angeles and New York was chosen for its experience in designing libraries. Legorreta + Legorreta of Mexico City was renowned for its community centers and housing, and Ellerbe Becket of Washington, DC had a track record in delivering large-scale sports centers. In addition, Carol R. Johnson Associates of Boston, in collaboration with Egypt's Sites International, was engaged as the main landscape architects.

Following the appointment of these practices, the design phase began in late summer 2001. During the process representatives of the firms visited Cairo to participate in workshops, sharing their designs, and receiving feedback from the buildings' end users, namely AUC administrators, faculty, and staff.

The AUC's own New Campus Development Office acted as the technical arm of the institution. "We were a bit afraid at the start," says Ashraf Salloum, "because you had all these star architects in a room, but it was very rewarding. There was a real dialogue, a collaborative process that enriched the whole design." Ricardo Legorreta of Legorreta + Legorreta, interviewed in 2002, also spoke of the challenge of collaborative design: "It's a fine balance of having an honest attitude, and being attentive to Egyptian culture and your fellow architects."

The design phase was completed in April 2003.

CONSTRUCTION

The formal ground-breaking ceremony for the new campus took place in early February 2003. This marked the beginning of the construction phase. Before anything happened above ground, there were months of site preparation. To early visitors in 2003, the site must have seemed more like a mining operation as workers excavated underground networks for natural gas, water, sewage, and irrigation. Most striking of all was a great canyon running across the site, two stories deep and the width of a two-lane road—this was the service tunnel that links all of the buildings on the campus (see pp290–91).

Incoming president David Arnold and his wife, Sherry, paid a $\gg$

**PRESIDENT #10
DAVID ARNOLD
(2003–10)**
Prior to joining AUC, David Arnold served as executive vice president of the Institute of International Education. He also worked in New Delhi as the Ford Foundation's representative for India, Nepal, and Sri Lanka. During his tenure at AUC he oversaw the construction and development of the New Cairo Campus. Under his direction, the LEAD program was launched, offering full tuition undergraduate scholarships to the top male and female students from each of Egypt's 27 governorates. On leaving AUC he became president of The Asia Foundation.

▲ The university as it was in May 2008, just three months before it would welcome the first students. At this stage the gardens are barren and large areas of the campus are still under construction

first visit to the site around this time. "We chose a day when there was a *khamsin*, so dust and sand were blowing all around us. There was no construction at that point, it was just excavation and digging. With the wind blowing the sand all around it felt like we were on the surface of the moon. And I thought, at the time, these people are out of their minds! This is never going to work. This is a crazy idea."

Above-ground construction began in August the following year, with multiple crews working simultaneously on different groups of buildings. The starting point was the main plaza and the buildings around it, and over time construction branched out east and west from this central point. On any given day there could be up to eight thousand workers on site and, at one point, there were nine tower cranes. In April 2005, the NCDO became the first AUC office to move to the new site. The first building to be completed was the library.

COMPLETION

Construction was due to be finished in time for classes to begin on the New Cairo Campus in fall 2007, but that deadline was missed. There were several reasons: delays in procurement of materials, labor issues,

◀ AUC president David Arnold and Egypt's minister of planning Faiza Abou al-Naga tour the rising campus in the company of architect Ashraf Salloum, November 2007

budgetary tussles over rising costs (by the end, the budget had risen to US$400m), even the discovery of unexploded ordnance on the site left over from when the area had been a range for tank manoeuvres.

Instead, it was 7 September 2008 when thousands of students flooded in through the campus gates to be met by information desks offering maps and floorplans. Student Union volunteers dressed in dark-blue T-shirts served as guides, helping students navigate the unfamiliar grounds in search of their classes.

Work was still not totally complete. The whole southeast side of the campus, including the campus center, student housing, and sports facilities was fenced off, while laborers rushed to get them finished. It was not until the start of the spring semester that dust finally settled and the official inauguration could take place on Saturday 7 February 2009, with guest of honor Egypt's then first lady Suzanne Mubarak ('77, '82), also attended by American ambassador Margaret Scobey, who delivered a special message on behalf of President Barack Obama. This launched a series of inauguration week events that included Egypt's minister of finance Youssef Boutros Ghali, AUC trustee Mohamed ElBaradei, and novelist Alaa Al Aswany. ✣

"We'll look back proud to have built this new campus and confident that future generations will be well served by what we've done."

AUC president
John Gerhart

87

A MOVING EXPERIENCE

Relocating a whole campus thirty kilometers was never going to be easy

▲ One of the custom-made moveable stacks used for the transfer of books

When AUC's library moved from Hill House to the Greek Campus in 1982, the books were put in plastic bags and passed from hand to hand along a chain of students down Mohamed Mahmoud Street, which was temporarily closed to traffic. "It wasn't a big library then," says Shahira El Sawy, dean of libraries and learning technologies. There was no way that was going to happen with the move to the New Cairo Campus. There is the little matter of the thirty kilometers distance between the two campuses (as opposed to the few hundred meters that separated the old and new libraries last time around), not to mention that by the time of the 2008 relocation, the number of books and periodicals had increased to over 400,000 items.

Instead of plastic bags, the move to the New Cairo Campus involved the library's books being placed on 170 custom-built, transportable shelf stacks. These were numbered so the books could be transferred directly to their correct shelving in the new library.

The books were just part of a greater transfer of the whole university, which involved some forty thousand cartons of equipment and five thousand computers that had to be shifted across the city to a new home comprising 136 classrooms, 145 science and engineering labs, fifty-five non-science labs and studios, and 727 faculty offices. Happily for the movers, the relocation did not involve much furniture, as all the interior fittings were designed and made especially for the New Cairo Campus.

The man responsible for overseeing the overall move was former AUC engineer Mohamed Abdel Gawad. "The original plan was to start moving at the beginning of June and finish by the end of July, which is two months. So I made a plan showing every room on the campus, where it's going to be moved, how it's going to be moved, and who is going to move it. It told you, if you are in room X, this room will be moved on this date, through this corridor and then by this elevator and then down this stair, and the same at the other end. It was a very big job."

▲ Movers load the transportable
shelf stacks onto a truck for
transfer to the New Cairo Campus

Everything was set to go for the summer of 2007, when the
university decided to postpone the move by a full year. Twelve months
later Mohamed Abdel Gawad's plans were finally put into action. AUC
appointed some fifty "move captains" from the various departments.
They attended regular briefings to learn about the procedures involved
in the move and then oversaw the arrangements for all their offices and
classrooms to be packed up and shipped out. Besides hiring carriers
and drivers to move boxes from one campus to the other, the university
brought in specialists to transport valuable electronic equipment such
as computers, printers, photocopiers, and fax machines, to ensure that
everything was disassembled and put together correctly. In some cases,
with the scientific instruments, for example, experts were flown in from
overseas to dismantle sensitive items and recalibrate them again once
they were in place in their new home.

An additional difficulty was that city regulations prohibit large trucks
from driving in Cairo during the day, so the whole move had to take
place between the hours of 11 p.m. and 6 a.m.

Despite this, the move itself was remarkably smooth, even if it
transpired that the new campus was far from ready for its new occupants.
Many elevators were not working, and entire buildings were not finished.
The library, however, was complete and the job of unloading the books
from their transportable stacks and placing them on the shelves was
carried out quickly. "We moved the library—the whole library—we
moved it in nineteen days. This was a miracle!" says Mohamed Abdel
Gawad. An achievement, perhaps, even to eclipse the human chain
along Mohamed Mahmoud Street. ⬡

88

THE NEW CAMPUS

AUC's New Cairo Campus weaves Egyptian architectural traditions into the design of a modern center of learning

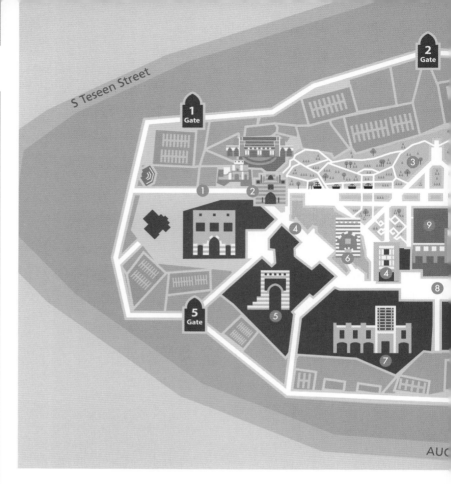

1. AUC SQUARE
At the end of a long approach from main Teseen Street, passing by a palm grove, AUC Square acts as an intermediary space. The public is on campus but they have not yet passed through security. From the square they can access the Dr. and Mrs. Elias Hebeka Building, Hamza Al Kholi Information Center, Sharjah Gallery, and Malak Gabr Theatre.

2. AUC PORTAL
The statement-making main entrance references both the rich Islamic heritage of Cairo and the neo-Islamic stylings of the Khairy Palace on the Tahrir Campus. The portal is roofed by an intricate arrangement of intersecting arches that form squinches to support a dome—except where the dome should be is open sky, symbolizing

that beyond this gateway, the sky is the limit. Directly beyond stretch the two main axes of the campus: the garden path and the urban avenue.

3. UNIVERSITY GARDEN
One of the stipulations in the brief for the design of the campus was that all schemes had to retain the natural features of the site. Consequently, the campus sits on two levels: the urban upper, or Plaza level, and the lower, or Garden level. The two are connected at multiple points by staircases.

4. THE AVENUE
Inspired by al-Muizz Street in Islamic Cairo, the Avenue forms the spine of the campus, interconnecting a sequence of open spaces. Off it branch streets and narrow alleys. It pivots twice, so the campus is only gradually

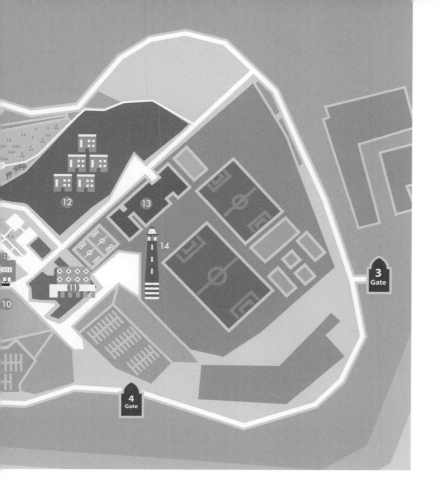

> "The campus should not be seen as individual buildings, but as clusters that make up neighborhoods."
>
> Architect Abdelhalim Ibrahim Abdelhalim

revealed. Arcades along the avenue provide shade and semi-private places to gather and sit.

5. PRINCE ALWALEED BIN TALAL BIN ABDUL AZIZ ALSAUD BUILDING

All of the structures in this lower part of the campus (including the portal) were designed by Aga Khan Award-winning Cairo architectural practice Abdelhalim CDC. The treatment of the Prince Alwaleed Building, home of the School of Humanties and Social Sciences, exemplifies CDC-founding architect Abdelhalim Ibrahim Abdelhalim's approach to designing the campus. Buildings are detailed on a human scale, with arched entrances, passageways, and terraces that invite exploration and interaction. Around and between the buildings is a warren of narrow alleys linking a series of shady courtyards. The feel is not so much of a campus but of an old city neighborhood. The courtyards have a dual function, as places in which people can pause and meet, while also ensuring that the interior of every room is naturally lit and ventilated. »

▲ The AUC portal, a modern update on classic tropes of Islamic architecture

265

> # "This is a liberal arts campus and the campus was envisioned to be a learning tool in itself."
>
> Architect Ashraf Salloum

6. ADMINISTRATION BUILDING

Another design by Abdelhalim CDC, the administration building is again rooted in the traditions of Islamic art and architecture. The interior

▲ The campus design encourages students to stop and socialize

features a series of courtyards that act as natural light wells and which link and facilitate interaction between the various offices. There is much use of traditionally inspired *mashrabiya* (wooden screens) for privacy and sun-protection, *malqafs* (wind catchers) on roofs to circulate fresh air, and *shukhshaykhas* (vented domes) to remove hot, stuffy air.

7. SCHOOL OF SCIENCES AND ENGINEERING

Many of the buildings in the middle section of the campus are the work of Sasaki Associates, including the School of Sciences and Engineering, the Abdul Latif Jameel Hall, and the Core Academic Center. Although based in Massachusets in the United States, Sasaki had previous experience in Cairo, being heavily involved in the creation of the city's award-winning al-Azhar

Park in the early 2000s. Its campus buildings feature lots of "in-between spaces" creating both architectural unity and a sense of community. A wide, shaded colonnade in front of classrooms shared by all the schools stimulates interdisciplinary interaction among both faculty and students. Plazas and courtyards connect visually to protected outdoor stairways, corridors, and bridges above, all of which encourage chance meetings and social connection—a key theme of the campus as a whole.

8. BARTLETT PLAZA

The campus's central space is vast, bigger than a football field and the main venue for outdoor events. It is typically filled with student organizations promoting their activities. Arcades around the edges provide shade and fountains set

▲ Bartlett Plaza, overlooked by the *mashrabiya* facade of the library

in the paving are there to provide additional coolness (when they are switched on). The original plan was to have a canopy on the square to provide additional shade but this has not been implemented.

9. LIBRARY

Designed by Hardy Holzman Pfeiffer Associates of the United States, the library is in some ways the climax of the architectural development of the campus. It takes a traditional architectural vocabulary and makes a very modern statement with it. Two dramatic *mashrabiya*-like screening walls of punctured concrete, for example, not only shade the library's large windows from the summer sun, but also create wide arcades that invite passersby to stop and converse. Meanwhile, links are made to AUC's own past: the processional staircase that connects the plaza to the lower level of the university garden deliberately echoes the popular steps and platform of the old Greek Campus. Inside, the building's purposeful open-floor-plan Learning Commons offers a space for interdisciplinary collaboration and scholarly discussion between members of the academic community.

▲ The apertures in the library facade are perfect for student nesting

>>

▲ An internal courtyard intended to foster a community spirit in the student housing complex

10. CAMPUS CENTER

The upper campus, which is the area south of Bartlett Plaza, is all about student life. This is where you find the Campus Center, the extensive sport facilities, and the student housing. Bold color starts to intrude into the southeast corner of the Bartlett Plaza with Legorreta + Legorreta's Campus Center.

Ricardo Legorreta established his architecture practice in his native Mexico City in 1963. When his son, Victor, joined him it became Legorreta + Legorreta. The practice's signature style is boldly modern yet deeply rooted in the traditional architecture of Mexico. Prior to its work on the New Cairo Campus, Legorreta + Legorreta had a wealth of experience with universities, designing student residences for the University of Chicago and Stanford University's School of Business. In 2000, Ricardo Legorreta received the highest honor the American Institute of Architects can give, the AIA Gold Medal; past recipients

▲ The distinctive shapes and colors contributed by Legorreta + Legorreta

have included Frank Lloyd Wright and Frank Gehry.

For their Campus Center, rather than create one large building, the Mexican architects have scaled the project down into a series of more human-scaled components. It begins on Bartlett Plaza with a

giant, shade-giving arch under which shelters a coffeestore. As the main avenue slopes away from the plaza, it is flanked by Legorreta's student services, international student, campus life, and career placement offices, and the AUC bookstore, printing services, food court, clinic, and the day-care facility. Buildings are low rise and faced in stone of varying tones, which adds texture and warmth. The natural stone is contrasted with planes and surfaces painted in an intense earthen orange.

11. BASSILY AUDITORIUM

Also by Legorreta + Legorreta, the Bassily and its three subsidiary lecture halls are connected by a central outdoor lobby. Shaded by an overhead canopy, this space has evolved into a popular meeting place and hangout for students. This open-air area also doubles as a gallery and event space. On the upper levels, where walkways connect rooms, narrow openings in the walls entice the sun to slice shadows with knife-like precision. »

▲ The Bassily complex, with the Legorreta mix of color, light, and strong shapes

12. STUDENT HOUSING

Legorreta + Legorreta's student housing takes the form of burnt-orange clusters of cubes. The internal arrangement has been designed to foster peer-to-peer learning with each four-bedroom "house" sharing a lounge, kitchenette, and study space. The houses then also share a common lounge, more study space, and a service center with a laundry. One set of houses is for men, one for women, but there is a common room where the two can meet. The intention is that the facility should function more like a village than a traditional dorm with long corridors lined with closed doors.

13. SPORTS COMPLEX

The sports complex comprises the single largest space on campus—and incidentally, boasts some of the best sports facilities in Cairo, including a 1,396-square-meter multi-purpose

◀ The Sports Complex, dominated by its 30m-high observation tower

▲ The multi-use ARTOC Sports Court that anchors the AUC Sports Complex

court. It is designed by Ellerbe Becket, which at the time of the new campus build was headquartered in Minneapolis with twelve offices worldwide, including in Cairo. It specialized in sports architecture, designing major athletic facilities for universities including Yale and Notre Dame. The majority of AUC's sports facilities are sunk below the level of the main avenue so as not to overwhelm the neighboring, smaller-scale housing. You only realise the scale of the building when approaching from the sports fields.

14. SPORTS TOWER

Positioned at the highest point of the campus, the thirty-meter tower is a navigational point for the campus, while also providing a bird's-eye view of the sports grounds below. At the time of writing, the plan was for the tower's multiple landings to be used as exhibition spaces. ❀

271

89

A LIVING, BREATHING CAMPUS

From day one, sustainability has been key to the design of the campus

The New Cairo Campus is as close to a living, breathing organism as a conglomeration of buildings can get. Sustainability was a core aspect of the masterplanning brief. Along with organization of the physical aspect of the campus and design of the buildings, the architects were tasked with developing a campus-wide environmental strategy to maximize natural ventilation and cooling.

To achieve this, buildings tend to be oriented east–west to reduce the amount of exposure to the sun. The large gardens on the north side of the campus are heavily planted to form a cool, low reservoir. Summer winds from the north move through the gardens and bring cool, moist air into the heart of the campus. On the southwest side of the campus, a shelter belt has been planted to block winter winds and act as a filter for wind-blown sand. Building facades on this side are heavily planted with deciduous trees to provide shade during summer, however allowing sun to filter in during winter.

Careful consideration was given to building materials: how sustainable they are, what kind of thermal qualities they possess. Much of the stone is sandstone, quarried in Egypt from a site near Aswan. This is a stone that was favored by the pharaohs and it has lasted pretty well for them. To reduce emissions transporting the stone, the architects even looked at sailing it down the Nile, just like the pharaohs did; unfortunately, this proved impractical.

It is common to build in concrete and clad with a thin, 2-centimeter layer of stone for an attractive finish. On this campus many of the walls use stone that is 10 centimeters thick. Behind it is a 5-centimeter air gap and 25 centimeters of blockwork, giving a wall that is 40 centimeters

thick in total. This prevents heat transfer, keeping out the worst of the sun in summer and keeping the interiors warm in winter. It is an expensive way of building but air-conditioning and heating costs are reduced by around 40 percent.

Similarly, all rooms have windows, not just for the views, but because natural lighting cuts down on the need for artificial lighting, which generates heat. Windcatchers and internal courtyards channel breezes for natural ventilation, reducing the need for air-conditioning.

The commitment to sustainable building and practices continues. AUC's New Cairo faculty housing includes green roofs where residents can grow things, solar water heaters that provide all of the development's hot water, and non-CFC cooling refrigerants for the air-conditioners. The faculty housing is used as an educational model for current students of architecture, so they can acquire first-hand understanding of green building practices and hopefully later disseminate the ideas far beyond the bounds of the campus. ⊕

▲ In 2009, the Washington-based Urban Land Institute recognized AUC's New Cairo Campus with a Global Award for Excellence. It commented on how the campus is "designed to be a tool and stimulus in itself for learning and to anchor community development around the university"

90

GREEN THINKING

There is more to the New Cairo Campus landscaping than just looking pretty

As stunning as the architecture is, arguably the real jewel of the New Cairo Campus is the university garden. As you walk beside the jacaranda, white mulberry, and ornamental pomegranates, past the bottlebrush to the splashing waterfall with its papyrus beds, the important thing to remember is that before 2008 all this was desert. Let me say that again, because it really is something quite extraordinary: before 2008 this was all desert. Erecting steel frames and pouring concrete in the sand is one thing, coaxing life out of it is something else entirely.

Greenery surrounds the entire campus. It is far from being just ornamental. In some parts, notably around the perimeter of the site, its purpose is to screen the campus from the surrounding highways and development beyond. Along the border with AUC Avenue, tall, evergreens also serve as a shelter belt against dust storms and the chilly southwest winds of winter. The oasis-like grove of over 350 date palms around the approach to the AUC portal is there to make a welcome gesture to the outside community in traditional Arab fashion. And then there is the university garden.

It sits at a lower level than the built campus, occupying the depression of a wadi (the site masterplan retained all original topographical features—no leveling, no filling). The first aspect to strike a visitor is the garden's beauty. The obvious inspiration is the Islamic gardens of Andalusia. There are the characteristic water features of fountains and channels, geometric patterns, symmetry, and architectural elements—here the water channels run along an axis that ends in the monumental arch of the AUC portal. The vista looking down from the terraces into the garden from the area between the food court and the Moataz Al Alfi Hall recalls some Ottoman and Persian formal gardens. All around are trees—lots of trees—and flowering and fruiting bushes and shrubs that provide year-round color and wonderful fragrance. There are immaculately manicured lawn areas, some rolling, some flat, although these are kept to a minimum because grass is notoriously thirsty. (The

gardens have been designed to require minimal water consumption and they use recycled rather than fresh water.)

Much of the garden is planted as a multi-canopied system. Palms are the top canopy, citrus and other smaller trees are the second canopy, and the ground covers (including seasonal ornamentals) are the third canopy. This mirrors the agricultural system found in Egyptian and Middle Eastern oases (palms, fruit trees, seasonal crops). There are several other notable features too, including a "Syrian hillside," which is a slope planted with varieties native to Syria, and Yemeni-style terracing in the area around L'Aroma coffeeshop.

But back to the trees. They serve as a marker for the ambition and sophistication of the garden. Everyone expects a garden to contain a variety of shrubs and flowers, but the AUC campus contains no less than around sixty different types of tree. These are a mixture of Egyptian and non-native species. The former category includes a couple of varieties of date palms (Zaghloul, with red fruit, and Samani, with yellow fruit), carobs, cypresses, olives, figs, and gum trees, among others; the internationals range from banyans and magnolias to mesquites and macadamias, lebbeks and acacias, and the wonderful "sausage »

▲ Water features have moving and recirculating water to minimize waste and evaporation loss. They lead the eye to the monumental structure of the AUC portal

275

▲ The university gardens are a vital part of the experience of studying at AUC

▶ All the plants for the gardens (except the palms) were grown at what was then AUC's Desert Development Center, starting in 2003. Transplanting began in 2005, three years before the campus received its first students

tree" (Kigelia africana), so called because of the long, tubular appearance of its hanging fruit. (Complementing the "sausages" you will find in the garden several species of yellow-and-red flowers from the Fabaceae family, more commonly known as "eggs-and-bacon" plants.)

There are regimented rows of citrus trees, as well as apricots, guavas, mangoes, peaches, and pomegranates. The citrus selected are varieties developed and introduced into Egypt by what used to be known as the Desert Development Center (DDC). These are primarily Valencia and Navel orange varieties with rootstocks adapted to Egyptian desert conditions, and also tangerines, seedless limes, and grapefruit varieties—also all introduced by the DDC (see pp202–05). The citrus orchards serve a living laboratory, in line with the original concept that the garden should not just be a nice place to walk through and sit in, it should also be productive. Fruit picked from these trees is sold on campus.

As a way of highlighting the richness of the inner campus landscape, the Desert Development Center drew up a self-guided AUC campus "Tree Walk". Laid out in a pocket-sized, folded pamphlet, it describes a two-and-a-half-kilometer route starting (with an Indian laurel fig) and ending (with a pomegranate tree) at the AUC portal. It is a pleasantly relaxing way to pass the best part of an hour, but the walk also fulfils another of the other important roles of the garden, which is as a tool for learning.

The garden (and tree walk) is a natural outgrowth of the concept of the campus as a "City for Learning." Scientific thinking, Egyptology, biology, and ecology programs all find educational content here, whether it is in the study of indigenous Egyptian plant life or examining the hunks of petrified wood that dot the garden—discovered on site during construction and retained. More generally, the garden also embodies the ideals of a liberal arts education by providing opportunities for chance meetings and open-air study. It also provides inspiration.

"Sometimes you find when you are teaching, the class is dead and you're dead," says Richard Hoath, senior instructor in rhetoric and composition. "So you say, okay, let's go outside. You lead everybody out to this lovely setting of grass, flowers, and trees and all of a sudden things liven up." ✸

91

A WALK ON THE WILD SIDE

Faculty member and naturalist Richard Hoath rhapsodizes over the campus's non-human residents and visitors

Flashback to the early 2000s, to before the foundation stone was planted, before there was a Road 90, when the New Cairo Campus was little more than an architectural vision appended to a newly acquired swathe of bare desert. The site, to be exact, was a northerly extension of Egypt's Eastern Desert, a sedimentary plateau scored by wadis, and with a flora and fauna similar to that still found in Wadi Degla, a few kilometers to the south. Early visitors to the site would have found nothing but sand and gravel. Yet the keen-eyed might have discerned life from the myriad tracks of nocturnal animal species, of jirds and gerbils, desert lizards, and desertic beetles. Looking up they may have spotted overhead Brown-necked Ravens and displaying Hoopoe Larks, Mourning and White-crowned Wheatears, and Common Kestrels (more of which in a moment). They may have witnessed a Brown Hare erupting from its form and bounding off in angled zig-zags. This was desert but even the desert has a few hardy inhabitants.

Forward to the present. As the architects' visions became actual bricks and mortar, the landscape architects' imaginings became real gardens, with trees, plants, and water features. What was arid has become agricultural—arcadian, even—and a whole new 'natural' community now blossoms among the flora, largely non-native and introduced by human agency. The desert ecosystem still exists in the peripheral parts of the new campus grounds but the desert habitat has now become a true oasis. The university garden, so recent and so alien, has already, in barely over a decade, developed its own seasonality and rhythm.

As the new academic year begins each fall, the gardens become a welcome stop-off for untold numbers of birds migrating south from European breeding grounds to wintering grounds here and farther afield. The palm and citrus groves, olives and acacias heave with warblers and chats, rarely visible but very much heard, a cacophony of chits, *tchaks*, and *tsks*. Woodchats and Masked Shrikes join the resident

Common Kestrel
Admin. Building

◀ A high window ledge belonging to the Administration Building has been sequestered by a pair of breeding kestrels who have chosen it as the perfect spot in which to raise a family, painted here by Richard Hoath

Great Grey Shrikes; Common Redstarts and Nightingales, sadly mute in transit, mingle with the newly fledged Blackbirds. Birds such as the White Wagtail and diminutive Chiffchaff will wait out the cold in the north and make the campus home for the winter. This pair weigh no more than around ten grams each, but both call way above their weight, the former a *pee-vitt*, and the latter a soft *huitt* or onomatopoeic *chiff-chaff*. In winter the gardens are not just beautiful to look at, they are beautiful to listen to. »

In spring the flypast is perhaps even more spectacular than fall. The Eastern Desert is a major flyway for the big birds, the flappers, and a glance skyward might reveal passing raptors or even a spiraling flock of Common Cranes. In just over ten years nearly fifty species have been recorded on the New Cairo Campus and at least a dozen now breed; an incredible colonization in such a short period of time. And it is not just the birds. An early pioneer was the Red Fox. In parts of Europe and the United States this is often an urban species but in Egypt it is the fox of the desert margins and farmlands. One caused a huge stir when it arrived unannounced on campus in 2008—and disappeared just as enigmatically.

In that same short time, ten species of butterflies have been recorded around campus—Plain Tigers, Yellow Pansies, African Migrants, Painted Ladies, Red Admirals, and more. When only sixty-one species have been recorded in the entire country ever, the impact of the university gardens becomes dramatically apparent. Dragonflies and damselflies patrol the beds and bowers. Crickets call and at night the Egyptian Toad serenades with the crickets and other creatures crepuscular. Night brings the moths—Death's Head and Oleander Hawk Moths, Large Yellow Underwings, and many smaller, less glitzy night fliers. It also brings the Little Owl, a pair having been recorded recently just off campus, and Egypt's iconic *karawaan*, in English known as the more prosaic Senegal Thick-knee.

The highlight of spring are the European Bee-eaters. Spectacular birds resplendent in turquoise, russet-orange, chestnut, black, and yellow, their *kroop kroop* fills the air for a few short weeks in April/May. Listen first, then look up and witness the kaleidoscopic fly-by.

Spring also means nesting—for the Blackbirds and Great Grey Shrikes, and for the Palm and Collared Doves. The male Blackbird sings loudly and mellifluously, arguably Egypt's finest songster, while the shrike belies its raptor-like bill with a subdued witter. The doves coo: the Collared soporifically, the Palm with more urgency, hence its alternative moniker 'Laughing.' Spring is also when the Common Kestrel nests. These small falcons—and falcons were worshiped in ancient Egypt as the god Horus—were first found nesting on campus in spring 2014 and every season since they have returned to rear their young on a washroom window ledge on the administration building, an urban substitute for the usually preferred cliff-face cavity. Two other nesting sites have since been found on campus, and the birds themselves may be seen wheeling and scything over the grounds "on wimpling wings."

By summer the migrants will have left and as the climate hots up, natural activity cools down. While the stalwarts last it out, the Common

Painted Lady

Bulbuls—the English name appropriately comes from the Arabic—and the House Sparrow are joined in the gardens by the Rufus Bush Robin, a stunning, bright chestnut bird with a graduated black and white-tipped tail. It is one of the very few species that only visits Egypt in summer to breed. The Common Bulbul is dull brown above, paler below, with a slight crest. What it lacks in flamboyance it makes up for in song, its conversational chortlings and chattering a constant companion. In the evenings, large flocks of House Sparrows commandeer the groves of trees to form large and noisy roosts.

And so once more to fall. The academic cycle renews, the natural cycle repeats. In addition to the fresh intake of students, some of us are also excited by the promise of new feathered species. Last fall a stunning male Rüppell's Warbler with matt-black throat and gleaming white moustachial stripe. Who knows what this fall might bring for those with open eyes and ears. ☺

▲ The Painted Lady—painted in this case by rhetoric instructor and keen naturalist Richard Hoath—is one of ten species of butterfly that have been observed around campus

281

92

WHO'S WHO ON CAMPUS

Many campus buildings and spaces are named for the sponsors, educators, and leaders who have contributed to making AUC what it is today

Names like Ewart, Hill, and Howard resonate with generations of alumni who studied on AUC's Downtown campus. For those who have studied and will study on the New Cairo Campus, there are a whole different set of reference points: Bartlett, Bassily, Malak Gabr, and Moataz Al Alfi among them. Who are these people whose names denote facilities ranging from buildings, departments, classrooms, laboratories, and lecture halls to courtyards, benches, and fountains? Like Ewart, Hill, and Howard before them, they are largely people whose monetary contributions to the university have generously funded facilities for the student body. What's different on the New Cairo Campus, however, is the welcome prevalence of Egyptian and Arab names.

ABDUL LATIF JAMEEL HALL

Mr. Yousef Jameel ('68) is a prominent Saudi Arabian business leader, long-time university supporter, and devoted alumnus. Mr. Jameel, chairman of Yousef Abdul Latif Jameel Co. Ltd (YALJ), supported the Yousef Jameel

▶ Abdul Latif Jameel Hall, which houses the schools of Business and Global Affairs and Public Policy

'68 GAPP Public Leadership Program, Yousef Jameel '68 PhD in Applied Sciences and Engineering Fellowships, Science and Technology Research Center (STRC), and named the Abdul Latif Jameel Hall. The hall, like the Jameel Center that was inaugurated in the Greek Campus Downtown in 1989, is named after Yousef's father who was a great believer in education. Mr. Jameel also supports a wide range of institutions and projects in the fields of education, scientific research, and the arts around the world.

ALLAM AMPHITHEATRE
AUC's outdoor amphitheatre is named in honor of Dr. Mohamed Abdel Khalek Allam, former vice president for student affairs, who was with AUC from 1966 to 2005.

ARNOLD PAVILION
Named in honor of former AUC president David Arnold (2003–10), see p259, by the university. It was during his term in office that the campus was built and inaugurated.

BARTLETT PLAZA
Named in honor of the Bartlett family. Thomas Bartlett was president of AUC from 1963–69, returning as interim president in 2002. His sons Richard and Paul are both members of the Board of Trustees; Richard currently serves as chairman.

BASSILY AUDITORIUM
The late Dr. Sarwat Sabet Bassily was a long-time AUC supporter. Dr. Bassily named the Bassily Auditorium, which is the main university auditorium. He spent

 The Arnold Pavilion fronts the university's daycare center, medical clinic, and other facilities

his career as a leader in the pharmaceutical industry, founding several companies, including Amoun Pharmaceuticals in 1998.

DR. AND MRS. ELIAS HEBEKA BUILDING
Dr. Hebeka had a long career in pharmaceuticals, including various senior executive positions at Revlon Inc. He has served on AUC's Board of Trustees and is now an advisory trustee.

DR. HAMZA ALKHOLI INFORMATION CENTER
Named for the chairman and chief executive officer of the ❯❯

Alkholi Group in Saudi Arabia, who, in 2017, was also appointed to AUC's Board of Trustees.

HATEM AND JANET MOSTAFA CORE ACADEMIC CENTER

The late Hatem Niazi Mostafa was an AUC trustee from 1992 to 2006. He contributed enormously to the university, notably through the Hatem Niazi Mostafa Public School Scholarship, and he supported the Theban Mapping Project and Thomas A. Lamont Endowed Scholarship. He and his wife, Janet, also endowed the new campus with the Core Academic Center.

KHALAF AHMAD AL HABTOOR FOOTBALL AND TRACK STADIUM

Dr. Khalaf Ahmad Al Habtoor, founder and chairman of the Al

Habtoor Group, is one of AUC's most generous and committed supporters. He established the Al Habtoor Endowed Scholarship Fund as part of AUC's centennial campaign, and named the Khalaf Ahmad Al Habtoor Football and Track Stadium. Dr. Al Habtoor is known for his extensive knowledge of international political affairs, his philanthropic activities, and his efforts to promote peace.

LA PALMIRA LODGE

Mrs. Suad Al-Husseini Juffali, AUC advisory trustee and chair of the Ahmed Juffali Foundation, is a philanthropist dedicated to social work in the Middle East, particularly Saudi Arabia. Mrs. Juffali named the female student residence, La Palmiera Lodge, and the Library Garden Reading Room—The

▲ Al Habtoor Stadium is a world-class, Olympic-standard facility boasting a full football field and a 400-meter track

Serenity Room—at AUC. She also established the Suad Al-Husseini Juffali Scholarship, the Tarek Juffali Endowed Fellows Program, and the Tarek Juffali Professorship in Psychology. Mrs. Juffali is the co-founder of the Help Center, a special education institution for children with intellectual disabilities.

LOUIS GREISS COURTYARD

Named for the Egyptian journalist, who died at the age of ninety in 2018. Born in Assiut in 1928, he studied journalism and literature at AUC, graduating in 1955. He was the university's very able director of public relations in the late 1980s and early 1990s.

MALAK GABR ARTS THEATRE

Mr. Shafik Gabr ('73), who is the chairman and managing director of ARTOC Group, is a loyal AUC alumnus and a major financial supporter of AUC. Mr. Gabr named the Malak Gabr Arts Theatre for his daughter Malak, as well as the Mohamed Shafik Gabr Department of Economics, the Mohamed Shafik Gabr Lecture Hall, and ARTOC Sports Court. He was the first to receive the AUC Global Impact Award, in 2015. Mr. Gabr is an international business leader and philanthropist; he is responsible for two foundations in Egypt and the US that provide diversified services in many areas including education, arts, and science. He is also a leading collector of Orientalist art.

MOATAZ AL ALFI HALL

Named for the chairman and CEO of Egypt Kuwait Holding Company, who played a large role in the fundraising for the New Cairo Campus. He established the Al Alfi Foundation for Human and Social Development, which, through education and training, helps to discover future leaders among Egyptian youth. He has also twice served as the vice chairman of the AUC Board of Trustees. The hall is one of the major public gathering spaces on campus.

MANSOUR GROUP LECTURE HALL

The Mansour Group is one of Egypt's top conglomerates spanning the automotive, banking, industrial, real estate, tourism, and agribusiness sectors. Its president, Mohamed Mansour, served on AUC's Board of Trustees from 2003 to 2010.

MARY CROSS LECTURE HALL

Mary Cross was a photojournalist and writer who spent most of her life traveling and exploring cultures around the world. She was a long-serving member of the Board of Trustees and later an advisory trustee. She died in 2016.

PAUL B. HANNON SWIMMING POOL

Paul Hannon is a retired lawyer who served on the Board of Trustees for more than twenty-five years, including seven years as chairman, before stepping down in 2004. He retains an involvement with AUC as an advisory trustee.

PAUL AND CHARLOTTE CORDDRY PARK

Paul and Charlotte Corddry are long-time supporters of AUC, supporting, among other things, the Charles J. Hedlund Distinguished Visiting Professorship in Business & Computer, Hermann F. Eilts Endowed International Scholarship, and the Paul I. Corddry Scholarship. The Corddrys have a shared passion for art and in 2015 they donated their multi-million-dollar collection to The Baker Museum on the Artis–Naples campus in Florida.

PRINCE ALWALEED BIN TALAL BIN ABDULAZIZ ALSAUD HALL

Prince Alwaleed bin Talal bin Abdulaziz Alsaud is a Saudi businessman, investor, and philanthropist, and a member of the Saudi royal family. He was listed on *TIME* magazine's annual list of the hundred most influential people in the world in 2008. Prince Alwaleed also sponsors the university's Center for American Studies and Research. The building that bears his name houses the School of Humanities and Social Sciences and is universally known as HUSS.

WATSON HOUSE

The president's residence is, of course, aptly named for AUC founder and first president Charles Watson (1919–44; see p13). ✿

▲ AUC's main auditorium, the Bassily, accommodates 1,255 people on two levels

93

VEILLON, BOGHIGUIAN AND SIRRY

The work of three women artists in particular provides the core of AUC's art holdings

O n 23 November 2009, AUC dedicated a gallery on the Tahrir Campus to honor the memory of artist Margo Veillon (1907–2003). Born in Cairo to a Swiss father and an Austrian mother, Veillon spent her whole life in Egypt—although she did plenty of traveling outside the country—and its people and landscapes were the primary subject for her vast output of drawings and paintings. During her life she had over fifty exhibitions, particularly in galleries in Cairo and Zurich. For a time, Veillon taught painting at AUC and the university organized a first major retrospective of her work in 1960. At the opening of the show, the university purchased a large piece called "Three Horses," which it put on public display.

Veillon also had a close relationship with the AUC Press and it published no less than six books dedicated to her work. It was obviously a meaningful relationship because when Veillon died she left all her sketches and paintings to the publishing house. Following on from that initial first purchase in 1960, AUC now found itself the guardian of over five thousand pieces by the artist.

Despite bearing her name, the Veillon Gallery does not have a permanent Veillon collection and instead hosts temporary exhibitions. The place to see her work is the New Cairo Campus. Approximately fifty pieces by Veillon hang in various offices, meeting rooms, halls, and other public spaces—and should you ever be invited to an event at Watson House, there are about the same number again distributed about the rooms of the president's residence. Specifically, there are six paintings in the Sullivan Lounge (room 1058) on the first floor of the Alwaleed Building, including a fine Nile scene "Unloading the Fodder" (1994) and an untitled representation of what might be the artist's studio (1988). Also worth seeking out is the breezy "A Street in London" (1988), which hangs in room 1072. On the main staircase in the Administration Building is the uncharacteristically violent "Against the Individual" (1966), and there are several more works in and around the president's office.

Also well represented around campus is Gazbia Sirry. Born in Cairo in 1925, Sirry is a senior Egyptian artist who is recognized internationally. As with Veillon, Sirry also served as a painting instructor at AUC and her longevity (she is still exhibiting at the time of writing) means that her work also reflects social and cultural shifts in Egypt for the best part of a century. What is also notable is the intense use of color. "I have a sensual relationship with color," she once told a journalist. "When I enter a paint shop, I want to swallow everything." Indeed, when the AUC Press published a book about Sirry and her work in 1998 its title was *Lust for Color*.

Her paintings have graced a range of prestigious exhibitions and collections in Egypt, the Middle East, Europe, and North America—she was the first Egyptian to exhibit work at the Metropolitan Museum of Art in New York. In 2008, Sirry donated sixteen of her oil paintings to AUC, saying, "I want the next generation to know about my art and about that period in Egyptian life. I have high hopes that AUC will achieve these objectives." At present several works by Sirry are displayed in the Administration Building, including two in the Plaza level entrance hall ("Life on the Embankment of the Nile I" and "II") and there is a beautiful, stylized portrait of a girl in a pink dress hanging outside room 1061 on the first floor.

Anna Boghiguian was born in 1946 in Cairo, the daughter of a Cairo watchmaker. Her mother and grandparents were all Armenians from Turkey. She came to AUC as a student in the 1960s and graduated in »

▲ In November 2009, AUC dedicated an art gallery to honor the memory of artist Margo Vellion (1907–2003) and launched it with an exhibition that included paintings the artist made during the 1991 Gulf War

▲ Margo Veillon's charming oil of characters on a blustery street in London, painted in 1988, now hangs on the New Cairo Campus

political science, before moving to Montreal in the early 1970s to study art and music. In a subsequent artistic career spanning half a century, writers, poets, and philosophers have frequently provided the inspiration for her work, particularly the Greek Alexandrine poet Constantine Cavafy, whose works she has illustrated. Now well into her seventies, Boghiguian has suddenly become a figure of the moment, honored with a solo show at Tate St Ives in Britain in 2019, which followed hot on the heels of major shows in New York (2018), Sharjah (2018), Nîmes in France (2016), and Berlin (2013). In among all that, she won the Golden Lion at the 2015 Venice Biennale for her Armenian Pavilion.

Like Margo Veillon, Boghiguian has enjoyed a long relationship with the AUC Press, which has published *Anna's Egypt* (2003), a collection of her writing and art, and commissioned illustrations for *Farewell to Alexandria* (2004), a collection of short stories by Harry Tzalas. She also created a series of twenty covers for the Press's editions of the novels and short-story collections of Naguib Mahfouz. In the 1990s, Press director Mark Linz also asked her to paint the entrance hall and stairwell of the publishing house's offices on Mohamed Mahmoud Street. In this unique painting/installation, dead writers, including Taha Hussein, converse with living ones. The mural was broken up when the Press moved but parts of it still hang in their new offices on the Tahrir Campus, above the

bookstore. The university has many other smaller works by Boghiguian in its collection.

As a quick footnote, while studying political science at AUC, Boghiguian also took painting lessons from a visiting African–American artist named Robert Colescott. He arrived at the university in 1965 from California, with a master's degree from Berkeley and two years spent studying painting in Paris with Fernand Léger. He joined the Department of English Language and Literature, although his main contribution to university life was in February 1967 when he launched the Corridor Gallery, an exhibition space—in a corridor, naturally—used to show emerging Egyptian artists. It was run as a commercial gallery, free to the artists, but they were asked to contribute ten percent of all sales to a special fund for buying paintings for the permanent collection of AUC. Colescott left AUC in summer 1967 when war broke out. He died in 2009 in Tucson, Arizona leaving many of his own vibrant, multicultural, and frequently politically, racially, and sexually charged paintings in the collections of many major American museums including the Metropolitan Museum of Art, Museum of Modern Art, and Whitney Museum of American Art. Recently one of his pieces sold at auction for just under one million dollars. Unfortunately, as far as we know, AUC never bought or was gifted anything of his. ❁

▲ Advertisement from the *Caravan* student newspaper for the AUC art gallery founded by American artist Robert Colescott

94

TUNNEL VISION

Supplying and servicing the campus happens without anybody noticing, right under everyone's feet

The New Cairo Campus is a mini-city with neighborhoods, streets and alleys, offices, housing, places to eat and shop, public spaces and gardens, and a pleasingly diverse array of architecture. But like any city, for it to function smoothly there is a lot going on behind the scenes. Only it is not so much behind as under.

Beneath the campus, and following the route of the main avenue, is a huge service tunnel, or underground roadway. Around 1.6 kilometers long, it begins in the no-man's-land that is Parcel 17, where the physical plant (the mechanical systems) and stores are located, and runs all the way to the Dr. and Mrs. Elias Hebeka Building, outside the main portal. The tunnel is six meters wide and five meters high, in other words, easily big enough for two lanes of traffic.

One side of the roadway has a raised platform that looks like a sidewalk but which is, actually, a trench for high-voltage electrical cables. Other ducting in the tunnel carries IT cables, hot and cold water pipes, cooling and heating systems, all sensitive utilities that

► The service tunnel was the very first stucture to be completed on the New Cairo Campus. It is essentially a concrete box buried in the sand

need constant monitoring and maintenance, and all of which are easily accessible. The only utilities that are not in the tunnel are the gas piping, which, for safety reasons, has to be buried, and the sewerage pipes; both of these are in their own separate trench.

As well as utilities, the tunnel is a conduit for people. The tunnel connects to loading docks under every building for all deliveries, everything from furniture to equipment to water bottles, and for trash collection. This is also how maintenance and housekeeping staff make their way around campus.

To get around the tunnel, staff use golf carts. AUC owns eighty-five of them. Some are passenger carts (and some of these are used like shuttle buses, running up and down the tunnel on a regular schedule, picking up and dropping off staff), but most are utility carts, used by maintenance, landscape, and construction. All drivers need to have passed an AUC cart driving test with theoretical and practical exams, and they need to adhere to strict speed limits. With just a few exceptions, which mostly involve driving guests around, plus two that operate as ambulances, the carts are not permitted "upside," meaning the campus proper is left to pedestrians. This was always a key part of the masterplan, to embrace the liberal arts idea, allowing students the maximum opportunity to circulate and interact with no interference whatsoever from vehicles.

Although it was the very first element to be constructed on campus, the tunnel was designed with the future in mind and has plenty of knock-out sections of wall awaiting links as other parts of the site are developed later. In years to come as AUC inevitably expands so will its unseen, subterranean under-city. ❀

▲ Running the length of the entire campus, the tunnel enables maintenance, delivery, and service staff to move around without disrupting the learning environment up above

291

95

FIVE PILLARS FOR THE FUTURE

After eleven years, the New Cairo Campus enters a new phase

A few months before AUC inaugurated its centennial celebrations in early 2019, the university marked another milestone—ten years since the first intake of students on the New Cairo Campus. In some senses, the first decade in New Cairo has been all about bedding in and adapting to the rhythms of life on a new campus. Some faculty and staff still harbor reservations about the daily commute from homes that were more convenient for Downtown, but almost everyone would agree AUC has gained a world-class campus, the like of which would simply not have been possible had the university remained as it was.

As the administration reflects on the last one hundred years and launches plans for its next century, it has also been assessing how the university and its campus have performed over the last ten years. Part of that process has involved assessing what changes need making in the short term. The results are summed up in a document titled *2019–22 Vision*, which sets out the next steps on the path of progress, succinctly summarized as a transition "From Good to Great."

This Vision document outlines five strategic pillars. The first of these is a commitment to "Quality of Education," which is very much a continuation of something that has been a mainstay since the day the first students enrolled back in 1919. "Quality in higher education is difficult to define," says Provost Ehab Abdel-Rahman. "But at AUC we have identified certain key elements, which are critical thinking, creativity, self-reflection, collaboration, academic integrity, balance of breadth and depth of content, high expectations of academic achievement, relevance, and return on investment. Enhancing the quality of education at any institution should be a life-long journey."

The second pillar is "Internationalization." As we've seen elsewhere in this book, AUC has always been the most global of universities, but that status has been challenged since 2011 by the perception abroad that Egypt is unsafe. The result is that in 2019, approximately 95 percent of students were Egyptian. Four percent were from other Arab countries,

most of them from the Gulf, Palestine, and North Africa. Only 1 percent of all students were of other nationalities, including Americans.

"Our challenge is to get the number of foreign students back up," says President Frank Ricciardone. "We need to bring the world back to Egypt, and that is very much our mission." The current goal is for international students to increase to 20 percent of the student body, with 50 percent of those international students to be Americans.

The third pillar is the "AUC Experience," which includes campus life. Back at the masterplanning stage, the vision for the New Cairo Campus was that it should be a "living campus." In other words, not like a school with students and staff arriving in the morning and leaving in the afternoon, but something more resembling a permanent community. Only now is that finally moving toward becoming a reality. "What has been interesting," says chairman of the Board of Trustees Richard Bartlett, "is just how rapidly New Cairo has developed. It no longer **»**

▲ Campus food services are in the process of receiving an upgrade, in terms of both the physical environment and the food offerings

feels like we're an outpost in the desert. The first time I stayed in faculty housing if you didn't have a car you would starve to death. There wasn't a grocery store within walking distance. That's changed so much and as a result the campus is very much coming alive."

Now that New Cairo has caught up, the aim is that AUC should move toward being less of a commuter campus and more of a residential campus. The task facing administration is to figure out how to have more students (as well as staff and faculty) living on or around the campus. "We have this spectacular space and it needs to be active all the time," says Bartlett. "And that's a real project."

One idea under consideration is to require that all first-year students live on campus. This is a radical move in a society in which sons and daughters generally only leave home when they get married. In a practical sense, if this were to happen then the current levels of on-campus student housing would be inadequate. There exists the option to repurpose plots off campus that were originally earmarked as faculty housing. If necessary, there is also plenty of land available on campus for new housing. The current university takes up only around half of the plot. Room for future expansion was built in to the original site masterplan.

One exciting idea to improve the experience of students living on or around the campus is a new university bicycle-sharing scheme. Many cities around the world have such schemes, where people can borrow bicycles from a dock and return them at another dock, with payment by mobile app. Not only would this help students get to and from campus in a clean and ecologically sound way, it would also help getting around on campus, where it can be a bit of a hike to go from one end to the other. The system should already be in place by the time this book is published.

PRESIDENT #12
FRANCIS RICCIARDONE
(2016–present)
Born in Boston, Ricciardone graduated from Dartmouth College. A subsequent career as a diplomat saw him serve as US ambassador to Turkey, Egypt, and the Philippines, and chargé d'affaires and deputy ambassador to Afghanistan. He was vice-president of the independent US-based Atlantic Council and director of its Rafik Hariri Center for the Middle East. Ricciardone taught at international schools in Italy and Iran, and speaks and reads Arabic, Italian, Turkish, and French, as well as elementary Farsi. "Egypt faces massive problems, climate, demographic, structural," says Ricciardone, "and yet there is an energy in this country. I see AUC being a part of this potential renaissance."

Other tweaks include the roll-out of AUC Coin, a cashless, tap-and-go way of paying for services and goods on campus linked to student ID cards; an upgrade of student lounge and cafeteria facilities; and the creation of more functional working spaces around the campus, including in the university garden, through the addition of shaded seating with improved wifi, and power points for charging laptops and phones.

The fourth pillar, "Institutional Effectiveness," mandates the effective use of university resources, with less dependency on tuition moneys and more on gifts and endowment. Pillar five is simply "Innovation." This is best expressed in the form of the Innovation Hub, an exciting new facility set to launch in spring 2020. "There is a trend in higher education to be more experiential," says alumna, trustee, and AI pioneer Rana El Kaliouby ('98). "The mission of the Innovation Hub is to bring more start-ups to campus so you have this cross-pollination between academia and industry." The Hub will provide individual workspaces for around forty multinationals, potentially including the likes of Microsoft and El Kaliouby's own Affectiva. The companies tap into the student and faculty resources of AUC, involving them in directed research. Students benefit from valuable work experience and the opportunity to prove their worth to potential employers. "We aim to ensure that innovation plays a prominent role in the students' and faculty's way of thinking," says Provost Ehab Abdel-Rahman. ⊛

▲ Scheduled for 2020, the Innovation Hub aims to "bridge the gap between what higher education institutions teach and the market demands by offering a platform for the two worlds to engage," says Provost Ehab Abdel-Rahman

◀ After studying how the student body uses the New Cairo Campus, changes are being made to the campus fabric in order to improve the user experience, including upgrading student lounges

295

96

ARTS FOR ALL

The historic Tahrir Campus is in the process of being reinvented as a vital cultural hub for Egypt

---

When, in 2008, the university moved from its Downtown campus on Tahrir Square to New Cairo, the big question was what would happen to the buildings and spaces that had been its home for the past eighty-nine years?

The palace on the square helped make AUC what it is. The central location, facing right onto Cairo's main square, a block from Parliament, two blocks from the American Embassy, across from the Nile Hilton, a jam of traffic from the Egyptian Museum . . . it embedded AUC in the national consciousness. Whenever events brought Cairenes out onto the streets—celebrations, protests, revolution—and the crowds swarmed, as inevitably they do, into Tahrir, there always was AUC as backdrop, witness, gathering point, forum, participant.

That location has always been one of the university's greatest physical assets. But when the decision to move was made, all options had to be examined and the cost benefits of selling the university's entire Downtown real estate were considered. "Part of the plan for paying for the new campus," says chairman of the Board of Trustees Richard Bartlett, "was a complete divestiture." In the event, it turned out that this was not necessary, and only peripheral parts of the Downtown campus were sold, notably the old AUC Press building on Mohamed Mahmoud Street and the villa housing the Rare Books and Special Collections Library. Other parts have been let out on long term leases, including the Greek Campus and the dormitory building in Zamalek.

So it was that in February 2019 Richard Bartlett found himself on stage at Ewart Hall delivering a speech to mark both the beginning of the university's centennial celebrations and the inauguration of the new Tahrir Cultural Center (TCC), which is the new role for the original campus. As Bartlett told his audience, from its founding AUC always looked for ways to contribute to the cultural life of Egypt, and turning the old home of the university into a center devoted to culture in all its forms guaranteed that the legacy would continue.

In preparation for its launch as a cultural center, the Tahrir Campus underwent three months of renovations, including a repurposing of some areas and a general sprucing up

Other speakers that day explained the mission of the TCC to become a venue for a wide variety of events, including dance, theatre, art, music, movie screenings, and conferences. Prior to this public launch there had been three months of renovations of the old buildings and a re-landscaping of the outdoor garden. The money for the work came from prominent businessman Naguib Sawiris, chairman of Orascom Investment Holding, and a long-time supporter of cultural and educational institutions in Egypt. He also spoke at the inaugural event. "If you ask me what connects me to AUC," said Sawiris, "frankly nothing, except I used to come and watch movies in this hall." However, he continued, as the owner of numerous companies, he was always happy to employ AUC graduates. In fact, he went so far as to say, that without AUC graduates he didn't know how his and other Egyptian companies would have managed. Financing the TCC, he said, was a way of saying "Thank you." His gift, however, did come with strings attached—in his speech he claimed he told then–president Lisa Anderson he would give his money only on condition that she buy some dynamite and persuade the Board of Trustees to demolish the university's 1960s

»

297

▲ French jazz trumpeter Erik Truffaz performing with drummer Artis Orubs and pianist SIG at the TCC in April 2019

Science Building, which, he said, was "the ugliest building in the world." The demolition duly happened, said Sawiris, and the TCC was born. (In fact, the demolition happened because AUC decided it was too expensive to refurbish the building and having a company dismantle it free of charge in exchange for scrap rights made sounder financial sense.)

The TCC launched with two exhibitions, *When Dreams Call for Silence* by former AUC professor Huda Lutfi, and *Bint al-Nil* by Sherin Guirguis. The latter was a celebration of Egyptian activist and poet Doria Shafik (1908–75), who in 1951 led "a feminist congress" from AUC's Ewart Hall. She gathered 1,500 women to march along Qasr al-Aini Street to the gates of the Parliament building, where they demanded that women be granted the right to vote. Coinciding with the launch of the exhibition, AUC president Frank Ricciardone unveiled a plaque to Shafik at the TCC, in the presence of her daughters, Aziza Ellozy and Jehane Ragai, both of whom are AUC alumni and faculty.

Since the inauguration of the TCC, events there have included a week-long festival of jazz with local and international artists, theatre and dance performances held in collaboration with the Downtown Contemporary Arts Festival (D-CAF), children's theatre as part of the Hakawy Festival, and weekly movie nights. One movie event, held in June 2019, was a special screening of *Kilo 64*, a documentary by AUC journalism and mass communications alumnus Amir al-Shennawi.

◀ The opening of the TCC Collective Visual Art Exhibition in March 2019, which involved the participation of 35 Egyptian artists

The TCC is very much a work in progress. Still to come are a new cafeteria space and a chic rooftop restaurant overlooking Tahrir Square. There are also plans to turn the former president's office and adjacent administration rooms in the old palace building into a businessmen's club. The idea behind this is to expose potential supporters of the arts to TCC's carefully curated mix of interesting voices, thrilling performances, and creative works of art. "We are trying to attract all classes, all ages," said Aly Mourad, director of TCC at the time of the launch. "Each class, each age will find something to do here." Mourad, incidentally, like Naguib Sawiris, originally came to know AUC through attending Thursday night movie screenings.

The center remains fully owned, operated, and programmed by AUC—unlike the former Greek Campus, which used to house the AUC Library, social sciences building, and Jameel Center among others, and which now operates as the GrEEK Campus, a hub for innovators and start-ups (including Egyptian franchises of Uber and Uber Eats), bankrolled by businessman Ahmed al-Alfi, who took the complex on a ten-year lease in 2013.

Meanwhile, in addition to its arts activities, café, and restaurant the Tahrir Campus continues to host university-related professional and academic programs, and it also remains home to the AUC Press and its flagship Bookstore. ◈

"I really believe in the potential of this place to bring light to the brains of the people."

Aly Mourad, launch director of the TCC

97

NOTHING VENTURED, NOTHING GAINED

AUC's V-Lab is helping launch Egypt's future businesses

Why pay thousands of pounds for a designer dress that might only be worn a few times? Why not just rent it? That is the idea behind La Reina, a couture service that allows customers to rent gowns for special occasions, whether it's a formal evening or a wedding. It follows the same path as businesses like New York–based Rent the Runway, which pioneered the rental concept back in 2009, and in the UK, Girl Meets Dress. To help ensure that the concept stood the best chance of successfully transferring to Egypt, La Reina founders Ghada ElTanawy and Amr Diab applied to join the mentoring program run by the AUC Venture Lab, or V-Lab for short.

V-Lab is Egypt's first university-based start-up 'accelerator.' Based at AUC since 2013, the lab's purpose is specifically to provide support to budding entrepreneurs. Each semester, the lab takes ten to fifteen start-ups, selected from the roughly four hundred applications for places that are made via V-Lab's Facebook page. Applicants do not have to be AUCians. They can be of any background, from anywhere in Egypt, and of any age. The criteria, explains Maureen Ayoub ('17, '19), one of the lab's program coordinators, are that they must have an original idea, along with a working prototype or viable product. "It must be something innovative and have the ability to quickly scale," she says. "Teams must have the right combination of business and technical knowledge, and there should be at least one team member who is committed full-time throughout the duration of our program."

The teams whose projects are selected then receive the benefit of everything V-Lab has to offer. There is an emphasis on business training, covering such vital skills as how to pitch and market effectively, exploring pricing models, dealing with legal issues, and how to attract investment. Teams have access to AUC's facilities and network, including workspace and the library, professors, lecturers, and even students, who provide a useful sounding board. In the past, the start-ups have even pitched their ventures to AUC graphic design students who, as part of their course

◀ Mostafa Kandil ('15), whose start-up, Swvl, is at the core of a revolutionary travel trend in Egypt. Kandil and his co-founders were early beneficiaries of AUC's V-Lab

"As AUC graduates, we have the opportunity to take risks."

Mostafa Kandil,
co-founder of Swvl

work, have created logos and corporate identities for them.

"This is a free service," says Ayoub. "We don't take any equity from the businesses, which is part of why it's so attractive to them." Instead, the costs of V-Lab are covered by sponsorship from the likes of the Commercial International Bank, Arab African International Bank, International Finance Corporation, and Drosos Foundation. "Sponsors also play a big part in supporting our start-ups with the right know-how," says Ayoub. »

▲ Maureen Ayoub ('17,'19) is a program coordinator and evangelist for V-Lab but, she says, success behind a start-up such as Swvl is driven by the passion and dedication of its founders

To date, V-Lab has assisted with more than 150 early-stage start-ups across different industries (ecommerce, energy and environmental sustainability, fintech, the creative industries, and more). Together they have created more than five hundred new jobs and raised more than LE 890 million in investments. "AUC Venture Lab has had a distinctive impact on Egypt's entrepreneurial ecosystem," says Ayman Ismail ('95, '97), director of V-Lab and the Abdul Latif Jameel Endowed Chair in Entrepreneurship, "not only by supporting innovative, high-growth startups, but also by connecting them with AUC's educational mission through experiential learning, where students and entrepreneurs work together and collaborate to create value for the startups."

"V-Lab was my first window to the start-up ecosystem," says Ghada ElTanawy of La Reina. "After I joined, I was mentored by many entrepreneurs and got to know them, and they helped me in my journey." Even though it is has been three years since La Reina launched, ElTanawy still benefits from V-Lab's support. "When I am faced with challenges or different opportunities and I need guidance, I always reach out to them. They follow up with me along the way and warn me if I have a blind spot in my business. I advise future entrepreneurs to get the most out the AUC V-Lab because it can really change your life."

Mostafa Kandil's ('15) life has already changed and he is only twenty-six. His start-up, Swvl, is at the core of a revolutionary travel trend in Egypt. If you don't already know it, Swvl is a mobile app that makes getting around easier. Users input their pick-up location and destination, and the app offers a set of routes and times from which to choose. Users pay online so that riding just becomes a matter of pick-up and drop-off. In the short amount of time since its founding in 2017 the start-up has seen impressive growth and in 2018 raised $8 million in its first round of venture capital financing.

When the application was first introduced in Cairo, the first few routes departed from AUC, where Kandil formerly studied petroleum engineering, but now where he and his partners, Mahmoud Nouh and Ahmed Sabbah, were participating in V-Lab's spring 2017 cycle. With its support, the team was able to launch the application before graduating from the program.

"V-Lab was instrumental in Swvl's early days," Kandil told *AUC Today*. "The team's mentorship and constant feedback on how to take Swvl from zero to one was key in how we shaped our marketing, operations, and other key functions. Being a V-Lab graduate was a stamp of confidence when we started fundraising." Kandil and his partners now dream of seeing Swvl as the first Egyptian tech unicorn, the term for a company that investors value at more than $1 billion. ⊗

98

A CULTURE OF GIVING

AUC owes its existence to philanthropy, and passing it forward is part of the university's philosophy

When the late John D. Gerhart, AUC's ninth president, addressed graduates at the 2002 commencement, a year before he died, his core advice was loud and clear: make a difference in the lives of others. "You cannot determine the length of your life, but you can determine its breadth and depth," said Gerhart. "I hope that you have learned that AUC is a privileged environment and that we have a responsibility to serve those less fortunate than ourselves, both in Egypt and in the world . . . We have the ability, the training, and the resources to make a difference, not just in our own lives, but in the lives of others. If we do not make use of those skills, we have failed in our responsibilities."

A long-time philanthropist, Gerhart believed that an essential aim of a liberal arts education is to instill values of service and civic responsibility among students. So, when in 2006 the university established an institute dedicated to furthering public service in Egypt and the Arab world, they named it the John D. Gerhart Center for Philanthropy and Civic Engagement.

Combining learning, research, and service, the center—later renamed to the John D. Gerhart Center for Philanthropy, Civic Engagement, and Responsible Business—works to strengthen philanthropic and civic practice, as well as nurture responsible

▲ Participants in a Lazord Academy mid-year retreat at Ardi, Dahshur in April 2019. The retreats aim to nurture the regional leaders of the future

**PRESIDENT #9
JOHN GERHART
(1998–2003)**

Almost as soon as Texan John Gerhart graduated (from Harvard then Princeton), he set out on a lifetime of philanthropy. He started with the Ford Foundation, where he worked for nearly thirty years. During his tenure as AUC president, he introduced policies to equalize treatment of Egyptian and foreign staff, expanded tenured faculty positions, and improved pension and retirement programs. He expanded community-based programs and introduced community service courses. Gerhart was most happy, however, when out of his office and interacting with students (or birdwatching). He died in July 2003 at the age of 59.

leadership and business practices. In the words of its founder, Barbara Ibrahim, the center aims to help create "outward-looking citizens." It looks to do this through a multitude of programs, the flagship of which is the Lazord Academy for Civic Leadership, which trains participants in volunteerism, civic engagement, and the inner workings of NGOs and non-profit organizations. "We are trying to create a pool of positive social agents," says director of the Gerhart Center, Ali Awni.

AUC students have always given freely of their time and money—look at the number of student clubs devoted to charitable causes. They have also always been quick to offer aid during times of war and emergencies. After the 1992 earthquake, for example, AUCians were some of the first to fill their cars with food, blankets, and flashlights and drive to villages on the Cairo outskirts that had been destroyed. However, the center's target extends far beyond the AUC community and involves the participation of other universities throughout Egypt and the region.

The fact that the students who took aid to the earthquake victims were met by soldiers, who turned them away because of the government's suspicion of just who might be providing aid and why, emphasizes another role that the Gerhart Center can play, which is advocating for private philanthropy at government level.

The Gerhart Center is part of AUC's policy of paying it forward, helping to foster the same philanthropic instinct in today's youth that nurtured the university in its formative years and that has sustained the institution ever since. Over the century of its existence, the AUC family has benefited from the largesse of donors, from the anonymous woman who funded Ewart Hall (see p184) to the Weyerhaeuser family who funded Hill House in the 1950s, and the numerous generous individuals who contributed to the creation of the New Cairo Campus.

That tradition continues. As part of the centennial celebrations, AUC launched a Centennial Campaign, part of which includes the Give 100 initiative, which encourages the AUC community to give 100 units of their country's currency to the AUC Fund. All proceeds go towards scholarships for deserving students from all walks of life — refugees, international students, athletes, students from populations that

are unrepresented in their field—who would otherwise be unable to access the high-quality education that AUC provides. This builds a new generation of broad-minded, forward-looking citizens and leaders.

"When I was at AUC, that's where my dreams were built," said Omar Khalifa ('08), CEO and founder of Shaghalni and member of the recently formed AUC Alumni Council. "I feel indebted to AUC. That's why I feel it's important to give back—whether it's financial, experience, mentoring new students . . . everything." ❀

▲ Board of Trustees chairman Richard Bartlett addresses the room at an AUC benefit dinner at the Metropolitan Museum of Art in New York in 2019, where more than $1.15 million was raised for Centennial Scholarships

99

STORING UP HISTORY

Without its
University Archives,
AUC would not
have quite so much
to celebrate

If there is one department that has truly embraced the marking of
AUC's centenary, it is the University Archives. In fact, this is the sort of
occasion the archives were created for.

"Part of the purpose of the archives," says Stephen Urgola, "is to
establish AUC's identity, capture it, and commemorate it—that's what
this whole Centennial book is all about." According to Urgola, who is
the university archivist and director of AUC records management, and
who came to AUC and Egypt from New York in August 2001, the archives
really only came into existence because of another, earlier celebratory
book. That book, *The American University in Cairo: 1919–1987*, was
written by Lawrence Murphy, a young American faculty member hired
to teach history, who then made the history of AUC his pet project. He
convinced the administration to sign off on a book on the subject, and
then commenced a search for sources. He discovered the files of Charles
Watson and other early records stashed in boxes on the roof of the old
palace building, preserved by what must have been a more forgiving
climate back then. He retrieved these, added material kept in the library
and other places, and so began the University Archives.

For a while the Archives were kept at the library on the Greek
Campus under the care of Kareem Helmy, then in 1992 they were moved
to the newly-established Rare Books and Special Collections Library in its
villa on Sheikh Rihan Street, where they were looked after by Mohamed
Abu Bakr, who these days is director of AUC's conservation lab.

Today Urgola heads a small but dedicated team, mostly based on the
top floor of the library. Nada Yassen joined the archives in 2004. "The
purpose of the Archives is to document and to preserve AUC history first,
and then Egypt's heritage and social life, and to make these materials
available for researchers at AUC and from around the world."

Over the years, the profile of the Archives has expanded dramatically.
It is frequently tapped by external researchers for academic topics, family
history, or quirky quests, such as the elderly lady who was searching

▲ The archivists. *Back row, left to right*: Emad Khafaga, Stephen Urgola, Ryder Kouba; *front left to right*: Nada Yassin, Natalya Stanke, Martha Tode

for evidence of a man she once knew, a fellow codebreaker in World War II, who said he once taught English at AUC. "One person," says Urgola, "contacted us about tessellations, which are tiles, because they were interested in a certain tile pattern found in Egypt that wasn't found anywhere else in the world and they'd seen this pattern in an image from AUC's old campus, Downtown." The Archives have gone from a handful of reference requests a year to hundreds—and in the run-up to the Centennial, possibly thousands.

Part of the reason for the growth in usage of the Archives is down to its presence online. Ryder Kouba has been the digital collections archivist since 2014, busy overseeing a program of scanning documents, placing them on the Archives website, and publicizing the collection via Facebook and other forms of social media. "We want people to use our material, not just people who live in Egypt but those who live abroad, so it's important to put things online." Currently, says Kouba, the Archives have around forty thousand items available to search and view digitally.

The size of the Archives means that even for those that know it best, it still constantly throws up surprises. "One of the stories in this book is about the vertical campus," says Urgola. "I'd never heard of this before but it's there in the Archives. So yeah, we're always making discoveries, all the time." ❦

> "Part of the purpose of the archive is to establish AUC's identity."
>
> Stephen Urgola,
> university archivist

100

THE NEXT 100 YEARS

The Bartlett family has been involved with AUC for over half of its existence. Richard Bartlett* considers what comes next.

* Richard Bartlett is currently chairman of the Board of Trustees, on which his brother Paul also serves. Their father, Thomas Bartlett, was president of AUC from 1963–69, returning as interim president in 2002.

It is tremendously gratifying that an institution that had not yet turned fifty when the Bartlett family first encountered it in the early 1960s is now celebrating its centennial. The occasion allows the AUC community to take stock of its remarkable history, and to contemplate its future promise.

Despite AUC's dramatic evolution during its first century, its founders would find AUC in 2019 to be a remarkably faithful fulfillment of their early aspirations. The university's program today is guided by principles they adopted during AUC's earliest days: a liberal arts focus—exemplified by today's Core Curriculum; an encouragement of critical thinking and reasoned debate; an emphasis on extracurricular activities like student clubs and athletics; and the provision of services to a public beyond its undergraduates. Even the new campus would resonate for the founders as a spectacular realization of their original hopes for a large suburban and partially residential campus.

AUC's whole-hearted embrace by Egyptian society is another achievement that would please the university's early leaders. Egyptians were understandably skeptical of a university funded originally by foreigners, but those suspicions gradually gave way to an appreciation that although AUC's roots were in the United States, Egypt is its only home. Critical to that acceptance has been the university's steadfast commitment that service to Egypt is the heart of its mission. By building its community without regard to politics, gender, ethnicity, or religion, the university earned its place in the mainstream of Egyptian society. The remarkable contributions of AUC graduates to Egypt provide ongoing validation of the university's work.

What might AUC's next century bring? If the past is anything to go by, then unforeseen events will inevitably play a role, but the current context suggests several influences. Unlocking the tremendous potential provided by the new campus will be central to AUC's next chapter. The new home creates space to support growth in its academic programs, and also allows AUC to develop as a residential community with dramatically expanded activities beyond the classroom. The development of Egypt's new administrative capital to the east of AUC places the university once again in the middle of a burgeoning corridor of Egyptian life.

A residential community will allow AUC to serve more students from more disparate parts of Egypt, and from a wider swath of socioeconomic backgrounds. A more diverse student body will enable AUC to fulfill its objectives as an engine of social mobility within Egypt, as well as broaden the array of perspectives represented on campus.

Higher education is increasingly global, and AUC must institutionalize its traditional role in bringing Egypt to the world and the world to Egypt. AUC's cross-cultural traditions implore the university to harness the creative energy generated by international engagement. Meanwhile, the digital revolution is transforming how intellectual information is produced, shared, and applied. AUC must be a leader in reshaping what it means to be a teacher, a student, a researcher—and a university.

Although AUC's century of experience cannot guarantee its future success, it provides a confidence that our founders would have envied. AUC has developed from an idea into a cherished institution. That position creates a stewardship responsibility for all members of the AUC community. AUC will continue to prosper provided we never lose sight of what a privilege it is to be part of it. ◈

▼ The AUC portal on the New Cairo Campus is a built representation of blue-sky thinking

NOTES ON SOURCES

AUC's University Archives (UA) were the major source for this book. Of particular value were the oral history recordings, in which archive staff interview long-serving faculty, administrators, staff, alumni, and students about their life and work at the university. This is an ongoing project, the results of which are available to all via the AUC Rare Books and Special Collections Digital Library. The interviews conducted by the author are not part of the archive.

For the historical pieces in this book the major references were *The American University in Cairo: 1919–1987* by Lawrence R. Murphy (AUC Press, 1987) and its supplementary volume *The American University in Cairo 1987–1995* by Thomas A. Lamont (AUC Press, 1995), also the minutes from Board of Trustees meetings. All additional references are cited below, organized in the following sequence: Interviews. Articles. Books.

5. THE PALACE ON THE SQUARE
"Story of a Palace" by Muriel Allen (*Places in Egypt*, November/December 1991); "The Building of the American University in Cairo: An Example of Mamluk Revival Style," an unpublished MA thesis by Hend Asaad Nadim (AUC, 1992); "Building the Past" by Cecilia Simon (*AUC Today*, Summer 1995). *Twentieth Century Impressions of Egypt: Its History, People, Commerce Industries, and Resources* edited by Arnold Wright (Lloyd's Publishing Company, 1909); *Cairo the Glory Years* by Samir Raafat (Harpocrates Press, 2003)

7. HOW AMERICAN IS THE AMERICAN UNIVERSITY?
Interviews with chairman of the AUC Board of Trustees Richard Bartlett (October 2018) and AUC president Frank Ricciardone (December 2018) by the author; oral history interview with former president John Badeau by Manucher Moadeb Zadeh, 1973 (UA); oral history interview with former president Raymond McLain by Lawrence R. Murphy, 1973 (UA); oral history interview with former president Thomas Bartlett by Caroline Foster and Stephen Urgola, 2005 (UA). *American Evangelicals in Egypt: Missionary Encounters in an Age of Empire* by Heather Jane Sharkey (Princeton University Press, 2008)

8. WHY A LIBERAL ARTS COLLEGE?
Interview with Robert Switzer by the author, May 2018. "If You Want to Run the World, Study a 'Useless' Subject" by Sarah Churchwell (*Financial Times*, 25 January 2018); "The Core Curriculum at the American University in Cairo: Legacy and Innovation" by Carol Clark, Amani Elshimi, Ghada Elshimi, and Robert Switzer in *Tradition Shaping Change: General Education in the Middle East and North Africa*, Al Hendawi, M., Ahmed, A., and Albertine, S., eds (Association of American Colleges and Universities Press, 2019

9. BRANDING AUC
Oral history interview with Carl Schieren by Stephen Urgola, 2008 (UA). "Making a Mark" by Peter Wieben (*AUC Today*, Fall 2008)

10. THE FREEDOM OF THE PRESS
"The Priceless Work of University Presses" by Matthew Walther (*The Week*, 30 January 2018); "Scholarly Publishing's Last Stand" by Samuel Cohen (*The Chronicle of Higher Education*, 22 April 2018). *The American University in Cairo Press 1960–1985* by Carolyn Niethammer (AUC Press, 1985)

11. SETTING THE PROTOCOL
Oral history interview with Tarik Saleh by Stephen Urgola, 2019 (UA)

12. THE STORM CENTER OF WAR

Cairo in the War 1939–1945 by Artemis Cooper (Hamish Hamilton, 1989)

13. MAKING FRIENDS IN THE NEW EGYPT

Oral history interview with Thomas Bartlett by Caroline Foster and Stephen Urgola, 2005 (UA). "Middle East Newsletter" by John Badeau, 18 October 1952; "American University Makes Friends in Egypt" by Raymond F. McLain (*The Christian Evangelist*, 13 May 1957)

14. SAVED BY THE INVENTORY

Oral history interview with Thomas Bartlett by Caroline Foster and Stephen Urgola, 2005 (UA). "American School Is Open in Cairo" by Jay Walz (*New York Times*, 9 October 1967); "American University Reopens" by Mary Hornaday (*Christian Science Monitor*, 17 November 1967)

15. THE DEATH OF MANSOUR

"Ex-Azharite Throws Molotovs at Tahrir Gate" by Nisreen El Tell, Lamya Gouda and Osama Abdel Rahman (*Caravan*, 12 April 1987); "Arrest Brings Menadi Problem to a Head" by Dina Farid and Ramy Anis (*Caravan*, 13 March 1988); AUC Student Stoned Near Campus by Menadi" by Ramy Anis (*Caravan*, 6 November 1988); "Menadi Adds 90 km to Student's Parked Car" by Tamer Abdelaal (*Caravan*, 18 December 1988); "Interior Minister Survives Assassination Attempt" (*Egyptian Gazette*, 19 August 1993); "A Sense of Security" by Islam M. Guemey (*Caravan*, 27 September 1993). *The Map of Love* by Ahdaf Soueif (Bloomsbury, 1999)

16. AND THEN THE REVOLUTION BROKE OUT

Email interviews with Lisa Anderson and Rick Tutwiler by the author, May 2018. Oral history interview with Brian MacDougall by Stephen Urgola, 2018 (UA). "And Then the Revolution Broke Out," a report by President Lisa Anderson to the AUC Board of Trustees (2011); "After Tahrir: Rebuilding the New Egypt" by Madeline Welsh (*AUC Today*, Fall 2011)

17. STUDENTS ON THE SQUARE

This piece draws from the series of "University on the Square: Documenting Egypt's 21st-Century Revolution" interviews conducted on behalf of the University Archives

18. IN THE MIDDLE OF IT

Interviews with Deena Boraie and Kevin O'Connell by the author, May 2018; oral history interviews with Mark Linz and Mokhtar Shalaby by Stephen Urgola, 2011 and 2015 (UA); "Serving through the Storm" by Dalia al-Nimr (*AUC Today*, Spring 2011)

19. MOHAMED MAHMOUD STREET

"Mohamed Mahmoud Demolition for Beauty, Not Politics, Says Cairo Official" (www.madamasr.com, 18 September 2015). *Revolution Graffiti: Street Art of the New Egypt* by Mia Gröndahl (AUC Press, 2013)

20. THE KEEPERS OF CONTINUITY

Interviews with chairman of the Board of Trustees Richard Bartlett, and board members Teresa C. Barger, Nathan Brown, Rana El Kaliouby, and Gretchen Welch by the author, October 2018

21. CHOOSING A PRESIDENT

Interview with Richard Bartlett by the author, October 2018; email interview with Tim Sullivan by the author, December 2018

22. THE HALF-CENTURY CLUB

Email interview with Mahmoud Farag by the author, January 2019; interview with Shahira El Sawy by the author, December 2018; oral history interviews with Abdel Messih Abdalla Meawad (2005), Pakinam Askalani (2012, 2014), and Mahmoud Farag (2014) by Stephen Urgola, (all UA); oral history interview with Farouk El-Hitami by Stephen Urgola and Jennfer Waxman, 2006 (UA). "164 Years of Loyalty" by Sally El-Sabbahy (*AUC Today*, Spring 2014)

24. MAKING RESEARCH PAY
Interviews with Rania Siam, Nageh Allam, and Ahmed Ellaithy by the author, March 2019. "Curbing the Epidemic" by Tessa Litecky (*AUC Today*, Fall 2015); "Pushing the Boundaries of Life" by Helen Albert (*The Biochemist*, December 2017)

25. ONE OF THE STRONGEST
"When Small Is Big" by Inas Hamam (AUC Today, Spring 2000); "Zewail Relays Vision of the Arab World" (*AUC Today*, Summer 2004); "Ahmed Zewail, Nobel Prize-winning Chemist," an obituary (*Daily Telegraph*, 8 August 2016)

27. FOR THE RECORD
Interview with John Baboukis by the author, April 2019; interviews with Joudi Abou Ayed and Wael al-Mahallawy by Martha Tode, March 2019. "Connecting with Egypt Through Music" by Katherine Pollock (News@AUC, 26 November 2017)

28. DESIGNING FOR LIFE
Interviews with Haytham Nawar (December 2018) and Bahia Shehab (email, January 2019) by the author. The lead to this story reuses text from "An Artist Amplified" by Tess Santorelli (News@AUC, January 2019)

29. NOT A SOFTER OPTION
Interview with Magda Mostafa by the author, April 2019; interview with Ahmed Sherif by Martha Tode, April 2019; email interviews with Mirette Khorshed by Martha Tode, April 2019, and with Nada Nafeh by the author, May 2019

31. THE FIRST COED
Oral history interview with Eva Habib el-Masri by

Manucher Moadeb-Zadeh, 1969 (UA). "The Path of a Pioneer" by Jeffrey Bellis (*AUC Today*, Spring 2009)

32. FOUR FEMALES FOR EVERY MAN
"Four Females for Each Man" by Mounira Habachi (*Caravan*, 9 April 1979); "Boy/Girl Ratio at AUC Surveyed" by Shahira Shaker (*Caravan*, 30 March 1981)

33. DON'T CALL ME "MUZZA"
Oral history interview with Gulmar Gidawi [Djeddoaui] Buttic by Manucher Moadeb-Zadeh, 1969 (UA). "Baheya Farag, First Queen of Beauty, Established Traditional Miss AUC Contest" (*Campus Caravan*, 2 March 1951); "Attiya Falaki Elected Miss AUC" (*Campus Caravan*, 20 March 1953); "Cairo Hairdressers Benefit Most" by Fatma Mashhour (*Caravan*, 30 November 1971)

34. I PROTEST
"Hostel Boys Walk Out in Food Strike" (*Campus Caravan*, 23 February 1945); "Dean Tells Students Food Will Improve" by Youssef Ibrahim (*Caravan*, December 1966); "AUC Teachers Lead Protest on Renewed US Bombing of Hanoi" (*Caravan*, 27 December 1972); "AUCians Protest the Israeli Raid on Tunisia" by Enas Shinawi (*Caravan*, 21 October 1985); "Israeli Flag Burned on AUC Campus" by Ousama Abdel Rahman (*Caravan*, 3 January 1988); "Protests Held as Jameel Center is Opened" by Ghadir al-Agabany, Rasha Zaki, and Shinda Aly (*Caravan*, 5 March 1989); "United We Stand" by Ghaydaa Fahim (*AUC Today*, Fall 2011); "AUC Survives a Difficult Semester" by Tanya Zaki, Mafdy Ramsis, and Khaled al-Amin (*Caravan*, 9 December 2012)

35. AUC'S OTHER PRESIDENTS
Interview with Saeed Zakaria by Martha Tode, March 2019; email interviews with Ahmed Alaa Fayed, Ahmed Atalla, Ahmed Ayoub, Ahmed

al-Bakry, Ayman Ayad, Beethoven Tayel, and Mohamed Ali by Martha Tode, March 2019

36. A FAMILY AFFAIR
This story first appeared as "It Runs In the Family" by Tess Santorelli in the "2019 Centennial Special Edition Issue 1" of *AUC Today*

37. READ ALL ABOUT IT
Interviews with Abdelhamid Mahmoud, Eynas Barakat, Firas al-Atraqchi, Lamees Elhadidy, and Dania Mohamed El Akkawi by Martha Tode, February 2019. "From the Archives: Student Journalism at AUC" by Margaret Epps (*AUC Today*, February 1993)

39. BACK AT THE OLD STOMPING GROUND
"Queen Rania Encourages Civic Engagement at AUC" by Ragia Mostafa (*Caravan*, 7 March 2010)

40. EGYPTIAN WOMEN CHANGING THEIR WORLD/41. GETTING ON IN BUSINESS/43. SOUND AND VISION
These stories draw on text written by Dalia al-Nimr, Claire Davenport, Nahla El Gendy, and Tess Santorelli and published as part of *AUC Today*'s "Alumni of the Century: 2019 Centennial Special Edition, Issue 2"

45. THE SENIOR ALUMNUS
Oral history interview with Wadei Philistin by Stephen Urgola, 2008 (UA)

46. THE PURSUIT AND EXPRESSION OF TRUTH
Email interviews with Lina Attalah and Maggie Michael by the author, May 2019

47. LEARNING TO SPELL "PHARAOH"
Interviews with Louise Bertini, Fayza Haikal, and Salima Ikram by the author (September and December 2018); email interviews with Mennat-Allah El Dorry, Monica Hanna, Kate Liszka, Leslie

Warden by the author (May 2019); "Digging Deep" (*AUC Today*, "Centennial Special Edition, Issue 2")

48. "17 AND IN AUC"
Email interview with Hassan Khan by the author, March 2019

49. DOWNTOWN DAYS
Most of these recollections come from the AUC Memories pages on the AUC website (archived in the RBSCL Digital Library), which is a collection of written recollections contributed by members of AUC past and present, and compiled by Mahmoud Farag. Some additional quotes come from "AUC in the Seventies" a piece of audio journalism created by Jasmin Bauomy as part of her graduation work in 2009. It won the 2010 Collegiate Broadcasters Inc Best Radio Documentary Award and can be found in the Digital Archive and Research repository of AUC University Archives

50. ROCK & ROLL HALL OF FAME
Email interview with Basil Philistin by the author, March 2019; Oral history interview with Raed Badder by Stephen Urgola, 2018 (UA). "The 'Mass' Attack" (*Caravan*, 6 April 1971); "Three of the Best" by Alya al-Mufti (*Caravan*, 15 January 1979); "Ladies and Gentlemen, the Gama Show" by Amr al-Kadi (*Caravan*, 29 December 1981); "Alpha, Beta, Gama: the Ups and Downs" by Basil Philistin (*Caravan*, 9 February 1982); "The Mass: From the 60s Music Scene" by Samir Raafat (*Egyptian Mail*, 4 October 1997)

51. CAMPUS CATS
Interviews with Rowaida Saad-Eldin and Ingrid Wassmann by the author, May 2018; oral history interview with Molly Bartlett by Stephen Urgola, 2013 (UA). "Homecoming Cats" by Eynas Barakat (*Caravan*, 31 December 1989); "Keeping Up with the Cats on Campus" by Yomna Marzouk (*The Insider*, 14 December 2017)

52. JOIN THE CLUB
"AUCians at Their Best: Trucks Packed with Humanitarian Aid" by Sara Hussein (*Caravan*, 12 May 2002); "AUC has a Legacy of Long Lost Student Clubs" by Mary Aravani (*Caravan*, 15 November 2014)

55. MAKING A SPLASH
Interviews with Louise Bertini (December 2018) and Reem Kassem (email, May 2019) by the author; email interview with Mariam Foum by Martha Tode, May 2019; oral history interview with Chuck Gordon by Stephen Urgola, April 2018 (UA). "Akher Kalam: Taking the Plunge" (*AUC Today*, Summer 2010); "On the Mark" (*AUC Today*, Fall 2010)

56. THE OLYMPIANS
Email interviews with Yossra Ashraf Helmy and Dina Meshref by the author, February 2019. "Returning from Rio" (*AUC Today*, Fall 2016)

57. A CULTURAL CENTER FOR CAIRO
Oral history interview with Ghali Amin by Lawrence R. Murphy, 1973 (UA); oral history interview with John Badeau by Manucher Moadeb Zadeh, 1973 (UA). "Ewart Hall in the Old Days: Memories of Dick Pedersen, Cynthia Nelson, and the Seminar" by Dan Tschirgi (UA); "The Renovation of Ewart" by Patricia Smith (*AUC Today*, May 1993). *Out of Place: A Memoir* by Edward Said (Knopf, 1999)

58. THE EWART HALL HOARD
"AUC's Hidden Treasures" a four-part investigation by Reem Gehad and Ahmed Aboul Enein (*Caravan*, April–June 2012); "AUC: A Story to Be Remembered" by Zahi Hawass (*Al-Ahram Weekly*, 3–9 August 2017)

59. THE NUBIA PROJECT
Oral history interview with Nawal al-Messiri by Stephen Urgola, 2017 (UA). "Marking 50 Years of Development Assistance: A Look at AUC's Social Research Center" by Lamia Tawfik (*AUC Today*, Spring 2004); text written to accompany an exhibition of Nubia images at AUC's Photographic Gallery in 2005 by Abdallah Schleifer and Barbi Bursch Eysselinck. *Nubian Encounters: The Study of the Nubian Ethnographical Survey 1961–1964* edited by Nicholas S. Hopkins and Soheir R. Mehanna (AUC Press, 2010)

60. A FAME OF SORTS
This story is largely a transcript of a talk given by professor of Arabic literature Samia Mehrez, on 8 February 2009, as part of AUC's 90th-anniversary celebrations. Additional material comes from an oral history interview with Gail Gerhart by Stephen Urgola, 2015 (UA)

61. HERE COMES THE SUN
Interview with Salah Arafa by the author, December 2018. "Sun Brings TV To Mud Village in Egypt's Delta" by Christopher S. Wren (*The New York Times*, 11 June 1978); "Salah Arafa Implements Sustainable Development Model in Sharqiya" (News@AUC News, 3 February 2014)

62. CONSERVING EGYPT
Interview with Philip Croom by the author, May and December 2018. "AUC's Rare Books and Special Collections Library Preserves Local and International Heritage" (www.menaherald.com, 28 February 2016); "Librarians Abroad: 'None of Us Thought We'd Grow Up to Be One'" by Denyse Woods (*The Irish Times*, 26 January 2019)

63. A BETTER ORANGE
Interview with Richard Tutwiler by the author, September 2018. "Adli Bishay: Opportunity Knocks" by Yasmine El Rashidi (*Al-Ahram Weekly*, 25–31 March 2004); "Sustainability on the Rise" by Marjon Momand (*AUC Today*, Fall 2013)

64. GOING PUBLIC

This story was first published as "Continuing the Legacy" by Veronika Edwards (*AUC Today*, Fall 2014); it has been updated via interviews with Alia Shoeib (May 2019) and Deena Boraie (May 2018) by the author

65. READING WRITING ON BUILDINGS

Email interview with Lobna Sherif by the author, March 2019. "Islamic Inscriptions: Reading Between the Lines" by Dalia al-Nimr (*AUC Today*, Spring 2012)

66. AL-SITT SINGS AT EWART

Oral history interview with Ghali Amin by Lawrence R. Murphy, 1973 (UA). *The Voice of Egypt: Umm Kulthum, Arabic Song, and Egyptian Society in the Twentieth Century* by Virginia Danielson (University of Chicago Press, 1997)

67. A VISIT FROM THE KINGS

Oral history interview with James A. Beshai by Katrina Righter, 2012 (UA)

68. A VISIT FROM THE POLICE

"Police Caught in the Act" by Arbaggy (*Egyptian Mail*, 29 March 1980). *Can't Stand Up for Falling Down: Rock'n'Roll War Stories* by Allan Jones (Bloomsbury, 2017). *The Police—Around the World* tour film (available on Vimeo)

69. HILLARY CLINTON

"The Bonds of Friendship" by Fayza Hassan and Khaled Dawoud (*Al-Ahram Weekly*, 25–31 March 1999); "Egyptians Pelt Clinton Motorcade with Tomatoes" by Arshad Mohammed (Reuters, 16 July 2012)

71. NOAM CHOMSKY

Adapted from "Chomsky in Tahrir" by Madeline B. Welsh (*The Cairo Review of Global Affairs*, Fall 2012)

74. WE ARE HONORED THIS EVENING . . .

"Gene Tunney Visits AUC and Addresses Students" (*The AUC Review*, 13 March 1931); "Dr Helen Keller Addresses Capacity Audience at AUC" (*Campus Caravan*, 2 May 1952); "AUC Follows Right Path Says Gamal Abdel Nasser" (*Campus Caravan*, 20 March 1953); "62 Degrees Awarded at 31st Annual Commencement; Adlai Stevenson Among Guests of Honor" (*The Chronicle*, Fall 1953); "A Week with Agnes Moorehead" (*Campus Caravan*, 16 March 1961); "Condoleeza Rice Calls for the Government to Have Faith in Its People" (*AUC Today*, Summer 2005)

75. GENUINE LITERARY CELEBS

Oral history interviews with Doris Shoukri (by Stephen Urgola and Pauline Wickham) and John Rodenbeck (by Stephen Urgola), both 2006 (UA). "The Visit That Isn't Possible" by Shahira S. Fahmi (*Caravan*, 5 March 1989)

77. FROM ALL CORNERS OF THE WORLD

This article was written by Elizabeth Lepro and first appeared in *AUC Today*, Fall 2017

78. TALK LIKE AN EGYPTIAN

Email interviews with Elisabeth Jaquette, Hebatalla Salem, and Paul Wulfsberg by the author, February 2019 (and thanks to Alice Duesdieker, Eleanor Ellis, and Denis Sullivan for email updates); oral history interview with John Swanson by Stephen Urgola, 2016 and 2017 (UA). "In the Heart of Cairo, the Language of Immersion" by Ursula Lindsey (*The Chronicle of Higher Education*, 27 July 2010); "CASA: 50 Years of Changing Lives . . . in Arabic" by Aliah Salih (*AUC Today*, Fall 2017); "For the Love of CASA: AUC's Benefit Dinner Surpasses $600,000" by Elizabeth Lepro (News@AUC, 14 May 2018)

79. INTERNAL AFFAIRS

Interviews with Rowaida Saad-Eldin, Frank Packard

(email), and 2018–19 presidential associates Aaron Blinderman, Claire Davenport, Erin Hayes, Kara Hoving, Grant Smith, Natalya Stanke, Meredith Sullivan, and Sarah Wylie by the author, December 2018

80. GOING GLOBAL WITH MAHFOUZ
Email interview with Martha Levin by the author, June 2018. "At the Ali Baba Café" by Christopher Dickey in *Vanity Fair's Writers on Writers* (Penguin, 2016). *The American University in Cairo Press 1960–1995: The 35th Anniversary Celebration* by the staff of the Press (AUC Press, 1995); *Jackie as Editor: The Literary Life of Jacqueline Kennedy Onassis* by Greg Lawrence (Thomas Dunne Books, 2011)

81. HANDS-ON EGYPTOLOGY
Email interview with Kent Weeks by the author, January 2019; "AUC at Luxor: Looking into the Past" by Howdy Stout (*AUC Today*, Summer 1994); "Secrets of the Tomb" by Howdy Stout (*AUC Today*, Fall 1995); "Secrets of the Lost Tomb" by Michael D. Lemonick (*TIME*, 29 May 1995); "Kent Weeks: Plotting the Past" (*AUC Today*, Fall 2000)

82. MODELING SUCCESS
Email interview with Tim Sullivan by the author, February 2019; interview with Marwan El-Sayed by Martha Tode, February 2019. "Modelling Success" (*AUC Today*, Fall 2010); "AUC's Model United Nations, Model Arab League Teams Win Top Awards at International Conferences" (News@ AUC, 14 May 2017). Thanks to Reem Al Salem for updated information

83. HELPING PEOPLE HELP OTHERS
This story is adapted from "From IDP Camp to Egypt's Top Universities: a DAFI Scholar's Journey" by Yasmine El-Demerdash, which ran on the UNHCR Egypt website on 9 Dec 2018. Additionally, email interviews with Dawood Mayom and Yasmine El-Demerdash by the author, May 2019. "GAPP Celebrates 10 Years and Plans for Growth" by Aya Aboshady (*Caravan*, 8 April 2019)

84. TIME TO GO
Oral history interview with Andrew Snaith by Stephen Urgola, 2014 (UA). "Moving Toward the Future" by Inas Hamam (*AUC Today*, Winter 1997)

85. THE VERTICAL CAMPUS
Email interview with Ashraf Salloum by the author, April 2019

86. A CITY FOR LEARNING
Interview with Ashraf Salloum by the author, September 2018; oral history interviews with David Arnold and Hussein el-Sharkawy by Stephen Urgola, 2016 and 2017 (UA). "The Search for Style" by Heba Kandil (*AUC Today*, Fall 1999); "Designing Voids" by Fawzeya El Sawy (*AUC Today*, Spring 2000); "Developing Design Guidelines" by Beth Turk (*AUC Today*, Fall 2000); "The New Campus Project: A Year in Review" by Beth Turk (*AUC Today*, Winter 2001); "A Firm Commitment" by Fawzeya El Sawy (*AUC Today*, Winter 2002); "Breaking Ground in New Cairo" by Dalia Al Nimr (*AUC Today*, Spring 2003); " Creating a Small-Town Home" by Dina Abulfotuh (*AUC Today*, Spring 2003); "Beneath the Surface" by Lamia Tewfik (*AUC Today*, Spring 2004); "Going Up: AUC's New Campus on the Move" by Lamia Tawfik (*AUC Today*, Spring 2005). *A City for Learning: AUC's Campus in New Cairo* by Dr. Hussein El-Sharkawy and Dr. Larry L. Fabian (AUC Office of New Campus Development, 2004)

87. A MOVING EXPERIENCE
Interview with Shahira El Sawy by the author, May 2018; oral history interview with Mohamed Abdel Gawad by Stephen Urgola, 2013 (UA). "A Moving Experience" by Leen Jaber and Peter Wieben (*AUC Today*, Summer 2008)

88. THE NEW CAMPUS
Interview with Ashraf Salloum by the author, September 2018

89. A LIVING BREATHING CAMPUS
Interview with Ashraf Salloum by the author, September 2018. "Keeping it Green" (*AUC Today*, Fall 2013); "Going Green with Architecture" by Tessa Litecky (*AUC Today*, Spring 2016)

90. GREEN THINKING
Interviews with Richard Hoath, Ashraf Salloum, and Rick Tutwiler by the author, September 2018

92. WHO'S WHO ON CAMPUS
"A Name That Lasts" by Sarah Topol (*AUC Today*, Fall 2009)

93. VEILLON, BOGHIGUIAN, AND SIRRY
"Anna Boghiguian at Tate St Ives: Pilchards, Salt and Philosophy" by Maya Jaggi (*Financial Times*, 6 February 2019). *Margo Veillon: Painting Egypt: The Masterpiece Collection at the American University in Cairo* edited by Bruno Ronfard (AUC Press 2003)

95. FIVE PILLARS FOR THE FUTURE
Interviews with Richard Bartlett (October 2018), Frank Ricciardone and Hanan Abdel Meguid (December 2018), and Rania El Tahan and Maha Farouk (June 2019) by the author

96. ARTS FOR ALL
Interview with Richard Bartlett by the author, October 2108; interviews with Aly Mourad by the author (December 2018) and Martha Tode (June 2019); speech by Naguib Sawiris at Ewart Hall, 9 February 2019 (Tahrir Cultural Center Facebook page). "Right at the Center: Launching Cairo's New Cultural Hub" by Claire Davenport (News@AUC, 9 February 2019)

97. NOTHING VENTURED, NOTHING GAINED
Interview with Maureen Ayoub Guirguis by Martha Tode, May 2019. "AUC Vlab Graduate SWVL Closes a Half a Million-Dollar Deal with Careem" by Maureen Ayoub Guirguis (News@AUC, July 2017); "Tech Unicorn" by Ionna Moriatis (*AUC Today*, Spring 2018); "AUC Venture Lab: Five Years of Changing Egypt's Entrepreneurial Landscape" by Aliah Salih (News@AUC, 13 June 2018)

98. A CULTURE OF GIVING
Interview with Barbara Ibrahim by Martha Tode, April 2019. "Fountain of Philanthropy" by Carolyn Vasquez (*AUC Today*, Fall 2016)

99. STORING UP HISTORY
Interview with Ryder Kouba, Natalya Stanke, Stephen Urgola, and Nada Yassen by Martha Tode, May 2019; additional information supplied by Stephen Urgola, May 2019 ✿

ACKNOWLEDGMENTS

Enormous thanks go to AUC's chief archivist Stephen Urgola who read the first drafts of the stories in this book, and supplied extensive notes and corrections. Steve frequently provided pointers to additional material and people to interview. If there are any mistakes in this book then it can only be that there was text I failed to run by Steve.

Thank you also to Steve's colleagues Ryder Kouba, Nada Yassen, and Ola Seif, and presidential associate to the Rare Books and Special Collections Library 2018–19 Natalya Stanke. This book is similarly indebted to project research assistants Caroline Benson and Martha Tode, and to long-term AUC faculty member Richard Hoath for his guidance throughout this project. Without these people this book would simply not have been possible. It also would not have been anywhere near as enjoyable to work on.

Thank you to AUC Press director Nigel Fletcher-Jones for the commission, and to his colleagues at the Press (past and present) Neil Hewison, Miriam Fahmy, and Sylvia Maher. Thank you to the members of the centenary book project steering committee: Deena Boraie, Lamia Eid, Richard Hoath, Ghada Sheba, Jennifer Skaggs, and Rick Tutwiler. Thank you also to Dalia al-Nimr and Lamia Al Naima, editor and designer of *AUC Today*, respectively.

Lastly, thank you to everybody—faculty, students, administration, alumni—who was kind enough to give up their time to answer our questions and help in our researches during the course of putting together this book. There are far too many names to mention (although many of you are cited in the Notes on Sources) but I hope we have done you, your work, and your university justice.

PICTURE CREDITS